The Landscapes
of Western Movies

ALSO BY JEREMY AGNEW
AND FROM McFARLAND

Healing Waters: A History of Victorian Spas (2019)

*The Age of Dimes and Pulps: A History of Sensationalist
Literature, 1830–1960* (2018)

*Crime, Justice and Retribution
in the American West, 1850–1900* (2017)

*Spanish Influence on the Old Southwest:
A Collision of Cultures* (2016)

*The Creation of the Cowboy Hero:
Fiction, Film and Fact* (2015)

*Alcohol and Opium in the Old West:
Use, Abuse and Influence* (2014)

*The Old West in Fact and Film:
History Versus Hollywood* (2012)

*Entertainment in the Old West:
Theater, Music, Circuses, Medicine Shows,
Prizefighting and Other Popular Amusements* (2011)

Medicine in the Old West: A History, 1850–1900 (2010)

The Landscapes of Western Movies

A History of Filming on Location, 1900–1970

JEREMY AGNEW

McFarland & Company, Inc., Publishers
Jefferson, North Carolina

Photographs and illustrations are from
the author's collection unless otherwise noted.

ISBN (print) 978-1-4766-7951-8
ISBN (ebook) 978-1-4766-4223-9

LIBRARY OF CONGRESS AND BRITISH LIBRARY
CATALOGUING DATA ARE AVAILABLE

Library of Congress Control Number 2020038131

© 2020 Jeremy Agnew. All rights reserved

*No part of this book may be reproduced or transmitted in any form
or by any means, electronic or mechanical, including photocopying
or recording, or by any information storage and retrieval system,
without permission in writing from the publisher.*

On the cover: countless movies, television commercials,
and still photographs have made the brilliant red sandstone
spires and buttes of Monument Valley on the Utah-Arizona border
into the iconic vision of "The West" (author photograph)

Printed in the United States of America

McFarland & Company, Inc., Publishers
Box 611, Jefferson, North Carolina 28640
www.mcfarlandpub.com

For Pat,
for all the hours we spend discussing
Western movie trivia.

Table of Contents

Milestones in Filming Western Motion Pictures on Location   1
Preface   3

One. Pre–1900: Romanticizing the Landscape   7
Two. The Early 1900s: Shaky Beginnings   26
Three. The 1910s: Growth of the Silent Film Industry   50
Four. The 1920s: Consolidation on the Coast   69
Five. The 1930s: The Rise of the B-Westerns   86
Six. The 1940s: Solidly in the Outdoors   109
Seven. The 1950s: Realistic Locations   138
Eight. The 1950s: Locations That Moved   165
Nine. The 1960s and Beyond: The Shift in Power   180

Postscript   203
Chapter Notes   209
Bibliography   216
Index   219

Milestones in Filming Western Motion Pictures on Location

Late 1800s—Interest in the outdoor beauty of the West is sparked by romanticized paintings, Wild West shows, stage melodramas, popular literature, and outdoor landscape photographs.

1890s—Some of the first motion pictures made on location record life in the West but are primarily documentaries of real events, such as travel, cattle round-ups, and Indian ceremonies.

1903—*The Great Train Robbery*, directed by Edwin S. Porter, creates a great interest in fictional Western crime films, most of which are filmed on location in New Jersey and New York.

1908—Formation of the Motion Picture Patents Company starts to drive filmmakers westward to escape prosecution for patent violation.

1909—Studios filming Westerns on location establish permanent facilities around Los Angeles.

1910—New York Motion Picture Company leases land in Santa Ynez Canyon near Los Angeles and hires Thomas Ince and the Miller Brothers Wild West show to make action-filled Westerns in outdoor settings.

Early 1910s—Broncho Billy becomes the first identifiable Western movie hero in films made on location in Colorado and California.

Late 1910s—William S. Hart popularizes the good badman hero in his movies and makes his outdoor locations look seedy and ramshackle.

1918—The Motion Picture Patents Company is disbanded by the federal government under antitrust action.

1920s—The dour hero of W.S. Hart gives way to the flashy image of Tom Mix, who films at authentic locations in national parks and in the West. Silent movies give way to sound, leading to technical difficulties for filming Westerns on location.

1923/1924—*The Covered Wagon* and *The Iron Horse* stimulate audience interest in epic Westerns filmed on location.

1928—*In Old Arizona* is a success in location photography with sound and helps to promote a resurgence of large-scale outdoor sound Westerns.

1929—The stock market crash in New York leads to the Great Depression, which also depresses movie attendance and financing for movies filmed on location.

Milestones in Filming Western Motion Pictures on Location

Early 1930s—Westerns go into decline as the novelty of sound fades and the Depression deepens. The needs and limited finances of low-budget B-Westerns mostly restricts location filming to studio back lots and movie ranches near Hollywood.

1939—The success of *Stagecoach*, the first film by John Ford to use Monument Valley as a location, revitalizes audience interest in A-Westerns filmed on location in the outdoors.

Early 1940s—Expanded filming in Technicolor produces new impetus for filming Westerns on location in the outdoors.

1948—The Supreme Court orders major studios to divest themselves of their theater chains, thus removing their guaranteed market for their films.

1950s—Decline of the studio system as studios cut back on location budgets due to the loss of revenue from theater chains. Location filming returns to back lots and movie ranches.

Early 1960s—Peak years for television Westerns filmed on studio back lots. Budget cuts force filming at less expensive locations in Mexico and overseas. "Spaghetti Westerns" made in Spain promote a new vision of the West as a dry desert.

1969—Violent Westerns return to filming at locations in the U.S. and Mexico with *The Wild Bunch* and others.

1970s—Audience tastes turn to science fiction, outer space, the occult, horror, and kung-fu movies.

1980s—Westerns decline further in popularity in favor of blockbuster franchise action-adventure productions with stunning computer-generated effects.

Preface

"TV you can make on the back lot, but for the big screen, for the real outdoor dramas, you have to do it where God put the West."
—actor John Wayne on location filming[1]

Filming a Western on location involves making the picture in the outdoors away from the main studio, as opposed to filming outdoor scenes on a sound stage or on a studio back lot. Much has been written about Western cinema, but there have been few studies that describe this fundamental element of the genre, namely the use of the wide-open spaces that form the landscape and natural background of the outdoor West of the United States. These wide-open spaces and the scenery filmed on location are among the defining features of the Western that appeal to movie audiences and give a feeling of authenticity to Western films.

Popular culture is dominated by visual images created by Hollywood. Thus, in Western movies, the average moviegoer perceives and judges the physical reality of the West to be that which he or she sees on the screen. As a result, the Western motion picture as a genre owes much of its continued appeal and longevity to the use of rugged, scenic Western landscapes for the backdrop to the plot.

Movie audiences have always been awed by the splendor of the scenery shown in Western movies. Filmmakers quickly discovered, however, that to incorporate these magnificent backdrops into their movies they had to film on location. The rugged outdoors and splendid scenery of the true West could not be found on a studio back lot or studio ranch, or duplicated on a Hollywood sound stage. As a result, Westerns were typically filmed in the wide-open spaces of the American West where, as John Wayne aptly put it at the beginning of this preface, they belonged. Western epics, in particular, had to be filmed on location to look suitably real. However, as a result, the movie theater audience's perception of "the West" has been strongly influenced by what has been seen on the screen and the particular locations used for filming Westerns.

Western movies appeal to adults and children of all economic and educational backgrounds and to people of all nationalities. Today there is a heightened interest among these viewers about the background details of how and where movies are made. Originally the major studios resisted documentaries about making movies as they thought that this would spoil the "movie magic" for the viewer and for this reason did not want to reveal background details and information. They quickly discovered, however, that the opposite was true, and viewers showed a high level of interest in seeing how and where the movies they watched had been made. This level of interest can be judged by the popularity of Special Features on DVD releases that show how and where a particular movie was made and by high attendance at tourist-oriented movie studio tours. Similar interest is shown in the popularity of movie websites, such as the Internet Movie Database (IMDb), which lists detailed background information for almost every motion picture ever made.

Many moviegoers are curious about the part of America, primarily the Western states, that form the backdrop to Western films. This book will help fill in some of the details as it describes a popular history of filming Western movies on location. The intent is to relate the development of Western location filming from its origins in filming on the East Coast in the early 1900s, through the glory days of location work in Utah, Arizona, and California in the 1940s and 1950s, to the trend towards filming Westerns in Mexico, Spain, and other parts of the world in the 1960s and afterward.

Before describing further what this book is about, I am going to start with a couple of comments on what it is not. First, this is not a book on criticism of Western film. I am not a film critic and that is not the purpose of this book. This is also not my area of expertise. Analysis and criticism of film is a highly subjective field and critics vary widely in their opinions.

It is also not my ambition to analyze movies and theorize what the director might have been thinking when he was filming. For the reader seeking critical commentary on Western movies, there are many excellent books that cover the entire genre as well as specific films.[2]

This book is not an attempt to analyze specific Western movies, the genre, or filmmakers' intent. Instead, my purpose is to present a history of outdoor location filming in Western movies. Though this might seem on the surface like an obvious, simple, and not-particularly-interesting specialized aspect of the Western genre, it is actually fundamental to what has been seen on the screen in countless Western movies and is what has formed most people's perception of "the West." This book will look at the places where our screen heroes really rode and how they relate to the myth of the West of the silver screen.

Interested movie buffs can find specific locations associated with a particular film and particular films that were filmed at specific locations at Internet sites such as IMDb or in encyclopedic reference volumes such as *The First Fifty Years of Sound Western Movie Locations (1929–1979)* by Kenny Stier or *A Century of Western Movie Locations* by Carlo Gaberscek. What I have tried to achieve, by contrast, is not a detailed listing of movie locations or the films made there, but a more comprehensive overall view of the history of the location filming of Westerns while using specific films as examples. Remember also that most movies are filmed at many locations, some of them often hundreds of miles apart, so references made to locations for specific films in this book are not necessarily inclusive of all the places they were shot.

The very first Westerns were filmed in the East, in New Jersey and New York. This presented movie audiences with a vision of the West that consisted of lush forests and placid lakes. Contrast this, however, with the image from 60 years later of the West of the Italian- and Spanish-made Westerns as a stark, barren desert with bleak, sandy arroyos and a distinct lack of water. How and why did our perception of the "reality" of the appearance of the West of the movies change so dramatically? And why were both of these perceptions seen as valid by audiences of their times? This, then, is the subject of this book: How our vision of the West was changed over the years by choices made by directors and producers of the locations chosen to film their movies and how and why these choices developed the vision of the West that audiences hold today.

In describing what happened over the years, I do not intend to rehash the plots of specific movies or specific movie history, but seek rather to focus on and relate the significance of location and scenery to popular cultural perceptions of "the West" gained from Western movies.

Though this book is not intended to be a review of specific Westerns, a selection of movies will be used to illustrate various points in the text. Many will be from those made from about 1940 to 1970, because that period contains an immense amount of material. For the most part these will be the major or popular films that the reader is most likely to have seen, either in the theater, on television (such as the Western Channel, Grit TV, Heroes and Icons, Encore, Turner Classic Movies [TCM], Turner Network Television [TNT], and others), via streaming, or on VHS tape, DVD or Blu-ray disc, and are the ones that are most remembered. Most of them are used as examples because of their ready availability for viewing, but some are mentioned because of specific points of interest. Most are considered to be classics of the genre.

Although this book is not, strictly speaking, intended to be a history of film, the story of how moviegoers came to perceive the lonely bleak landscapes of the southwestern American deserts as "the West" is reflected in the history of the film industry, and the filmmakers' choices and eventual evolution of the use of certain locations for filming. Thus, the history of location filming is unavoidably intertwined with the history of the development of Western movies and of the motion picture industry, and the two will be presented together. The choice of outdoor locations was often forced on directors and producers by factors beyond their immediate control. Thus, by necessity, this book will be a history of film to the extent of describing how conditions prevailing in the studios and the motion picture industry at the time affected the choice of locations used, and thus directly affected the audiences' perception of what constituted the "Real West."

As we will see, this image changed with time, leading to today's perceptions of the "Real West." So the text will generally follow how the history of the motion picture industry evolved as related to the choice of locations used and how changes in the film industry and studios were, and still are, linked to the choices of various locations around the country, and eventually the world, used for Western films. This format will hopefully place into perspective what has been portrayed on the silver screen as "the West."

Because important developments in the motion picture industry and changes in Western location filming occurred roughly every 10 years, individual chapters have been divided into decades. This timeline will not be exact and certain subjects will necessarily overlap into and through several chapters and over many years, but this grouping will serve to roughly categorize the advances in the motion picture industry and location filming.

This history of location filming of Westerns will follow a journey across the country from New Jersey, to the Midwest, then to locations on the West Coast and California, and finally to Spain and Mexico. Along the way, movie-makers also filmed at many scenic locations around the West and Southwest. For example, Monument

Valley in Utah was a favorite location used for filming many of the Westerns of director John Ford.

Though Western movies have been filmed in almost every state of the Union, for most people the iconic vision of the West remains the magnificent desert scenery of the Southwest states of Arizona, Utah, New Mexico, and Southern California. Moviegoers have always been awed by the splendor of this type of scenery in Western movies, and their perception of "the West" has been strongly influenced by how these locations were used for filming Westerns. Many locations, such as Golden Gate Mountain and the adobe buildings of Old Tucson Studios in Arizona or the Alabama Hills with the backdrop of the Sierra Nevada mountains near Lone Pine, California, are easily recognized by fans of Western movies. Whether a movie is set in the Plains, the Mountains, or the desert country of the Southwest, the raw background scenery of the Western has awed and inspired its audiences. Monument Valley alone receives a large number of European visitors because to them this valley is their image of the American West.

Each chapter starts with one of a series of 10 photographs under the general heading "Iconic Images of the Movie West," which shows the most notable locations that appear in Westerns. These images show the vastness of the Western landscape as well as the diversity, from lush woodlands to mountains and deserts, of what has been considered to be the West of the movies. Many readers will know movies in which these locations have appeared and how they relate to the iconic images of the movie West seen by film audiences.

All this having been said, I have to confess that I am a fan of Westerns and have always been fascinated with the mythic aspects of the movie West and its scenery. When I was young I was brought up by my grandfather on Western movies, often a double-feature twice a week. When I grew older, I wanted to find and enjoy the West that I had seen portrayed in the movies. After I reached adulthood and traveled the real American West as a history writer and vacationed in it with my family, I never could quite find what I had seen on the silver screen. Though many of the locations I saw in movies as a boy were indeed real places in the West, the ambience of the movie West always seemed to be elusive. Where was the "real" West that I saw on the screen? Eventually I came to fully understand the myth behind the reality of the Old West. As cowboy film star Tom Mix aptly put it in 1938, "The Old West is not a certain place in a certain time, it's a state of mind. It's whatever you want it to be."[3]

In two of my other books, I have explored the background and people who created the mythic West of the movies, along with its cowboy hero and his lurid tales from western dime novels and pulp magazines. This present book will explore the myth of the place that was "the West" of the movies. Though elusive, the magnificent open spaces of the West used for locations to film the old Westerns were real places that formed the background to the plots that conveyed the Western state of mind.

So let us return now to the days of the dimly-lit movie palaces of the double feature, along with its accompanying cartoon and newsreels. As the lights of the theater slowly fade down, the great red velvet curtains sweep aside to reveal the silver screen, the music comes up, and the hero rides into town, ready to deal out justice to the bad guys.

Somewhere on location in "the West."

CHAPTER ONE

Pre–1900
Romanticizing the Landscape

Western films have always been a favorite of the movie industry and of its audiences. The popularity of the Western has risen and fallen over the decades since the first faltering images appeared in darkened nickelodeons around the turn of the 20th century, but the genre has always maintained a strong relationship with American culture. Nachbar, writing in 1974 in *Focus on the Western*, commented, "Risking the charge of overstatement, Westerns, especially Western movies, are thus far the single most important American story form of the twentieth century."[1]

The Western is a national myth, a global icon, and a fundamental building block of American identity. One revealing fact is that more than 4,000 Western movies were made during the 75 years between 1910 and 1985.[2] Another telling statistic is that about 25 percent of all the films produced by Hollywood from 1910 through the end of the 1950s were Westerns.[3]

Arguably the Western film is the most potent myth in America. It is a way in which America views its history and depicts an idealized representation of how we view ourselves. Perhaps, as suggested by Raymond White in *Shooting Stars*, that is because "the Western film hero's innocence and simple codes of justice provided Americans with a link to their past."[4] Some of the power of this myth may also be due to the potency of nostalgia, which is fueled by a desire to remember that things in "the good old days," in another time and another place, were somehow better. However, as humorist Will Rogers succinctly put it, "things ain't like they used to be—and they probably never were."

The myth of the West as retold in Western movies is mostly standard melodrama. It typically tells the tale of a dramatic triangle consisting of a hero, a heroine (often the victim of something), and her persecutor, the villain. This formulaic story is set against authentic backgrounds in the open spaces of the West, which consist of mountains, pine forests, plains, and sunbaked deserts. The plot is highlighted by action-packed chases and fights between the hero and the villain, played out against these scenic outdoor backgrounds.

From its earliest representations, the public image of the Western landscape that formed the background to these plots was influenced by artists, such as the romanticized images of painter Albert Bierstadt and others, by early photographs of the West, and later by written details in dime novels and pulp Westerns, such as Zane Grey's vivid descriptions of the blue, cloudless skies and red sandstone buttes of Utah.[5]

8   The Landscapes of Western Movies

Iconic Images of the Movie West #1: Abiquiu, New Mexico. **Vast open landscapes, brilliant blue skies, and puffy white clouds characterize movie images of the Southwest. These are the cliffs, canyons, and grassy flats around Abiquiu, used for** *Silverado* **(1985),** *City Slickers* **(1991),** *Wyatt Earp* **(1994),** *3:10 to Yuma* **(2007),** *Cowboys and Aliens* **(2011),** *The Magnificent Seven* **(2016), and others.**

From the beginning of Western cinema, the plot has been complemented by these landscapes in the background, the spectacular outdoor settings where Westerns were filmed.

Reality Versus Myth

The Western has become part of the national drama of winning the West from the wilderness. However, this concept applied not necessarily to the geographical western United States, but to "the West," which, as author John Hamilton aptly pointed out, is "a timeless never-never land of great expectations and grand illusions."[6]

To understand why Western film presented such a powerful cultural image, and its magnificent scenery has awed audiences for decades, it is important to first understand why the landscapes of the West held such an interest for the general public and how the West became such a strong symbol in our national consciousness.[7]

The Homestead Act of 1862 allowed every American adult to claim 160 acres of land in the public domain in the West, if the settler cultivated and made improvements on the property for five years. Boosted by this dream of available land for everyone, the boom in westward expansion across the country towards the Pacific Ocean started to mushroom at the end of the American Civil War in 1865, and lasted until about 1890. Historians vary in their assessment of the supposed closing of the West, but most feel that the end of the expansion of the Western frontier occurred in 1890, either with the end of the Indian Wars between the U.S. Army and the Sioux Indians at the battle of Wounded Knee in South Dakota, or when historian Frederick Jackson Turner and the U.S. Census Bureau stated that the American Frontier was gone.

Surprisingly, then, the real era of the classic Old West depicted in movies lasted for only about 25 years. Even though some Western movies have portrayed the earlier times of the fur trappers on the frontier, and some have been set as late as World War I and more modern times, most Westerns are even more narrow in scope and concentrate on the classic period of the cowboy era from about 1870 to 1875.

The Western story is typically set at a point in history where savagery and lawlessness are in decline as the frontier is being settled, but before the advancing wave of law and order has brought civilization to the West. This concept is expanded in the movies to a permanent state of the defenders of the law standing up against lawlessness and savagery. The scenic backdrop to these conflicts between lawlessness and social order is the grandeur of the Western landscape. The specific location where the story takes place, or is filmed in reality, is usually not identified.

Romantic Images of the Landscape

The myth of the landscape of the Old West that forms the background to Western films was created initially by paintings, literature, photographs, and then probably most importantly by Westerns themselves. The lurid dime novels, the spectacle of the Wild West shows, the vivid paintings of artists such as Frederic Remington and Charles Russell, popular books such as *The Virginian* (1902) by Owen Wister, and the Western pulp magazines of the 1920s, 1930s, and 1940s were major catalysts that helped to popularize and mythologize the landscape of the American West.[8]

The myth was boosted by paintings made during the popularity of the Romantic Movement. Romanticism originated in Europe in the early 1800s in art, literature, music, and intellectual thinking, as a departure from the Classical style that had previously been present in art and literature. Romanticism was perceived as a way to portray an imaginative view of the natural world while stressing its primitive aspects. Paintings of the West were characterized by huge landscapes of spectacular scenery. They emphasized emotion in their glorification of nature, and expressed the feelings of the artist as he let his imagination run free.

Some critics have claimed that these romanticized views of the West were a distortion of reality that created a false sense of history. To an extent this is true; however, it is also a misunderstanding of what the Romantic artists were trying to portray. Photographs and paintings are created by artists to communicate feelings that they wish to evoke in the viewer. The romantic paintings of Western scenery that became popular during the late 1800s were intended to interpret the artist's vision and point of view, based on how the particular artist wanted to portray them, rather than to simply document reality. These were artistic viewpoints of romantic scenes that provided a vision of the past, even though it was an idealized past that never was. The goal was not necessarily to portray the West as it really was, but to use the landscape as one component of a story and make it part of an enduring myth. Even today, artists often take this same approach and deliberately omit what they consider to be extraneous undesired features of the landscape, such as roads, power poles, and houses, in favor of a more pristine view.

Romanticism, in general, is still tightly woven into the culture of our society and particularly plays a significant role in the selective view with which we view nationalism and patriotism. The "Western" movie became one of the greatest of these myth-makers. It modernized the myth of the knight-errant and good-conquering-evil in a form of American morality play. The knight figure was mutated into a heroic movie cowboy who did not work with cows (even though he did in the real West), and who went around righting wrongs and rescuing damsels-in-distress.

The West in Art

Early interest in the West was stimulated by painters who created a romanticized and idealized version of the Western landscape. Before black-and-white photography caught the public's attention around the mid–1800s, the only way that Easterners who might not be able travel to the real West could "see" the Western landscape was through the eyes of these artists. Painters and their images soon turned the American view of the West into a mythological place, even before filmmakers added to it with their own images.

In the 1860s and 1870s, artists such as Albert Bierstadt and Thomas Moran created a mythic Western landscape with a series of huge romanticized inspirational paintings in the style of Thomas Cole and Frederick Church, and the earlier Hudson River School of painting in the East. Painters created magnificent views of the Rocky Mountains and Sierra Nevada scenery on giant canvases that idealized the full majesty of these mighty mountains. These artists depicted vast, sweeping Western landscapes with atmospheric effects, such as majestic gatherings of storm clouds with brilliant shafts of sunlight piercing the center of the composition. They created huge scenes of pastoral lakes, soaring waterfalls, and majestic, snow-capped peaks, portraying the magnificence of the mountains as evidence of their creation by a Supreme Being.

Painter Albert Bierstadt was a driving force in what was called the California School of Art, concentrating on the magnificence of the scenery of the West and Far West. Bierstadt painted stylized representations of idyllic Eden-like landscapes, fully reflecting the romanticism of the mid–1800s that was sweeping paintings and literature at the time. Examples of his magnificent landscapes were *Thunderstorm in the Rocky Mountains* (1859), *The Rocky Mountains—Lander's Peak* (1863), *A Storm in the Rockies—Mt. Rosalie* (1866), *Sunset in Yosemite Valley* (1868), *Yellowstone Falls* (1881), and *Geysers in Yellowstone* (1881). Many of these painting were huge. The canvas for *The Rocky Mountains* measured six feet high by 10 feet long. Another important artist in the California School was Thomas Hill, who produced stirring expansive landscapes, such as *Yosemite Valley from Below Sentinel Dome, as Seen from Artist's Point* (1876).

One of Thomas Moran's best-known paintings was titled *The Grand Canyon of the Yellowstone* (1872), an immense 7-foot-by-12-foot oil painting of the Lower Falls in Yellowstone National Park from Artist Point. The view shows the falls surrounded by steep and jagged walls, cascading 300 feet into the lower canyon, with the base of the falls enveloped in mist. Like other awe-inspiring Romantic paintings of the time, this was not one view from one specific location, but was a composite image that combined the most picturesque elements of the scenery into one composition. Paintings such as this attracted great interest among the public and were partially responsible for promoting Yellowstone and other parts of the West as tourist attractions where people could enjoy the unspoiled wildness of nature for themselves. Even today, the Lower Falls still inspires artists to produce enormous landscapes, such as Jim Wilcox's *Canyon Frosting* (2001) and Stephen Hannock's *Flooded Cascade, Yellowstone Dawn* (2011).

These paintings of the scenery of the Rocky Mountains and the Sierra Nevada mountains of California, created from the vision and imagination of Bierstadt, Moran, and others, became the dominant contemporary image of the West and thus shaped America's attitude towards Western scenery. Bierstadt's vision of the ideal landscape was linked with Manifest Destiny and the surge of westward expansion that was taking place in the nation at the time.[9]

Bierstadt and Moran tried to capture an ideal interpretation of the places they were painting, and did not intend to document the reality of the scenery in photographic detail or exactness. In Bierstadt's paintings of Yosemite, particularly *Sunset in Yosemite Valley* (1868), he rearranged some of the prominent features of the valley, such as Half-Dome, Bridal Veil Falls, and El Capitan, to conform to his vision of an ideal image. Other paintings were similarly pieced together from multiple views. In Thomas Moran's gigantic *The Mountain of the Holy Cross* (1890) the artist rearranged some of the elements of the foreground and added an almost perfect kneeling angel of snow on the side of the peak. This type of modification of reality was not unusual at the time and was an accepted practice among painters. Artists also often rearranged the relative sizes of various features of the landscape and their perspectives, and altered their natural colors, to meet the painter's artistic vision. In this way their subjects became transformed into mythical landscapes.

In a similar way, idealized—almost sentimental—images of the West were sketched and painted in enhanced dramatic ways by artists Charles Russell and Frederic Remington. Both Remington and Russell helped to create the elements of the Western myth as they emphasized galloping horses, blazing six-guns, and dramatic Indian encounters. These artists and others were among the premier myth-makers of the West, creating images of what they felt the West should have been, instead of what it really was. Frederic Remington, in particular, was fascinated by the conflict between the white settlers and American Indians, and he sketched and painted these fierce men under equally fierce conditions to create his vision of the Western experience. Cavalry scenes were one of Remington's favorite subjects and out of this came such paintings as *Cavalry Charge on the Southern Plains, Forsythe's Fight on the Republican River, Through the Smoke Sprang the Daring Young Soldier, A Dash for the Timber*, and *Last Cavalier*.

Remington, like other artists of the period, did not intend to be a reporter of the real West, but considered himself an image-maker who wanted to pre-

Romanticized paintings such as this one, *Mountain of the Holy Cross* by Thomas Moran, from 1890, helped to create a high degree of interest in the public in the spectacular landscapes of the West in the mid- to late-1800s. Like other artists of the time, Moran took artistic liberties with the scenery, rearranging the geographical features of the creek in the foreground to place it in front of the peak, a view not found in reality. Note also the perfect kneeling angel he created with snow to the right of the perfect cross, which is not quite so perfect on the real mountain (Library of Congress).

sent drama more than authenticity. Remington did not record facts, but depicted a carefully-constructed imaginary image of the West of action, tragedy, and violence.

After 1899 Remington turned more frequently to cowboy subjects in paintings such as *The Fall of the Cowboy* and *The Stampede*, noting at one time that "cowboys are cash."[10] His cowboys were often portrayed in clothing that real cowboys didn't wear, as can be seen by comparing his paintings with photographs of contemporary cowboys. But his success told him what people wanted to see, so he continued to paint his romantic action heroes in romantic settings of Western landscapes.

Frederic Remington and Charles Russell were among the premier mythmakers of the West as they created images of what they thought the West should have been. Remington created 2,750 paintings and drawings that portrayed the West as a world of melodrama and violence. Film director John Ford later said that he studied Remington's paintings and tried to reproduce the artist's images and use of color in his films. To evoke this feel when he was filming *She Wore a Yellow Ribbon* (1949), Ford asked cinematographer Winton Hoch to also study Remington's paintings.

Dime Novels and Pulp Literature

The years that preceded Western films were filled with books about the West as well as dime novels and other Western pulp literature. Much of the public's love affair with the West started with the publication of lurid tales in sensationalist Western pulp literature that started to appear in the mid–1800s. The invention of the steam-powered rotary press stimulated the mass production of printed books at very economical prices, which allowed these lurid fictional accounts of the mythic Wild West to be published and sold for five cents or a dime, hence the name dime novels. These books, also called pulp novels and pulp magazines because of the cheap pulp paper they were printed on, churned out sensationalized accounts of life in the West. The fictionalized exploits of real-life characters, such as Buffalo Bill Cody, Wild Bill Hickok, and Kit Carson, or fictional ones, such as Deadwood Dick or Denver Dan, thrilled the reading public with sensationalized tales.

Buffalo Bill was first made famous in the pulp writings of Ned Buntline (real name Edward Carroll Zane Judson), a dime novelist who wrote over 400 novels and stories, many of them under pseudonyms. Buntline's first Cody story was *Buffalo Bill, The King of Border Men*, which appeared in serial form in Smith & Street's *New York Weekly* between December 23, 1869, and March 10, 1870. Buntline followed this with 14 more lurid dime novels about Buffalo Bill, then was surpassed by writers such as Prentiss Ingraham, who wrote over 120 lurid stories about the plainsman and contributed the script of a stage play about Cody. These dime novels helped to establish Cody's mythic show-business persona and expanded both his personal legend and that of the Wild West.

Dime novels, such as those of Buntline and other prolific authors with vivid imaginations, sold hundreds of thousands of copies, many read by youngsters and adults in the big cities of the East who longed for a life on the open range of the romanticized West. The Western pulp story was the recounting of bravery, chivalry, romance, and excitement, with cover art that evoked the myths of the Wild West. During the 1880s and 1890s even the high-quality popular magazines for middle- and upper -class readers, such as *Harper's*, *Scribner's*, *Atlantic*, and *The Century Magazine*, published increasing amounts of Western fiction and accounts from travelers to the West. *Collier's* and *The Saturday Evening Post* started to include adventure tales of the West among their other dramatic stories.

One of the influential Western writers was future president Theodore Roosevelt, who published a series of articles on life in the West based on his experiences as a rancher and sportsman. They were first published in *The Century Magazine* and later collected as *Ranch Life and the Hunting Trail* (1899), illustrated by his friend, artist Frederic Remington. Roosevelt was so enthusiastic in writing about the West that his descriptions helped to create the mythology. He presented the cowboy as a heroic figure struggling with the wildness of the West, not as the common laborer that he really was.

Another influential book about the West was Owen Wister's novel *The Virginian*, first published in 1902. Wister brought the cowboy into new prominence in what is generally considered to be the first serious Western novel, though it also contained plenty of melodramatic riding, shooting, and fighting. Wister blended the new cowboy hero with Wyoming's past and added adventure, love, action, and good versus bad. Wister created a West that was a land of freedom, honesty, and integrity, where the wicked received their appropriate punishment.

Another highly influential Western novelist was Zane Grey. Grey was one of the most successful of all Western authors, and was one of the most popular Western writers of all time. Grey wrote from 1912 until his death in 1939, publishing over 90 books, most of them about the West, recounting the simple virtues of Western life. Zane Grey specialized in the larger-than-life hero, the innocent heroine, the chase, the duel, and the triumph of good over evil in melodramatic novels that were full of atmosphere. Grey's most popular novel, *Rider of the Purple Sage* (1912), sold over a million copies and helped to define the Western genre for later authors.

Zane Grey's books also influenced the reading public's perception of the Western landscape. A shift in public taste occurred at the end of the 19th century in which the mountains of the literary West were replaced by the deserts and canyons of Utah that were lavishly described in Grey's books. Grey's novels also stimulated tourists to visit the West to see the places he so vividly portrayed in his novels. Though there were certainly many others, Wister, Roosevelt, and Grey were among the prime creators of the myth of the West and the Western landscape.

Western Stage Melodramas

In the late 1800s stage plays set in the West preceded similar movie plots and glorified the Western way of life. One of the first promoters was Ned Buntline, who saw an opportunity for profit by bringing the real Buffalo Bill Cody to the public by way of the stage, after the success of his first dime novel about Buffalo Bill.

Buntline wrote a play based on his pulp novel *Buffalo Bill's Last Victory*. He reportedly churned out the script in four hours and called the result *The Scouts of the Prairie; or, Red Deviltry as It Is*. The play was not informative, factual, or educational, but was a fanciful, imaginative interpretation of the mythology of the West. It contained all the features associated with later Western novels, movies, and television, such as brave heroes fighting overwhelming odds, skill with guns, fighting off the villains (in this case Indians), and saving the beautiful heroine. The play was more music-hall entertainment than legitimate theater. The audiences loved it.

The principals of this melodrama played themselves, supported by a group of "Indians" recruited from locals in Chicago. The play was somewhat loose and amateurish, because Cody and the other were not experienced actors, and was marred by cheap theatrics, such as the use of pieces of red flannel for scalps. The play opened in Chicago on December 17, 1872, then went on to St. Louis, Rochester, Buffalo, Boston, and the Midwest. In spite of wooden acting and an improbable plot, the drama was a rousing success and played to packed crowds. Cody and his buckskin-clad fellow actors toured for the next 10 years in various other interchangeable shows based on Indian lore and rescuing settlers from Indian attacks.

The Wild West Show Spectacles

Another major contributor to the myth of the American West was the Wild West show, which paved the way for Western movies, and turned the cowboy into a leading male hero. Many of the scenes from these shows were duplicated in early Western films.

Wild West shows started in June of 1843 when showman P.T. Barnum purchased 15 buffalo calves to stage a "Grand Buffalo Hunt" and display of Western roping skills at a racetrack in Hoboken, New Jersey. The terrified calves broke out of the arena and promptly vanished into a nearby swamp, prematurely ending the show.

Other promoters presented Western shows over the succeeding decades, but none was particularly successful until the extravaganzas of William F. "Buffalo Bill" Cody in the late 1800s. Buffalo Bill's entry into the Wild West show business began in a minor way in 1882 when he organized a Fourth of July celebration named the "Old Glory Blowout" in North Platte, Nebraska. The show included displays of cowboy skills in which cowboys competed for prizes in marksmanship, riding, roping, horse racing, and bronco busting. The North Platte celebration was such a success that Cody teamed with W.F. "Doc" Carver to put together the *Hon. W.F. Cody and Dr. W.F. Carver's Rocky Mountain and Prairie Exhibition*, which opened on May 19, 1883, in Omaha.

Cody's show business career eventually developed into Buffalo Bill's *Wild West*, the largest and most popular of the Wild West shows. The *Wild West*, publicized as "America's National Entertainment," was Cody's primary myth-making enterprise. Different acts and scenes were presented as typical frontier history. The presence of real cowboys, horses, buffalo, Indians, stagecoaches, and shooting brought gripping entertainment to audiences for thousands of performances. But it blurred the lines between reality and entertainment, history and myth. Cody did not like his spectacle to be called a Wild West "show," as he felt that it represented real history rather than being a show, so it was always called simply the *Wild West*.

The *Wild West* continued to be a successful popular entertainment for more than

30 years and was a major influence on the public perception of the real American frontier West. Though Buffalo Bill wanted everything in the show to be authentic, he only featured the elements of the West that contained action, adventure, and spectacle. Audiences believed that they were being educated as well as entertained and perceived the show to be real history. Thus Cody's entire presentation became part of the powerful myth of the West.

Before the *Wild West*, Americans didn't know much about cowboys or really care about them. Though real cowboys were only common laborers who happened to work with cattle, Cody created a clean-cut image for the cowboy and made him glamorous. Cody's version of the truth was that cowboys worked and played hard, and helped to expand and settle the West, which in reality they didn't. The show's cowboys were represented as being as rough and tough as they had to be on the frontier, but underneath they were gentlemen from a cultured society. These cowboy performers dressed in show-business costumes, hats, and chaps that real cowboys never wore.[11]

More than any other person, Buffalo Bill portrayed the West in mythical terms, expanded the legend of the frontier and Western heroism, and turned the cowboy into a romanticized national hero. His show offered fast-paced entertainment full of animals, smoke, dust, and shooting, played in front of panoramic painted backdrops of the West, with rousing visual action, stirring spectacle, and fights between cowboys and Indians on horseback. Cody took a few elements of the West, such as Indians, buffalo hunts, stagecoaches, and cowboy action, and created an illusion that audiences thought was the reality of the West. This made the public believe that life in the West was a series of death-defying adventures, where cowboys continually rode bucking horses, roped steers, and rescued the Deadwood Stage from Indians.

The show's publicity men shaped Buffalo Bill's *Wild West* around what experience had taught them that the public wanted. Audiences were presented with cheap and convenient entertainment, and they loved the sensory stimulation of the sound, smell, and feel of galloping horses and pounding hoof-beats, with gunshots echoing around the arena. Riders in the show never walked but always galloped, creating a fast tempo to the entire experience.

The public was eager for heroes and by the time Buffalo Bill created the *Wild West*, his reputation as genuine Western hero was well-established. Cody combined elements from stage plays, circuses, and rodeo to create a historical pageant that blurred the lines between entertainment and education, fact and myth, history and melodrama. The show was a sensation and was extremely successful from 1883 to 1916, and helped to create an increased interest in the American West during the last two decades of the 19th century. As a result, at the turn of the 20th century, millions of Americans and Europeans thought they remembered the real West because they had seen it in Buffalo Bill's spectacle.

Though most of Cody's performers had personally experienced the Old West and its lifestyle, Cody's interpretation of the West was drawn from dime novels and contemporary melodramatic journalism. These hazy recollections of national memory were supported by the contemporary combination of Western literature and art, and the popular culture of dime novels and sensationalist magazines. Though the show claimed historical authenticity, it used the theatrical conventions of showmanship and melodrama, including stirring music and colorful costumes. Audiences loved the simulated bloodshed, violence, conflict, and galloping horsemen that personified Cody's show. The Western theme of the program and the apparent uniqueness of frontier life in the nation's history appealed to the patriotism of the audience.

By this time, paintings, photographs, and magazine illustrations had made the scenic landscapes of the West familiar to most Americans, so audiences who attended the *Wild West* easily absorbed the images presented in the show. Other similar shows also promoted the myth of a glorious and romantic American frontier that had never really existed. Among these were *Buckskin Ben's Wild West and Dog and Pony Show, Cherokee Ed's Wild West, Diamond Bar Ranch Wild West, Tiger Bill's Wild West, Hulberg's Wild West and Congress of Nations of the World*, and *Texas Bud's Wild West*. These shows ran the gamut from large spectacles, such as Buffalo Bill's *Wild West*, to small shows that presented only a few broken-down horses and fewer performers.

More than any other showman, Buffalo Bill converted the West into mythical terms, extended the myth of the frontier and Western heroism, and portrayed the cowboy as a national hero. Author Paul Reddin succinctly summed the result up when he said, "The Wild West show reduced the western saga to a morality play in which Cody, along with scouts and cowboys, represented the forces of good and civilization and Indians and a few errant white road agents symbolized evil and barbarism."[12]

The Wild West shows started to lose their appeal in the early 1900s and declined in popularity from about 1905 to the end of the traveling shows in 1917. There were no major Wild West shows on the road by 1918, though an attempt was made to replace the concept with shows that featured cowboys backed by circus and vaudeville acts.

Much of the reason for the decline was the public's changing tastes in entertainment. The competing entertainment form of motion pictures that had arisen in the meantime was a novelty that could provide similar elements with convenient excitement for audiences without having to transport a huge show of horses, riders, and scenery all over the country. The Wild West shows had evolved to meet the demands of American audiences but, like other forms of entertainment, the public eventually started to lose interest and turn to something else.

The West in Photographs

At the same time, photographs of the West perpetuated and magnified the romantic image of the landscape. The visual impact of these photographic images was one of the most powerful tools that helped to create and perpetuate the romantic view of the Western scenery.

One of the early uses of photography was to bring images of places and landscapes to people who were unable to visit them in person. From the very beginning of photography, images of exotic landscapes were extremely popular. Photographs of colorful foreign lands, such as India and Africa, Egypt and its pyramids, and Palestine and Syria in the Middle East, were extremely popular.

At the same time, photography was used to document the natural resources of the American West during early government survey expeditions in the 1860s and 1870s. Photography was important for John Fremont's Western explorations, Ferdinand Hayden's surveys, and the surveys of Clarence King. In this way, the West's spectacular scenery, such as the Yosemite Valley in California and the Yellowstone area in Wyoming, was available for viewing at home by the average person in the East and, at the same time, photography helped to open the public's eyes to the wonders of the Western landscape. The unspoiled West with its fast-flowing rivers, deep canyons, and towering mountains could now be brought into the living room.

Photography was first used in Colorado, for example, in 1853 by the exploratory expedition of John Charles Fremont, which used photographs to document his journey across the continent. Photography was an additional important tool in the 1860s when railroad companies and government geological survey teams wanted to document the immensity of the region and promote the unknown Western terrain. Photographs helped the public to understand and enjoy John Wesley Powell's expedition down the Colorado River in 1871. Viewers were inspired by the enormous scale of the pristine wilderness of the West, with its strange rock formations, steaming geysers, and spectacular waterfalls, along with barren deserts and soaring mountains.

After these expeditions returned home, landscape photographers sold copies of their images to the public. The sales of scenic views was a large part of the early photographic business, before mass-printed postcards became available. These photographs, which showed the most spectacular features of the West, created high levels of interest in the untamed landscapes of the western frontier.

Another use for photography was for publicity and to document the rapidly-expanding railroad system, as photographers such as W.H. Jackson recorded dramatic images of the railroads forcing their way through the rugged mountain country of the West. The railroad was the symbol of westward expansion and the powerful forces of Manifest Destiny. The locomotive itself was a symbol of power, progress, and the country's growing industrialization.

The first permanent photographic image had been created several decades earlier on a small metal plate in 1826 by an experimenter in Paris named Joseph Nicéphore Niépce. It was a photograph of the courtyard of his house. The exposure time required to create the image was about eight hours, thus making the process lengthy and obviously only useful for a stationary subject. But it was a beginning.

Major advances in photography started to take place about 10 years later. In 1839 Louis Jacques Daguerre announced the daguerreotype, a fixed image that was created on a thin copper plate with a polished coating of silver that had been sensitized by iodine fumes. After exposure, the plates were "developed" with hot mercury vapor, then "fixed" with a wash of sodium thiosulfate (photographer's "hypo," still used for fixing negatives).

By now the exposure time required to successfully make photographs had been successively reduced, but was still relatively long, requiring from 20 to 45 minutes to create an image. By 1843 improvements in the sensitization process for the plates had reduced the exposure time to between five and 30 seconds, depending on the intensity of the light illuminating the subject.

The daguerreotype produced a photographic negative that was sharp, clear, and realistic-looking; however, because of the complexity of the process and the highly toxic chemicals involved, daguerreotypes were generally produced only by professional photographers. Another limitation of the daguerreotype was that the process created a single unique image, unlike later photographic negatives which could be used to subsequently produce multiple photographic prints. Multiple copies of a daguerreotype could only be made by re-photographing the original as many times as the number of copies desired.

This limitation could be avoided by using other processes. For example, in 1835, William Henry Fox Talbot in England had succeeded in creating a photographic image on cotton-fiber paper, which he called a calotype, though he did not perfect the process for another four years. The calotype, also referred to as the Talbotype after its inventor, allowed duplicate copies to be made by exposing the created image to another piece of sensitized material. However, the images of the calotype were not as sharp and clear as the daguerreotype due to the rough surface of the fibers in the paper. Also, the image was brown, rather than black and white.

In 1851 Frederick Scott Archer in England announced a method of coating glass plates with a wet collodion emulsion that was sensitive to light to create photographs with what was called the "wet plate" process. Collodion was a solution of cellulose nitrate (gun cotton or cordite used for making explosives) dissolved in 60 percent ether and 40 percent alcohol. The plate was then exposed in a camera and the image developed while the emulsion was still wet. The resulting image was a highly-detailed photographic negative.

Other photographic processes quickly appeared. In 1854 James Ambrose Cutting patented the ambrotype process. The ambrotype was a negative produced on glass. After the image was created, the reverse side of the glass was painted black or backed with a dark surface, such as black velvet, to create a positive image when viewed. Ambrotypes were generally not as clear as daguerreotypes, but were easier and cheaper to produce, though they were quite fragile. The ambrotype image was reversed from left to right by the camera, as were daguerrotypes.[13]

In 1856 Hamilton Smith in the United States patented the tintype process, in which a positive photographic image was formed directly on a thin sensitized plate of iron. By the 1860s tintypes were popular because an experienced photographer could produce one in about a minute. Because of their low cost, they were made to fill the need for cheap photographs, typically for portraits. One disadvantage was that the image was also reversed from left to right.[14]

Though the wet plate process was a major step forward in photography and allowed photographers to take superb photographs of Western landscapes, the process was still cumbersome and delicate, and required practice and experience. It was thus rarely the hobby of amateurs and was almost wholly the work of professionals.

The glass plate was sensitive to light only as long as the chemical coating remained damp. Once the plate had dried, it could not be used. The glass plate had to therefore be prepared just before use and had to be exposed within about 20 to 40 minutes after coating it with the light-sensitive material. Exposure times were anywhere from one to 60 seconds, depending on the brightness of the light illuminating the scene being photographed.

The plate also had to be developed very soon after it was exposed to light. Thus the photographer had to travel with a portable darkroom tent or light-proof wagon for preparation of the plate and for developing it on-site right after it was exposed. Pioneering photographers of the West often pitched a small darkroom tent on a mountain top, prepared a wet plate, exposed it in the camera, then developed it on the spot. Photographers on Western surveys also had to haul along a large number of glass plates in a wagon or on the back of a mule during long journeys over difficult, unexplored terrain.

Many professional landscape photographers used an 11" × 14" camera (the dimensions denote the size of the glass plate). A large size of camera was often used to capture the grandeur of open landscapes because suitable methods of making enlarged prints from negatives had not yet been perfected. The enlargements that were available were poor in quality due to the lack of high-quality lenses. Thus the size of the final print was generally determined by the size of the negative used to make it. Positive prints were made by what was called the contact process, where the negative was placed in contact with light-sensitive paper and the combination exposed to the sun. This resulted in excellent detail and resolution in the final print.

Though mastering the wet plate process was difficult and cumbersome, the process resulted in clear, sharp images and took less time to produce than the daguerrotype. The wet plate process was used almost exclusively in photography for the next 30 years because of its ability to produce sharp detail and an excellent range of tones. As a result of the complexity of the process, however, creating photographs was mostly limited until around 1880 to professional photographers, scientists, and wealthy amateurs who had spare time, could afford the equipment, and could set up a darkroom.

Relatively long exposure times meant that subjects had to remain still. Running horses or buffalo, for example, could not be suitably photographed. The process was therefore ideal for landscapes. Outdoor scenes and architectural photographs were extremely popular and good subjects for the long exposure times required, because they did not move.

The gradually increasing ease of use of photography increased the desire of the public to capture the grandeur of the Western landscapes for themselves. Photographs of Western scenery were not only used for scientific documentation by photographers who accompanied survey expeditions, but also by photographers who wanted to capture the sense of wonder at the grandeur of the wilderness. Similarly, in Europe, taking photographs of alpine landscapes became all the rage.

One of the noted photographers of the West was William Henry Jackson, who documented the Rocky Mountain landscape from 1870 to 1878 as part of Ferdinand Hayden's expeditions. Jackson produced some of the finest photographs of the West, many of them later reproduced by the Detroit Photographic Company. Jackson made negatives in black and white, but advances in printing later allowed the images to be printed in color.[15]

Towards the end of the 1800s, an increasing interest in the landscape of the West created a large demand for Jackson's scenic photographs. In 1902 Detroit Photographic Company sold over seven million scenic photographs, from postcard size to large panoramas. In 1904, Fred Harvey, who managed the restaurant concession on the Santa Fe railroad line, commissioned the Detroit Photographic Company to produce scenic postcards of the West for sale in his restaurants and hotels.[16]

Photographic equipment was heavy and bulky, and Jackson was accompanied by two pack mules to carry all his supplies and camera equipment. On one expedition, Jackson had with him a 5" × 8" camera, an 11" × 14" camera, a stereoscopic camera, and two camera tripods. One of the cameras he used on the Hayden survey of 1875 used a glass plate that was 20" × 24". One mule was burdened down by the huge camera and another was required to carry all the glass plates for it. The rest of his outfit consisted of a darkroom tent, bottles of chemicals for preparing and developing the glass plates, various developing trays, and 400 glass plates. Among the supplies were several rubber bags filled with water, in case none was available at the photographic location.

For making photographs in the mountains, Jackson used a tent that was just big enough for him to crawl into to prepare his plates and then develop them. Jackson's typical time to make a negative was 30 minutes, but he said he could sometimes accomplish the task in 15 minutes. The most negatives that Jackson shot in one day was 32, but he said he was able to do that only because he was in an easy shooting location.[17]

Dry Plate Photography

In 1871 a major advance in photography was made by Richard Leach Maddox, a British physician, who developed a negative film material that used a thin layer of gelatin to bind a light-sensitive emulsion to a glass plate. These new "dry plates" could be prepared ahead of time and could be stored for long periods before they were exposed to light. A further advantage was that they did not have to be developed immediately after exposure. Now that plates could be used anywhere without further preparation and then developed after exposure at the photographer's convenience, photographers no longer needed to take a portable darkroom into the field with them. This advance resulted in a turning point in the ease of photography, which became even more popular when Albert Levy mass-manufactured the first ready-made gelatin dry plate negatives in 1880. The dry plate process made photography easy and practical for amateur photographers.

Several other developments contributed to the exploding growth and popularity of landscape photography. One was when inventor George Eastman founded the Eastman Dry Plate Company in Rochester, New York, to manufacture dry plates. The company was very successful and eventually evolved into Eastman Kodak Company, the world's leading manufacturer of film and photographic supplies.

In 1880 Eastman further developed the dry plate process, resulting in negative film in rolls that used a flexible celluloid base, instead of a rigid glass plate. Cellulose acetate was used as a support base for the film.[18] These two advances, the dry plate process and flexible roll film, were combined to revolutionize photography and eventually led to motion pictures.

In 1888, Eastman patented and started selling the Kodak camera, a small, relatively inexpensive, hand-held camera that used the new flexible roll film. Eastman said that the name Kodak was short, easy to remember, and started with the first letter of his mother's maiden name. Supposedly the name "Kodak" had no meaning and was just a catchy name, but the name is also anecdotally said to have come from the sound that the camera made when the shutter opened and closed to expose the film.

The camera sold for $25 which, put in perspective, was about what a good carpenter earned in a week. The first Kodak cameras had one shutter speed, a fixed focus, and a fixed aperture. The quality of the lens was so poor at the corners that photographic prints were masked into a round shape to eliminate the bad corners.[19] Basically there was no flexibility in exposure, but the camera was easy and fast to use. The camera came from the factory loaded with enough film to produce a hundred photographs. When all were exposed, the user sent the camera back to the factory, along with $10. The processed photographs, along with the camera reloaded with film, were returned to the owner.

The popularity and availability of personal photography increased even more when Eastman's company started selling the Brownie camera in 1900. The Brownie was an extremely popular inexpensive camera. Intended to introduce children to photography, it had a simple, box-like construction and sold for only $1. The Brownie camera continued in production until the 1960s.

The development of roll film and the introduction of inexpensive cameras for home use, like this one from Kodak, eliminated the need for the complicated wet-plate process and thus helped to fuel the craze for landscape photography among amateur shutter-bugs. First introduced in 1900, the Brownie was in production until the 1960s. This model is a Kodak Brownie Junior model Six-20 that uses 620 roll film; the cost of this simple camera in the late 1930s was less than $2.

Eastman's goal was to bring photography to the average man so that everyone could take photographs of whatever was important to them. As a result, photography became easier and more affordable for the average person. Amateur photography became very popular and numerous clubs sprang up to pursue the hobby. For the majority of amateur photographers in the West, the primary subject was landscapes and photographs of the mountains. Camera clubs and groups made outings on trains, hoping to outdo each other with spectacular landscape photographs. An increased use of photography in scenic locations was used to stimulate tourism by stimulating the desire to visit them.

Stereograph Images

The stereoscope and stereograph formed one of the most popular forms of visual entertainment in the home in the late 1800s. The stereoscope was a simple viewing

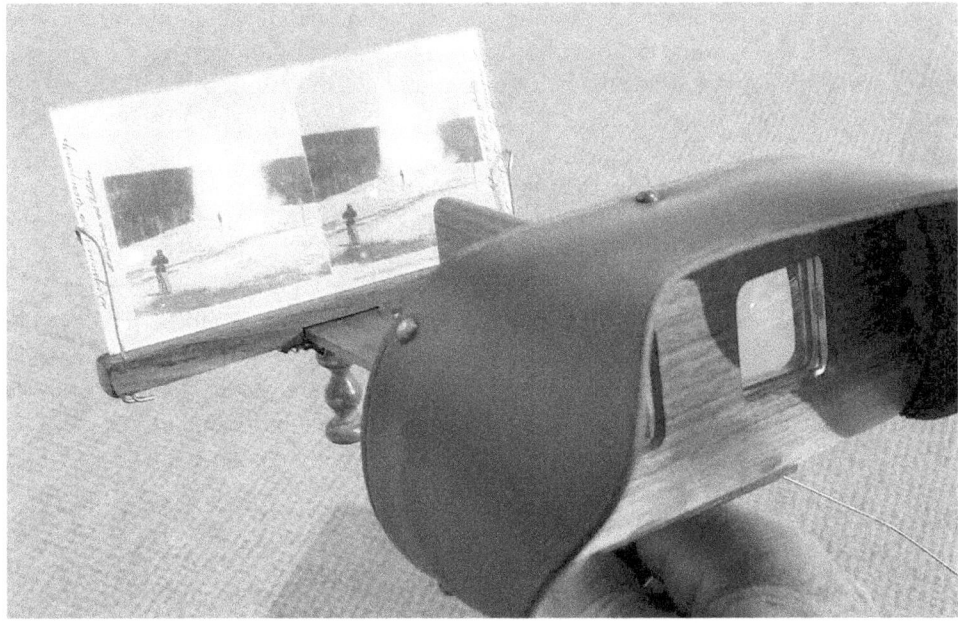

The stereoscope is a device for viewing photographs using a separate lens for each eye to view side-by-side photographs taken from slightly different camera angles. This was a tremendously popular way to view landscape photographs and allowed viewers to see the wonders of the West pop out at them as three-dimensional images in their own living room at home.

device that allowed two side-by-side photographic images (the stereograph), taken at the same time with a special camera that viewed the scene from slightly different angles, to be viewed as a seemingly three-dimensional image.

Each of our eyes sees an object from a slightly different point of view, creating the perception of depth. The stereograph created the illusion of three dimensions on a flat surface by photographing the subject simultaneously from slightly different vantage points that corresponded to the distance apart of the human eyes. When the pictures were viewed on a stereoscope, a slightly different image was presented to each eye, and the brain recombined them to create the illusion that made objects in the photograph appear to have depth. Stereographic cards of the natural wonders of the world, and especially of the American West, became very popular beginning in the 1860s. During the last half of the 19th century, more than five million stereographic postcards were made in the United States.[20]

During 1870s, 1880s, and 1890s, stereographs were probably the most popular and largest selling type of photograph, with landscapes and views of exotic foreign lands around the world being among the most popular.

Color Photography

Although many of the first photographs of the Western landscape were magnificent, they reproduced the image in various shades of grey. Photographers immediately sensed that they needed something more and the search was soon underway to find a process that would result in photographs in color for greater reality.

In 1903, the Lumière Brothers, Auguste and Louis, in France, patented one of the first processes for color photography, called Autochrome Lumière. Their invention involved a method of recording color images on glass plates coated with, of all things, particles of Irish potato starch. The microscopic grains of starch were dyed with each of the three primary colors (red, green, and blue), and spread onto a glass plate. The material was then coated with a photographic emulsion for exposure. The resulting color photograph was similar to a transparency, and had to be viewed by transmitted light. This limitation, however, was not insurmountable, as it could be projected in a magic lantern, which was similar to today's slide or overhead projectors. The film speed was equivalent to about 0.5 ASA.[21] The Autochrome process became popular with professional photographers and remained in use until the 1930s.

The West in Motion

By the 1920s, steady advances in photographic technology had made photography easy, fast, and inexpensive, and resulted in realistic depictions of its subjects. As a result, photography became the dominant visual medium of the world and it has remained so ever since. Once sensitized film on a flexible base could be manufactured in long rolls on an inexpensive commercial scale, the essential tool for motion picture photography was established.

Further advances in still photography, such as advanced camera features, snapshot photography, instant photography, digital photography, and photographs made with cells phones and electronic tablets, have simply been technological improvements on the basic concept of capturing an instantaneous visual image for later use and enjoyment.

The real challenge was to create pictures that moved. This was accomplished first in a crude way by Eadweard Muybridge, an English photographer who created a process for taking a series of photographs of a moving subject from a fixed camera position in rapid succession, one after the other, and then displaying them to a viewer. The slight amount of movement that took place between each photograph gave the illusion of seeing the subject (originally a galloping horse) in motion. The same basic principle later created moving pictures, which are also fundamentally a series of still photographs taken in rapid sequence, stored on a strip of flexible gelatin film, and then projected back at a rate faster than the eye can discern the individual frames, thus creating an illusion of motion. In fact, when moving pictures were first developed, they were often referred to as "living photographs."[22]

The arrival of moving pictures brought a profound change to the nation's culture, and produced a permanent impact on the public's leisure and entertainment activities. Movies also affected how the nation saw itself and its history. Early film audiences believed that they were seeing a true educational and historical part of the nation's past. In reality filmmakers deliberately manipulated the past, just as had the presenters of the Wild West shows, and reconstructed historical events into stories designed to lure crowds of paying audiences into theaters.

Even though the Western film supposedly depicts American history, the Old West of the movies is not so much a part of actual American history bounded by geography and time, as it is a legendary period that represents a state of mind. Most Westerns do not identify the year in which they are set and each decade of the existence of the real Old West, from about 1865 to 1900, is often portrayed as almost exactly resembling all the others. The typical timeless Western of our dreams has become stuck somewhere in our minds in the 1870s. This Hollywood version of the West included gunfights, cowboys, cattle drives, Indian Wars, discovery of gold and mining camps such as Deadwood and Cripple Creek, and the building of the railroad. These stories were particularly popular with males who looked to Westerns and the cowboy as the ideal of American manhood.[23] Filming Westerns reflected the sentiment of *The Man Who Shot Liberty Valance* (1962) as the editor of the *Shinbone Star*, Maxwell Scott (Carleton Young), declared, "This is the West, sir. When the legend becomes fact, print the legend."[24]

Just as "the West" became a generic mythic place and history somewhere in the western United States, moviemakers created a mythic landscape for the American Western. "The West" was thought by many people to be the area around Kanab or Monument Valley in Utah, Old Tucson Studios in Arizona, or Lone Pine in California, because these were popular locations where Westerns were filmed and are what audiences have seen. Over a 70-year period, movie-makers invented a "Western" geography that progressed from the "wilds" of New Jersey, to the canyons and hills of California, to the rocky desert country of Red Rock Canyon north of Los Angeles, to Monument Valley, and then the bleak desert country of southeast Spain.

Westerns managed to integrate the literary and historical tradition of the myth into a blend of fiction and history. As a result, Western films became the primary vehicle for transmission of the myth and had a major influence in shaping Hollywood and the motion picture industry. The Western terrain inspired movie makers with its splendor. Filmmakers used the natural dramatic background of the Far West to add to the visual image of the real West. The vast starkness and grandeur of the plains, deserts, and mountains each have an individual beauty and majesty, and gave a sense of importance to melodramatic plots.

All this, then, formed the background to the public's love affair with the majestic beauty of Western landscapes, and was the prelude to the use of spectacular background scenery of the western United States in Western films. This high level of interest in a romanticized Western landscape laid the groundwork for the public to accept the motion picture myth of the outdoor West.

CHAPTER TWO

The Early 1900s
Shaky Beginnings

The Western motion picture was a further extension and development of a long tradition of Western art, literature, and photography that dominated the mass entertainment tastes of late 19th-century America. The Western film, like other genres of movie, was shaped by contemporary social conditions, audience acceptance, demographics and tastes, the current state of moral attitudes and censorship, and business developments in film manufacturing and production, exhibition, and distribution.

Westerns portrayed part of the national American drama of the winning of the West. Westerns in essence were simple morality plays with background music, dramatic photography, effective lighting, good stunt work, capable direction, and (hopefully) good screenplays, set against the scenic outdoor background of the Western landscape.

One of the ways a Western film is identified is by its setting in the rugged landscapes of the West. In fact, a large part of the appeal of the Western is the exotic beauty of the wide-open plains, mountains, and deserts of the western states. But this did not appear until later. The first Westerns were filmed in the East.

Technology Overcomes Motion

In 1891 inventor Thomas Alva Edison patented the Kinetoscope for entertaining the public with moving pictures. It consisted of a box about four feet tall and 18 inches wide, with a viewing port and lenses at the top for the viewer to look through. The Kinetoscope was a peep-show type of machine, consisting of a mechanical system that rapidly ran a strip of film containing a series of still images in front of the viewer's eyes to create the illusion of motion. Though not a movie projector as we now know it, but more like viewing Eadweard Muybridge's galloping horse photographs, the concept was popular with viewers as it created apparent movement in pictures. The pictures, which could only be viewed by one person at a time, were contained on a strip of photographic film, about 50 feet in length, that continuously repeated itself. This type of machine could be found for many years in penny arcades and in the back of cigar stores. Edison later developed a projection version of the Kinetoscope, but it was not a commercial success.

Chapter Two. The Early 1900s

Iconic Images of the Movie West #2: Dover, New Jersey. This somewhat grainy postcard view of Shongum Lake in 1908 typifies the Eastern locations that were used for filming early Westerns. Scenery like this near Dover, New Jersey, created the first images of the Wild West for movie audiences as the wooded forests that were reflected in *The Great Train Robbery* (1903).

The first true motion picture projector was developed by brothers Auguste and Louis Lumière in France in 1895.[1] They patented their machine as the "Cinématographe Lumière." They also produced the first movie ever shown to the public, a 50-second black-and-white documentary titled *La sortie des ouvriers de l'usines Lumière* (*Workers Leaving the Lumiére Factory*), which showed workers coming out of the door of the Lumière factory. The debut was December 28, 1895.

Then Thomas Edison introduced the Vitascope projector in the United States and, by doing so, changed the face of popular entertainment. Though Edison is traditionally given credit for the invention of the Vitascope, he did not create the device, but merely secured the exclusive manufacturing rights from its inventors, Thomas Armat and Charles Francis Jenkins. The first projected showing of "moving pictures" using the Vitascope was at Koster and Bial's Music Hall, the biggest vaudeville theater in New York City, on April 23, 1896.[2]

Vaudeville entertainment at the time consisted of a series of eight to 12 unrelated variety acts that lasted from 7 to 20 minutes each, and were continuously repeated. These short, fast-paced acts followed each other in rapid succession, so if the audience did not like a particular performance, they only had to wait a few minutes because the performers would soon be followed by something else that they might prefer. Typical vaudeville acts consisted of singers, dance routines, magicians, fire-eaters, animal acts, acrobats, ventriloquists, jugglers, sword-swallowers, male and female impersonators, and comic sketches. Vaudeville was thus an ideal outlet for showing the new novelty of motion pictures. In fact, vaudeville provided the most important outlet for the exhibition of films for the infant motion picture business during the first decade of the industry's existence.

By late 1896 short films were commonly being shown in vaudeville theaters as part of the regular program. Movie operators traveled the vaudeville circuits, like any other vaudeville act, with a projector and films. By the early 1900s most vaudeville theaters had installed their own projectors, and 10- to 15-minute films were standard features on their programs. Film length was typically one reel, or about 10 minutes, which was the length of a typical vaudeville act. Movie subjects consisted of wholesome family material, such as travelogs, news films, comic narratives, and trick films, thus providing the type of varied entertainment that would appeal to a vaudeville audience.

In 1902, for example, the Sears, Roebuck Company sold a moving picture projector called the Optigraph for $64 through their mail order catalog. To accompany it was a full range of filmed subjects, such drill exercises of the Illinois National Guard, the arrival of the Overland Flyer train at La Junta, cattle in the Union Stock Yards in Chicago, and Indians riding through Cheyenne Canyon, Colorado. Each of the films sold for $7.50 and were advertised as being 50 feet in length.[3] A package deal of projector and films was available for purchase by exhibitors who wanted to travel around offering one-night shows in small towns that could not afford a permanent projection setup.

The Nickelodeon

Movies soon broke away from vaudeville and became a separate entertainment form. The nickelodeon appeared in 1905 and soon became the primary exhibition venue for movies. The nickelodeon was a type of early movie theater that consisted of a simple room with chairs, a screen, and a projector for showing films. The admission price was five cents, a nickel, hence the name nickelodeon. It was a popular form of cheap amusement for adults and families who had little money to spare for entertainment.

In 1906 there was a sharp increase in the number of nickelodeons as entrepreneurs rushed to convert empty building space into these popular movie theaters. Most were small storefront businesses with less than 200 seats, and most presented a mixed program of short features. Shows typically ran for a total of about a half-hour, then were repeated. Estimates are that by 1908 there were between 8,000 and 10,000 nickelodeons in the United States.[4]

Early movies were filmed in black and white and were silent because a workable method of recording and synchronizing sound at the same time as the visual image had not yet been developed. However, this was not all bad as in this way silent movies presented no language barrier to the incoming flood of immigrants from Europe to the East coast who spoke only their own languages. Another advantage of the silent era for filmmakers was that it was easy to substitute foreign language titles and dialogue cards for the English versions for use in overseas markets.[5]

To successfully attract audiences, the proprietor of a nickelodeon needed 20 to 30 new films every week. Thus the rapid increase in nickelodeons and the growing competition between them created an increased demand for films and a need for longer programs.⁶ Helping to fill the need, films with Western themes quickly became very popular with audiences. This was perfect as film manufacturers could make Western movies relatively easily and inexpensively.

The Beginnings of Film

The increasing demand for more films for exhibition naturally led to an increased requirement for someone to manufacture them. In 1893 Thomas Edison and his assistant W.K.L. (William Kennedy Laurie) Dickson built the world's first movie studio in West Orange, New Jersey, to produce movies. This was an ungainly tarpaper-covered structure that was given the slang name of the "Black Maria," because it was cramped, stuffy, painted black, and looked vaguely like a police paddy wagon. It was essentially a small, dark, cramped, overheated shed, but it was America's first movie studio. The roof was retractable and the entire structure was mounted on a circular track to allow it to rotate in place to follow the maximum amount of sunlight during the day.

In 1894 Edison's crew filmed Buffalo Bill Cody in this tiny, cramped studio. He was accompanied by sharpshooter Annie Oakley, who was filmed shooting at glass balls and plates tossed into the air. Some of the American Indians touring Brooklyn with Buffalo Bill's *Wild West* were also filmed in the studio. Existing short films show

The Black Maria, Edison's hot, stuffy, tar-papered film studio in New Jersey. The roof could be opened up as shown here to let in the maximum amount of sunlight, and the circular track in the foreground was used to rotate the entire structure to follow the maximum amount of light while the sun moved across the sky as the day went on (Glenn Kinnaman Colorado and Western History Collection).

bare-chested men wearing beads performing against the black background of the interior of the studio. This setup was common to all the early films shot in the Black Maria. Most of these short films were vignettes lasting for about 20 seconds.

By the end of the 1890s, films with Western themes had expanded to cover the landscapes of the West. These were short documentaries that showed some activity filmed in the Western outdoors, such as scenes of American Indian life, railroad trips, cattle branding, cowboys at work, or buffalo grazing. These short films were called "actuality films" or "actualities," as they depicted a real happening. They were filmed from a single position in a single continuous take that typically lasted from one or two minutes.

Western themes in these films usually had self-explanatory titles, such as *Cattle Fording Stream* (1898) and *Lassoing Steer* (1898). These short films were typically exhibited in vaudeville houses, so some films were sold as a package with an accompanying script for narration so that traveling lecturers could go on the vaudeville circuit completely prepared. Similar films were used by railroads and local chambers of commerce to show off local scenery as part of a way to market the West and attract potential visitors.[7]

Many of the earliest films that showed the scenery of the West were based on tourism. They showed off the landscape in actualities such as *Coaching Party, Yosemite Valley* (1901); *Panoramic View, Lower Kicking Horse Valley* (1901); and *Arrival of Train, Cheyenne* (1903). These short movies with Western themes attracted large audiences across the country, but at the same time they perpetuated the myths that had arisen about the West. Nevertheless, the increased use of actualities shot in scenic locations in the West stimulated the desire for tourists to visit them.

Some of these early documentary films focused on American Indians and recorded their culture. One surviving example is *Serving Rations to the Indians* (1898), probably filmed in Utah and lasting about 30 seconds. Another was titled *Carrying Out the Snakes* (1901), filmed in New Mexico, documenting part of a ceremony performed by Hopi Indians. Another of the early representative Western actualities was *Sioux Ghost Dance* (1894) filmed by an Edison crew.[8]

The first known film shot in New Mexico, and one of first films made by the Edison Company, was *Indian Day School* (1898) filmed at the Isleta Pueblo, about 12 miles south of Albuquerque, showing Indian children leaving school. It was 50 seconds long. While the film crew was in the area, they shot additional film at Santa Clara Pueblo, nearby to the north.

These semi-static views of the West were popular, but this type of short actuality film eventually started to become boring to audiences who wanted to see more than simple Western scenes and scenery. Filmmakers soon realized that they had to show more than just a fixed documentary view, and started to introduce people and plots into their Western movies.

These first fiction-based American Westerns were shot in New Jersey, New York, and Connecticut, so they featured background scenery of lush woodlands, lakes, and streams. With no precedent to go by, the landscape was treated as it would have been in the theater or in a photograph. Following the rules of scenic composition as used by theater set designers, early moviemakers commonly filmed in forest landscapes with small clearings, which formed natural theatrical spaces open to the light and were framed on both sides by overhanging dark tree branches.

More action scenes with rudimentary plots started to appear. In *Poker at Dawson City* (1898), four people sit around a table playing and cheating at cards, which results in a fight breaking out.

This recurring theme of gambling in Westerns was popularized in *Cripple Creek Bar-Room Scene* (1899).[9] This short movie, made by the Edison Manufacturing Company and directed by Edison's assistant W.K.L. Dickson, was one of the first identifiable fictional "Westerns." It was not long enough to be really even called a movie, but was more of a short vignette that lasted about 50 seconds.

The film starts with several stereotyped Western characters, represented by a cowboy, a miner, and a gambler, sitting at a table playing cards in a primitive saloon, supposedly in the contemporary gold-mining town of Cripple Creek, Colorado (but in reality inside Edison's Black Maria). A drunk lurches in through the door and starts to pester one of the patrons sitting next to the bar minding his own business. A homely female bartender throws both of them out of the door, then dusts off her hands with satisfaction and treats the remaining patrons to a drink.[10] It was a short film, but to the point.

The Western theme of card-playing also showed up in *Bluff from a Tenderfoot* (1899), where a newcomer wins in a poker game with a group of cowboys who become upset at losing to him. Retaliating when they become angry, he suddenly appears to draw his guns. However, this movie contains a joke, as the audience quickly realizes that he has "drawn" a couple of fans as he would guns and proceeds to fan his face to cool off.

Another theme that was to become very familiar to fans of Westerns was contained in *Cowboy Justice* (1904), in which a barroom gambler guns down a cowboy. He is quickly dragged outside by the cowboy's friends to meet his fate, and in short order is hung and then shot full of holes. This film was more advanced than most for the time as it contained two separate film shots, as opposed to just one. However, the film used obvious theatrical fakery for the outdoor location, as the background contains a lake painted on canvas and the tree the cowboy is "hung" from is obviously a painted image. However, the innovation in this film is not to be discounted and was considered quite novel at the time it was made.

The 12-minute *Life of a Cowboy* (1906) was filmed by Edwin Porter on Staten Island. The rudimentary plot line was an obscure story that contained an uneasy mixture of Wild West rope and horse tricks, a man beaten up for offering an Indian a drink, and a bandit and a band of Indians robbing a stagecoach but being thwarted by a heroic cowboy.

Unfortunately many of these early films have been lost. Part of the problem was that filming used nitrate-based film stock, which was highly flammable and subject to spontaneous combustion. Archived film had to be stored in specially-ventilated vaults at a low temperature to prevent fires. Before this was properly understood, the film vaults of several major studios literally went up in smoke when they spontaneously caught fire and the studio's total output was destroyed. Nitrate film was also subject to self-deterioration, and literally crumbled away with time. Nitrate film stock was finally phased out in 1951 and less-combustible film with an acetate base was used.[11] Modern film uses a polyester-based stock.

Another reason for the loss of these films was purely economic. Many of the archives of early film studios were recycled on purpose to reclaim the silver in the emulsion. Only later was the cultural worth of these early films understood and archival copies made for future study.

Early Success

Early fictional Western films promoted a sense of morality, freedom, and rugged individualism in the outdoors that resonated with movie fans. Their plots were the classic theme of good versus evil, and they were played out against scenic outdoor landscapes.

One of the early landmark Westerns was *The Great Train Robbery* (1903). This was not the first "Western," as has been often claimed, but it was the first to use novel cinematic techniques, such as cutting between action scenes, to advance the narrative. The movie was made by the Edison Company with director Edwin S. Porter, was one reel long, and was made at a cost of $150.[12]

The plots for Western melodramas like this came from dime novels and from stage dramas that played at low-class theaters, with the filmmakers adding as much sensationalism as they could. *The Great Train Robbery* (1903) was based in part on a stage melodrama of the same name by Scott Marble from 1896. The basic elements of the plot, repeated through many later Westerns, were a train robbery, pursuit of the bandits on horses, and a final shoot-out between the bandits and a pursuing posse.

The exterior scenes of *The Great Train Robbery* (1903) were filmed in the woods of New Jersey, on a siding of the Delaware and Lackawanna Railroad, near Dover, New Jersey. Interior scenes were filmed at the Edison studio.

The movie opens on a set of the interior of the railroad station that uses painted flats (pieces of theatrical scenery on a flat frame) for a backdrop. One innovative technique was the creation of the impression of a train rushing by in the background through an open window. This technique was used again for the interior of the express car on the train as scenery flashes by in the open doorway. The train was made to seem to be in motion by means of a moving painted background seen through the open door of the mail car.[13]

Early in the film the plot goes outside on location in New Jersey to a water tower and a real train. When the bandits take over the locomotive, the scene is shot from the tender of the moving train, which was quite a novel idea and innovative technique for the time. Later on the posse chases the bandits through the wooded New Jersey landscape to end in a final shootout among the trees.

The popularity of *The Great Train Robbery* (1903) and its use of outdoor locations helped to shape the image of Westerns and Westerns filmed in the outdoors. Though this wasn't the first Western film, it was first Western story that combined the classic plot structure of the Western (crime, pursuit, and retribution), with suspense, excitement, and emotional stimulation for the audience.

Audiences were very impressed with the train robbery itself, and the chase and final shoot-out that all took place on location in the outdoors. As a result, other filmmakers rushed to copy them and *The Great Train Robbery* (1903) was subject to sequels, imitations, and plagiarism in *The Great Bank Robbery*, *The Bold Bank Robbery*, and Biograph's *The Hold-Up of the Rocky Mountain Express*.[14] In 1905 Porter made a parody of his own film, also for Edison, with *The Little Train Robbery*, where child bandits rob a toy train.

Selig Polyscope

One of the film producers who had major impact on early movies and filming in the outdoors on location was Col. William Nicholas Selig. Selig, a pioneering Chicago-based film manufacturer, was a former entertainer, both as a stage magician named Selig the Conjurer, and later touring with his own traveling minstrel-show.

In 1895 Selig realized the commercial possibilities and financial potential of the new business of movies after seeing a demonstration of Edison's Kinetoscope in Dallas. With the assistance of a mechanical tradesman in Chicago he developed his own camera and projector, the Selig Standard Camera and the Selig Polyscope. He named his first version the Multiscope and later versions the Polyscope.[15]

With the equipment for filming in hand, Selig established a company to make short films and distribute them to vaudeville houses. By 1896 Selig had rented space in Chicago for a studio and started to produce films under the name Selig Polyscope Company. In 1904 Selig founded National Film Renting Company to sell motion pictures to traveling showmen.[16] By late 1909 Selig's company was one of the largest film producers in the country.

Like other filmmakers, many of Selig's early productions consisted of films of scenic landscapes, newsworthy events, and documentary short films of interesting wonders of the industrial world, such as dams, factories, and railroads. The expanding railroads were important corporate clients for Selig and he made commercial films in the outdoors for various railroads to help promote rail travel and tourism. Selig also produced non–Western fictional films, among which were *The Tramp and the Dog* (1896) and an early version of *The Count of Monte Cristo* (1908).

In his work producing films for the railroads, Selig met photographer Harry H. Buckwalter, one of Colorado's pioneering photographers. Buckwalter was a commercial photographer in Denver who had worked as a reporter and photographer for the *Rocky Mountain News* in the 1890s. He had photographed and filmed such diverse subjects as bolts of lighting, the Denver Fire Department's engines rushing to a fire, and photographs from a balloon ascent high over the city. He was also a pioneer in X-ray and medical photography. Among other subjects, Buckwalter made publicity photographs for Denver Union Gas Works to reassure the public that gas was safe and convenient for household use.[17]

Buckwalter was recognized as a skilled still photographer. In 1903 he won both the first and second prizes from the London Photographic Society for *Panorama of the Royal Gorge*, a scenic railway route used by the Denver & Rio Grande Railway, and for *Panorama of Ute Pass*, a road that ran up a scenic mountain pass west from Manitou Springs, Colorado, into the foothills of the Rocky Mountains.[18]

Buckwalter had also made moving pictures of rodeos, Indian dances, and local scenic attractions in order to promote Colorado's natural wonders and scenic beauty, and to boost tourism and promote railroad travel. Among his other capacities, he was the official photographer for the Colorado Midland Railroad.[19] He made documentary movies to promote various railroads, such as *Trip Over Colorado Midland* (1906) and *Trip Over Cripple Creek Short Line* (1906).

Like other early motion picture producers, Buckwalter also made Indian films, such as *Indian Fire Dance* (1902), *Ute Indian Snake Dance* (1902), and *Indian Hideous Dance* (1902). Also like other movie makers, many of his promotional films were shown in vaudeville halls and nickelodeons.

Over the course of his association with Selig, Buckwalter exposed thousands of feet of film of the outdoor scenic wonders of Colorado. In a Selig Polyscope advertising circular titled "Special Supplement of Colorado Films" of November 1, 1902, the company proudly stated, "We have had our special photographs corps in Colorado for several months. Our list of subjects from this grand state, with its gorgeous scenery and most wonderful attractions, is quite complete.... No other concern has ever made so many nor such good pictures in Colorado and we offer an entirely new line to all who want to take this golden opportunity of giving their audiences what they demand."[20]

Meanwhile, at the same time that Western subjects filmed in the outdoors were becoming popular in American nickelodeons, British film directors were producing an increasing number of films that concentrated on crime. These lurid movies were very popular and did well at the box office. These were not Westerns, but they set a new trend in entertainment by introducing violence and chase scenes into their plots, such as *Daylight Burglary* (1903) made in Sheffield, England, using members of the Sheffield Fire Brigade as actors.

Seeing the success of Edison's *The Great Train Robbery* in 1903, which resulted in dramatic changes in the cinematic presentation of the outdoor West, American filmmakers rushed to copy this new trend of sensationalism in films. Selig, in particular, wanted to produce what he thought would be distinctive entertainment by combining the new sensational depiction of crime with the best of the background scenery of the West. These added scenes of violence were part of what made Westerns popular.

Selig made arrangements with Buckwalter to make Westerns that combined the spectacular landscape of the West with the popular British type of stories of crime and violence, so that he could meet the increasing needs of the vaudeville circuit and expand his film output. Though the violence of the West had already been romanticized and sensationalized in previous dime novels, Wild West shows, and the melodrama of the cheap theater, this was a creative twist in films and the frontier's historical reputation for violence and conflict made the West a natural setting for these movie dramas. So the next generation of Westerns became filled with violence, guns and knives, abductions, robberies, chases, fights, and similar lurid plot elements.

Among the films Harry Buckwalter made for Selig were two notable fictional crime movies set outdoors in the West: *Tracked by Bloodhounds; or, A Lynching at Cripple Creek* (1904) and *The Hold-Up of the Leadville Stage* (1905). Both films combined crime action with scenic outdoor backdrops, and were characterized by violence, a hold-up, wild riding, chases, drinking, gambling, and random shooting sprees. This formula was a great success. By putting this combination of crime and violence together with plots derived from lurid stage melodramas and the Wild West shows, and setting them against scenic Colorado landscapes, it could be said that Buckwalter created some of the first real Westerns.

Tracked by Bloodhounds; or, A Lynching at Cripple Creek (1904) was a four-minute-long movie. It was mostly filmed in the outdoors, but contained a short sequence at the beginning that was shot on an interior set backed by theatrical flats with painted walls and doors. Selig promoted the film as "the most sensational film ever made," and added, "The scenery is grand, making the film one of more than usual interest."[21] Apart from the plotting, the use of an outdoor location made the story seem all the more credible.

The plot was not very complex. A shifty-looking character is invited inside by the lady of the house, where he subsequently attacks her and then flees. The woman's child and husband enter and find her lying on the floor. The action then moves outdoors on location. A posse with a group of bloodhounds is hastily assembled to track the perpetrator down. After a thrilling chase through wooded terrain and a fight in the water, the villain is captured. The posse grabs him, strings him up from a nearby pine tree, and then just for good measure blasts him with a shotgun. This was pretty strong stuff for 1904.[22]

To promote the sensationalistic aspects of *The Hold-Up of the Leadville Stage* (1905), Selig ran a story in the local newspaper about how a party of tourists had come across the motion picture crew during filming. The story claimed that they had thought there was a real crime in progress, so they drew their guns and started shooting at the supposed bandits. Reportedly even Selig himself was wounded in the volley of gunfire.[23]

Selig Polyscope continued to film movies set in Western landscapes in Colorado. In *The Girl from Montana* (1907) the company publicized the "magnificent scenic effects." *Western Justice* (1907) was praised by the press for its stunning backgrounds and stirring chase scene, and was publicized in *Moving Picture World* as set "in the wildest and most beautiful scenery of the western country."[24]

Buckwalter's films were very popular and on December 13, 1907, Selig sent a telegram to Buckwalter that said, "Prepare immediately to make at least 10,000 feet new Colorado subjects. Enormous sudden demand."[25] The fledgling motion picture industry was realizing that part of the popularity of these new Westerns was because they were filmed in the great outdoors, thus escaping the confines of the stage of live theater and a single fixed point-of-view documenting a static audience vantage point from the center of the theater seating. The vast open landscape of the West had become a significant element of Western films, just as important as the actors and the plot of the movie.

One of the important directors for the Selig Polyscope Company was Francis Boggs, a former leading man and stage director who was hired to produce Westerns. Boggs stayed at Selig's Chicago headquarters only long enough to learn the process for making Westerns, then he moved to Colorado to work with Harry Buckwalter. Boggs was good at filming in the natural outdoors and he combined melodramatic stories with the West's natural landscape. He made simple Western melodramas in beautiful outdoor landscapes that were made possible by location shooting. The Colorado mountains made a magnificent backdrop of scenic elements, and Boggs used this natural background scenery to enhance the actors. In fact, Selig's advertising at the time promised that his films contained "scenery that the world's artists gaze at in amazement."[26]

From Aronson to Anderson

Meanwhile, the man who was to have one of the strongest influences on Westerns and the early use of movie photography on location was just entering the business. His name was Gilbert Max Aronson, later to be known better as the Western film star "Broncho Billy" Anderson. Aronson, born in Little Rock, Arkansas, in 1880, had taken acting lessons and performed extra parts in Shakespearean plays, but found himself unable to land serious acting roles. He changed his name to Anderson, hoping to further his career.

Anderson joined the Edison Company in 1902, and talked director Edwin Porter into letting him perform in *The Great Train Robbery* (1903). To help secure the part, he told the director that he was born on a horse and could ride like a Texas Ranger. In reality, Anderson could not ride a horse and knew so little about them that he tried to mount from the wrong side. The animal didn't like it, threw him off, and Anderson had to walk back to the studio.[27] In the final film, as the bandits are mounting up (onto their English saddles!) for a fast escape, one of the bandits can indeed be seen mounting his horse from the wrong side.

Nevertheless, Porter cast Anderson in several roles in the film. The future Broncho Billy played one of the train robbers, the railroad passenger on the train who is shot as he tries to run away during the robbery, and the tenderfoot who has to prance to shots fired at his feet during the dance scene.[28]

After seeing the completed film, Anderson decide that he wanted his future to be in the movie business. In spite of his limited experience in *The Great Train Robbery* (1903), Anderson had fallen in love with filmmaking, but was more interested in the production side of the business than being in front of the camera. He went to work for Vitagraph Studios in Brooklyn making Westerns. He stayed there only a short while, leaving when the owners refused to let him buy a part of the company.

In 1906 Anderson traveled to Chicago and met with William Selig, who hired him to make films for Selig Polyscope. After Anderson went to work for Selig, he persuaded Col. Selig to let him go to Colorado to work with Harry Buckwalter on Western films with what he considered to be authentic location filming. The two of them made several simple one-reel films in Golden, Colorado, in December of 1906 and January of 1907. Anderson's first Western films by were met with a distinct lack of enthusiasm by audiences, so Selig stopped him from making any more.[29]

The turning point for Anderson occurred in May of 1907 when he left Selig. Unsure how to proceed with his goal of the movie business, Anderson looked up his old friend George Spoor, one of Selig's rival film distributors, who had invented the Kenodrome, an improvement on Edison's early machine and Selig's Polyscope.[30] The result was that Anderson and Spoor formed their own film manufacturing company.

Essanay Film Manufacturing Company

Like Selig, George K. Spoor was a Chicago-based film distributor who was also overwhelmed by the success of the nickelodeon and the demand for more and more films for exhibition. Thus the timing was ideal when Anderson approached him with the idea of forming a film production company to fill Spoor's increasing need for films.

Spoor and Anderson formed their film manufacturing company in Chicago in May of 1907. The partnership was named Essanay Film Company from their initials S and A, the "Ess" for Spoor and the "Ay" for Anderson. Their trademark for Essanay was the head of an Indian wearing a feathered head-dress.

Spoor and Anderson converted a storage room behind Spoor's office into an open-air studio in order to save the money that would have been required to build an outdoor set. They also made outdoor pictures on location using natural lighting, to avoid having to build a larger studio.

Initially the company made comedy films. Then in 1908 the two principals decided to make Westerns, as the genre was becoming very popular at the time. Anderson insisted that all his Westerns should be shot in the real West, so he moved his location filming to the mountains of Colorado in search of authentic outdoor backdrops for his movies. This time Anderson succeeded and audiences liked his Western films.

Selig Polyscope was the first film manufacturer to send a location crew out West to film. Then an Essanay film crew followed Selig to Colorado in 1908 and both Selig and Essanay filmed there.[31] Their competitors continued to make Westerns in the East, but were criticized in the trade press, which was of the opinion that Western films should be made in proper authentic scenic backgrounds in order to appear to be real. Also many of the actors were recruited from local Eastern theaters, and were not particularly representative of the authentic "Western" type.

Then suddenly competition reared up and everyone was filming Westerns. Other established film companies, such as Biograph, Edison, Kalem, Lubin Manufacturing Company, and Vitagraph followed Essanay's lead with Westerns films, hoping to exploit the popularity of the emerging genre. At first there was little competition to use Western scenery, but Westerns that were shot in the East could not compare with the authentic look of the productions of Selig and Essanay that were filmed in the West. Therefore the use of Western locations became essential for genuine-looking films.

When the weather turned cold in the fall, Anderson and his Essanay crew moved further west to Niles Canyon, near Niles, California, a little over 20 miles southeast of Oakland. The Colorado Selig crew also decided to look for warm weather and sunshine where they could continue to film in the winter.

Although New York was still the center of the film industry and films continued to be made in studios in New York or in the woods of New Jersey, Chicago started to become a major motion picture center. Chicago, however, was not any better a location than New York for filming Westerns, so companies making Westerns eventually relocated further West, to California, to take advantage of the constant filming weather found there.

Fans of Western movies can still find and recognize old filming locations, such as this one in the Southwest of the United States. This find is south of Santa Fe in the little town of Cerrillos, New Mexico, which was used as the location for several sequences in *Young Guns* (1988), a retelling of the story of the outlaw Billy the Kid. The town was dressed for the movie as Lincoln, New Mexico, the site of the real Lincoln County War of 1878. For the movie, this building in Cerrillos was turned into the dry goods emporium owned by Lawrence Murphy and James Dolan, two of the businessmen on one side of the conflict, and the store name painted by Hollywood on the outside wall for the movie is still visible at the top. At one time the Wortley Hotel in Lincoln was owned by Sheriff Pat Garrett, who permanently ended the crime career of Billy the Kid.

"Broncho Billy" Anderson

During his first three years of making Westerns, Gilbert Anderson did not have a dominant hero figure in his films. His intent was simply to make rousing action films that took advantage of the unique and authentic scenery of the West. Most of these simple short films consisted of setting up an initial conflict situation, such as a bank holdup or train robbery, which then led into an outdoor chase sequence, and finished with a fight at the end.

The domestic market, however, soon started to become flooded with Westerns that were very similar. As Anderson thought about it, he realized that Essanay's audience was identifying more with the characters in his films than with the Western landscapes, so he decided to create a central figure for his plots. Anderson thought that this would make Essanay films different from the Westerns that other companies were making. In this way he could differentiate his product, increase his audience, and increase profits.

When Anderson couldn't find what he felt was a suitable type of actor, he cast himself as the star and returned to acting, creating a cowboy persona named Broncho Billy as the central character for his films. The first of the long Broncho Billy series was *Broncho Billy's Redemption* (1910), based on Peter B. Kyne's story "Bronco Billy and the Baby," which had appeared in *The Saturday Evening Post* magazine.[32]

Gilbert Anderson's Broncho Billy character was the first hero that the audience could identify with. To everyone's surprise—including Anderson's—he turned out to be immensely popular as a character and thus became the first Western cowboy film star, under the name of "Bronco Billy" Anderson. Partly as a result of Anderson's success, cowboys became a popular subject of single-reel movies in the 1910s.

Broncho Billy was the first recognizable, repeatable Western hero, and was the first to help solidify the cowboy as a hero in the mind of the public. Anderson played his Western character in a simple, standardized costume of baggy denim pants, a dark shirt, leather gauntlets, boots, and a wide belt. The Broncho Billy character was part drifter and loner, part country bumpkin, part crime fighter, and part detective. But as a central character he interested the audience.

Anderson cranked out nearly 400 formula two and three-reel silent Westerns between 1903 and 1920.[33] These were not, however, necessarily connected narratives. Anderson played a good man in some films and a badman in others. He died in some of the movies, but returned to life in the next. Generally he was an outlaw who was converted by an act of goodness into a reformed citizen.

Anderson didn't use gunfighting, Indian battles, or wagon trains in his plots. Instead, he tried to create entertainment for families and be a role model who taught a moral lesson to children. He usually played an outlaw who underwent reform during the plot. He emphasized Victorian moral values, with a sense of responsibility towards women and children, and made the movie theater a place for middle-class family entertainment. He usually started with no script or particular plot, but made the film up as he went along. Anderson's first films were budgeted at $800 and often grossed up to $50,000.[34]

What distinguished Anderson was his characterizations. He typically portrayed a bad man with "heart of gold," such as in *Shootin' Mad* (1918), in which he played a rough and tough, but loveable, character who came to the rescue of a girl who had been tricked out of her land.

Anderson made 349 short Westerns in which he was the main actor. But soon Anderson and his Broncho Billy character couldn't single-handedly meet the increased demand for new Westerns, and Essanay was forced to use other directors to make the same type of popular crime westerns that Selig was making. One was Lawrence Lee, a former producer of stage melodramas, who made Westerns for Essanay in Chicago. Though the scenery around Chicago obviously wasn't the West, Lee made *The James Boys in Missouri* (1908) about the real outlaw Jesse James, in Chicago's Riverside Park. Another fictional film he made about a real family of outlaws was *The Younger Brothers* (1908), which he filmed at Berrien Springs, Michigan.

In the meantime, Selig Polyscope continued to be active in making Westerns. Francis Boggs, who had been making Westerns with Harry Buckwalter in Colorado, moved west to Los Angeles with a cameraman and a small production company of actors.

Boggs set up a small studio in the back of a Chinese laundry on Olive Street, where he could use the laundry's clothes lines to hang up background scenery for filming. Painted backdrops were often used for the backgrounds of films, a common practice of the time that was derived from stage productions. Huge paintings were set up at the rear of the stage, with small props, such as trees, saddles, or a wagon placed in the foreground to create an illusion of depth, and to allow the action in the foreground to blend back towards the backdrop.

The same technique was used by the Wild West shows. Buffalo Bill Cody often used huge painted scenic canvas backdrops behind the performance arena. These gigantic backdrops, which sometimes measured as much as 40 feet high and 150 feet long, contained vivid paintings of forests, prairies, and mountains. Stage entrances were cut into the canvas so that performers on horseback could appear to be entering from behind the immediate foreground. The backdrop to Buffalo Bill's recreation of "Custer's Last Rally" was 49 feet high and 440 feet long. On a clear, cloudless day, the painted sky at the top of the canvas blended with the real sky overhead to make the scene appear even more authentic. This combination of reality and illusion can be seen in some of the arena sequences in Robert Altman's *Buffalo Bill and the Indians* (1976).

In a similar manner, Selig directors integrated Wild West show types of staging with melodramatic stories and a scenic background. Large canvas paintings, which were as large as 12 feet high and 18 feet long allowed filming in a supposed Western setting while blocking out unsightly elements in the background, such as modern buildings and telephone poles.

After 1909 the number of Westerns increased. As the decade drew towards a close, many producers filmed plots centered around American Indians. These Indians were portrayed in the "noble savage" tradition, with sympathetic characters faced with racism and assimilation, though in somewhat mawkish stories. Typical sentimental titles of this period were *The Aborigines Devotion* (1909), *Her Indian Mother* (1910), *A Redskin's Bravery* (1911), *For the Papoose* (1912), and *Hiawatha* (1913). Curiously this took place at a time when real Indians were not particularly visible in American culture. Part of this emphasis on Indian stories was due to the growing popularity among audiences for films placed in Western settings, thus filmmakers sought out any suitable plots that they could film on location in the West.

The number of Westerns also increased because action, sensationalism, and scenic splendor were popular with audiences. Audiences wanted films of cowboys versus Indians, and plots that contained spectacular pitched battles between Indians and soldiers. And film producers provided them. Part of this may have been fueled by previous stage melodramas and dime novels, but also partly because Westerns were cheap to produce, were reliable in attracting audiences, and met the demand of audiences.

Noted director D.W. (David Wark) Griffith followed this trend in pictures with Indian themes, such as *The Redman and the Child*, *The Girl and the Outlaw*, *The Red Girl*, and *The Call of the Wild*, all filmed in 1908. These movies retained the popular theme of crime, and some were indeed quite violent. In *The Redman and the Child* (1908), for example, the protagonist strangles a man underwater and stabs another to death.

D.W. Griffith's birth name was Lawrence Griffith. He was hired by Edwin Porter at Edison to play a mountaineer in *Rescued from an Eagle's Nest* (1908). After acting in several other Edison films, Lawrence changed his name to D.W. Griffith and moved to Biograph as a director.[35]

Biograph had been founded in 1895 by William L. Dickson and Henry M. Marvi, who had invented their own camera. They began production as American Mutascope and Biograph Company, then shortened the name in 1908 simply to Biograph. At first the company did not have a director, but the cameraman and actors made up the story as they went along. Griffith's first Western for Biograph was *The Redman and the Child* (1908). Griffith's method was to come up with an idea, then start filming and embellish the story as he filmed. Out of a total of 571 films made by Biograph between July 1908 and November 1912, 74 were Westerns.[36]

The main Biograph studios were located in New York, but in October of 1910 Griffith traveled to California, searching for more suitable weather and stronger light for filming.[37] After that, until he left Biograph in 1913, Griffith regularly took a crew to California for the winter and returned to New York in April or May of the next year. One of Griffith's most successful Westerns, *The Last Drop of Water* (1911) was shot in the desert in California. Another, *The Battle of Elderbush Gulch* (1913), was an epic film of cavalry versus Indians that was filmed near Los Angeles.

Meanwhile, filmmaker William Selig made one of the early attempts at creating and filming the outdoors on an indoor stage, a practice that later became common in making Westerns. The event occurred after former president Theodore Roosevelt went to Africa on a big-game hunting expedition in 1909. Selig asked to accompany the group to film the adventure, but was refused permission. Not to be foiled, Selig found an elderly lion and hired an actor who looked somewhat like Roosevelt. He created a tropical scene in his studio with some potted plants and trees, and found some local actors to portray African tribesmen. Then he had a crew film the Selig version of Roosevelt's expedition. After news arrived back in the United States that Roosevelt had shot a lion, Selig released his film as *Hunting Big Game in Africa* (1909) creating the illusion that his cameraman had been there.[38]

The film was met with modest success and encouraged Selig to make more films with animals. Sensing another business opportunity, he sent camera crews to film stock footage of exotic places and animals for use in future films. This idea ended up being significant for location filming and the future of the Western film industry when a Selig film crew went to the Miller Brothers 101 Ranch in Oklahoma to film cowboys in action.

Miller Bros. 101 Ranch

To understand the importance of the Miller Brothers and their contribution to making Westerns in the outdoors on location, it is necessary to look at the origin of the Millers' famous ranch.

The Miller Brothers' 101 Ranch was a real Western ranch, started by Col. George Washington Miller in the Oklahoma Territory in 1893. Before Miller died in 1903, he urged his sons, Joseph (Joe), Zack, and George, to acquire more land. They did and the ranch and its associated farming operations eventually grew into an immense cattle empire that covered 110,000 acres near Bliss, Oklahoma. As well as raising livestock, the Millers farmed wheat, corn, and oats. Their 300 ranch and farm workers ate one beef cow a day, plus the eggs from 1,000 chickens.

The ranch grew so big that it contained its own schools and churches, and a complete road system. Lush orchards grew apples, cherries, and peaches. Dairy cows provided milk and butter, and meat came from cattle, pigs, and chickens. A ranch store on the property was a combination of department store and trading post. The ranch supported a cider mill, a cannery, packing plants, poultry farms, a dude ranch, a tannery, a power plant for electricity, an oil refinery, an ice plant, dairy operations, woodworking shops, a laundry, and a cafe. The Millers even operated their own train with 150 freight cars. The entire operation was nicknamed by its residents "The Hundred-and-One" or "The One-oh-One."

The Miller brothers wanted to keep the image of the Old West alive. As early as 1905 they hosted visitors from big cities who wanted to learn how to ride, rope, and live like a cowboy. It was not, however, an easy vacation. Guests purchased their own hats, boots, chaps, and Western shirts, and helped with roundups, breaking horses, fixing fences, and de-horning cattle, under the direction of the Miller cowboys. Guests could fish and hunt, and eat at a chuckwagon or could take their meals in the dining room and clubhouse. They could do as much cowboy work as they wanted—or not. Before the Millers built a series of guest cabins, early dudes and dudesses (dudines) lived in tents. The dude ranch complex, called Riverside Camp, drew guests from around the world and became a profit center for the ranch.

The Millers had previously been in show business in 1882, when Col. Miller staged a "roundup" (really a rodeo) in Winfield, Kansas. Their new idea was to promote demonstrations of Old West ranch life, including rodeos and a Wild West show. The concept of showcasing the ranch and its workers as the idealized image of the West was so successful that the Millers decided to develop a show that would make the ranch a monument to the days of the Old West.

In 1905, the Millers staged their first large-scale Wild West show for several conventions groups. The show, which included a roundup and buffalo chase, started with a parade of ranch employees and local Indians, and included cowboys displaying rodeo skills, such as roping and riding bucking broncos. Other parts of the program showed Indians hunting buffalo and an attack on a wagon train. The Millers followed the contemporary trends in Wild West show entertainment and did not try to develop new ideas, but included sharpshooters, herds of buffalo, Indian battles, trick riders and ropers, and bucking horses.

In 1907, the Millers took their show to Norfolk, Virginia, to the Jamestown Exposition. It was so successful that they decided to become professional showmen and present the show on a regular basis. Their show opened in Ponca City, Oklahoma, in 1908. Publicity said that the performers were employees who worked on the ranch, but in reality many of the performers were professional entertainers hired specifically for the show.

The performance opened with a grand revue, followed by acts of sharpshooting, bronco riding, and bulldogging. The show contained some violence, including a rather gruesome piece of drama where a group of cowboys supposedly captured a horse thief and dragged him to death behind a horse. They also performed re-creations of Indian massacres and scalp dances.

The show was so successful that the Millers decided to develop the *Miller Brothers' 101 Ranch Wild West Show* to feature their ranch as the idealized image of the West. It was a showcase for their many skilled riders, ropers, and bulldoggers. Over time, the show matured, featuring costumes, performances, and sensationalized acts that helped to further promote the cowboy as a romantic hero, and included Indian battles, sharpshooters, herds of buffalo, trick riders and ropers, and bucking horses. The Millers also added the typical sideshow staples of the times, including sword-swallowers, giants, midgets, snake-handlers, and temperance lecturers.

The years between 1908 and 1916 were the best and most lucrative years for the Miller's Wild West show. Their show was so appealing that kids, and even grown men and women, dreamed of running away from home and becoming Wild West performers or working as cowhands at the 101 Ranch.

Through their show, the Millers helped to promote the cowboy and his way of life as a romantic image, and their pageant became a showcase for riding, roping, and bulldogging. Over time, the show matured into sensationalized acts performed by cowboys and cowgirls in gaudy show-business costumes, including trick shooters, wranglers, ropers, and wild horse riders. The Millers hired the best band director they could find, as music was important in Wild West shows to set the mood. Stirring marches and up-tempo music helped to create tension during various acts.

So when Col. Selig approached the Millers about filming their cowboys, the brothers saw a possible opportunity. Selig crews filmed cowboys at work on the ranch for three films in the spring of 1909.

Among the ranch cowboys at the time was a wrangler named Tom Mix, who had spent the past three years with the Miller's Wild West show. When Selig needed someone to ride a horse over a cliff into the nearby Salt River for one action scene, Mix offered to do the stunt.[39] That was the beginning, and Mix eventually became one of the top Western motion picture stars of his time. He did not gain superstar status until after he went to work for Fox Studios in 1917, but the type of action hero that he developed for earlier Selig films affected the characteristics of the Western film hero of the 1920s and was instrumental in changing location filming.

Back in California

Meanwhile, Selig had decided to keep Francis Boggs and his southern California film crew in Los Angeles. By August of 1909, Boggs had converted a small suburban house into a studio in Edendale, an area northwest of downtown Los Angeles that was later known as Echo Park and Silver Lake. By doing this, Selig established the first permanent motion picture production facility in Los Angeles.[40]

Shortly afterwards, New York Motion Picture Company opened their own studio nearby, and Edendale became by default the hub for filming Westerns. The town also housed the first film lab in Los Angeles when Selig built a processing plant in his Edendale studio.

The new California-based filmmakers found it difficult to recreate the reality of the Old West on sound stages and studio backlots, so they used the nearby valleys, canyons, and foothills of Southern California for filming locations. The area around Edendale was ideal for outdoor location filming as it contained plenty of open spaces at the time, along with wooded areas, lakes, and rivers, and buildings from California's Spanish past. The little town was also convenient to Los Angeles, with a streetcar line to transport legitimate stage actors working in Los Angeles out to the studios for film work.

Selig Polyscope was also not standing still at home and Selig built a new three-story headquarters and studio building in Chicago. The first two floors of the building contained the film processing plant, along with the carpentry shop, the props department, and dressing rooms for the actors. On the top floor was a new film studio with glass walls to allow in the maximum amount of light for filming.

In spite of the trend towards filming Westerns in Los Angeles, Essanay's Chicago facility was also not forgotten. In 1909 Spoor upgraded the facility with a new studio and film processing plant.

By 1910 both Essanay and Selig had turned Chicago into the global center of motion picture production, responsible for 20 percent of the world's production of films. Two hundred workers were employed at each facility. At the same time Selig made more improvements to the Edendale studio, which employed a hundred workers.[41]

Broncho Billy Anderson continued his pattern of nomadic location filming all over the West. He followed his own ideas and continued to specialize in light-hearted Western comedies. Thus he did not need a large cast, complex props, or large herds of livestock. His costumes were practical and serviceable. The practice at the time was that there was no script and the director simply improvised as he filmed. Vague plots were derived from stories or magazines, or were "borrowed" from plays. This practice, however, was not without its hazards. For example, when Anderson filmed *Broncho Billy's Redemption* (1910), based on Peter B. Kyne's "Bronco Billy and the Baby," unfortunately he didn't obtain the screen rights to the story, which was also a common practice at the time. Luckily Kyne liked the movie and didn't sue, though he did demand a royalty.

Anderson and his film crew traveled all over northern and southern California looking for scenic locations. Once Anderson found one he liked, the crew stayed in a local hotel and rode around on horseback as they filmed in the outdoors. When Anderson was operating at full speed, he produced a one-reel Western every few days, at a cost of around $700 to $800. He seldom stayed more than three months at any one location.

Anderson's nomadic shooting tours typically started in Chicago, then traveled to Colorado where the production company worked until the fall. When the weather turned cold, they moved south to Texas and worked their way over to southern California, filming in places such as Los Angeles, Santa Barbara, and San Diego. By early spring Anderson and his crew were back in Colorado, which he considered to be the best place in the country to film Westerns.

Anderson filmed extensively in and around Golden, Colorado, which was only 12 miles west of Denver and was easily accessible by street car. He also liked to film in the scenic canyons, streams, caves, and mountains around Morrison, about seven miles south of Golden. Anderson recruited many of his actors on a temporary basis from Denver's vaudeville houses and theater companies. American Indian actors for Westerns came from Wild West shows during their off-season.

In 1909 Anderson constructed a large portable studio with a canvas roof that could be disassembled when it was time to move to the next location. He also purchased a portable lighting system to supplement natural light when the outdoor weather did not cooperate. The equipment for processing film was too bulky to take on location with the film crew, so he shipped exposed film back to the main factory in Chicago for processing.[42]

In 1910 Anderson modified a railroad car to house processing equipment so that he could develop his film on-site and re-shoot any "bad" scenes, such as those that did not match due to different lighting conditions on different days. With this addition, Anderson was able to develop and edit his own film, which he then sent to headquarters in Chicago for mass duplication and distribution.

During the 1909–1910 filming season, Anderson completed 52 one-reel pictures.[43] Critics and audiences liked his films as they felt that the location scenery and acting were authentic.

New York Motion Picture Company

The third important player in movie production of Westerns on location was New York Motion Picture Company. The company was founded in 1909 by Adam Kessel, Charles O. Baumann, and filmmaker Fred J. Balshofer at the height of the nickelodeon boom. Kessel and Baumann provided the capital and Balshofer contributed his knowledge of the motion picture business. Balshofer was originally a photographer who made stereographs, but he went to work in 1905 for film manufacturer Siegmund Lubin making motion pictures for Lubin Manufacturing Company, a major film company based in Philadelphia. Balshofer left Lubin in 1907 and started to make his own films under the name Crescent Film Company.

Balshofer sold his films to Empire Film Exchange, run by Adam Kessel and Charles Baumann.[44] Kessel had previously been a bookmaker for horse-racing tracks throughout Brooklyn and Long Island, and acquired the exchange after the original owner defaulted on a loan Kessel had made to him. Kessel expanded the business and went into partnership with his friend Charles Baumann, who had been a former streetcar conductor. When Crescent went out of business, Kessel, Baumann, and Balshofer went into business together, the result being New York Motion Picture Company. One of their subsidiaries was Bison Moving Picture Company, which used the image of a bison as a trademark.

Western films were in high demand at the time, so Balshofer started to produce them. He hired some actors and rented the necessary props, horses, and costumes. He took them and a film crew across the Hudson River and made Bison's earliest one-reel Westerns on location in New Jersey, filming in the open countrysides near

Coytesville and Fort Lee. Balshofer's first Western films were a success, so he went on to make more, and the company soon became an important producer of Westerns.

Fort Lee, which was known as the "American Movie Capital" long before Hollywood had that name, was a popular filming location that soon became overcrowded with production crews. Balshofer wanted a different look for his films than the others, so he moved his crew to Neversink, a small town in the Catskill Mountains. He used a barn for a studio and filmed Westerns with the local mountain scenery for backgrounds. When winter came, he and the crew returned to New York.

In November of 1909, looking for better weather for filming and for more realistic Western scenery, Bison followed Selig and Essanay to Southern California. Balshofer intended to stay for only a short time, but he ended up creating a permanent studio in an abandoned feed and grocery store on Alessandro Street in Edendale, just down the street from Selig.

Bison's original Edendale facility was not large. There were only two rooms, one consisting of an office and shooting stage, with the other used for storage of scenery, props, and costumes. Like other film producers, Balshofer chose Edendale for his western headquarters because of the variety of scenic locations nearby and the convenience of the little town to nearby Los Angeles.

Bison added a West Coast film developing plant to their facility in 1910. Film was processed and edited in Los Angeles, then was sent to New York for the addition of title cards and final duplication for distribution. Bison's Western films became very popular and required expansion of the New York manufacturing plant to handle the increased production.

Balshofer did not build an indoor studio at the Edendale facility for the first few years of West Coast operation. Instead, he made most of his pictures directly on location in the outdoors. Horse chases, gunfights, and stage holdups were filmed in the Hollywood area from their studio in Edendale. Balshofer filmed many of his Westerns around the existing old adobe buildings near La Brea Avenue and Hollywood Boulevard. He also used tree-covered Griffith Park, a large city park in Los Angeles, for location filming in the park's scenic hills, canyons, and streams. Griffith Park became a popular outdoor location for Westerns and after a few years as many as five film companies might be filming there at the same time.

Biograph was another of the companies that filmed in Griffith Park. Hoping to find new outdoor locations that had not been previously used, they also filmed in Big Bear Valley and at Big Bear Lake, which was then a very remote location in the San Bernardino Mountains north of Los Angeles. Travel to reach there was still primitive and could only be accomplished by wagon, instead of by automobile. Cast and crew lived in rustic cabins during filming. The location was excellent for Westerns as it contained a lake for Indian canoes, the lake shore, giant fir trees, scenic meadows, and snowcapped mountains for beautiful backgrounds. Many movie reviewers praised these settings with enthusiasm.

The most prosperous independent company at the time was Carl Laemmle's Independent Moving Picture Company (IMP). Laemmle, Kessel, and Baumann formed the Motion Picture Distributing and Sales Company, the first company to coordinate the production and distribution of independent films.[45] They contracted with other independent film manufacturers to create a balanced program of films that they sold

Chapter Two. The Early 1900s   47

A familiar sight around Gallup in the 1950s as a movie crew on location films a cavalry troupe of extras riding out of one of the red rock canyons (Glenn Kinnaman Colorado and Western History Collection).

as a block to exchanges. Though they did not know it at the time, their actions would foreshadow later anti-trust actions by the government to break up this practice and spell doom to the major motion picture studios.

The Decade Draws to a Close

The most commercially successful motion picture manufacturers during the period when the studio system was developing were Edison Manufacturing, Biograph Company, and the Vitagraph Company. They were also the most technically and artistically innovative of the production companies. However, these manufacturers initially avoided the routine production of Westerns, and were not the leaders in the production of the cowboy-and-Indian pictures that popularized the genre. They all made films on location in the West, but left production primarily to their crews based in Chicago.

These companies were also not the pioneers in locating permanent film production facilities in California. By the end of the decade, the four most important companies making Western films on the West Coast were Selig Polyscope Company, Essanay Film Manufacturing Company, New York Motion Picture Company's Bison subsidiary, and the Biograph Company. These companies sent crews to the West to shoot pictures and, by doing this, established Los Angeles as the center of American filmmaking. Kalem, Nestor, American, and Pathé West Coast were also important producers. Other smaller and less influential manufacturers followed, primarily to make cheap Westerns.

Westerns had been produced only sporadically before 1909 when film manufacturers turned the genre into the nation's leading film type. *Moving Picture World* commented in its November 11, 1909, issue that Western subjects were immensely popular with audiences. Westerns could be produced relatively easily and were inexpensive to make in the outdoors, thus becoming an important genre of film that met the increased demands for product due to the large increase in the number of nickelodeons.

This large demand for new movies spurred manufacturers, particularly Selig and Essanay, to regularly film more Westerns, and Essanay and Selig became the leaders in producing them, both in terms of quantity and quality. Both were headquartered in the Midwest, in Chicago, rather than in New York, thus making it easier for both of them to send film crews to Colorado, the Southwest, and to California. Some of their film units did not stay in one place, but were constantly on the move, looking for the best light and the most spectacular scenery in scenic and unphotographed locations in the West. Echoing earlier productions filmed in the East, though, both still tended to use lush valleys, and lakes and rivers for locations.

Essanay and Selig were direct competitors, both competing for the market for Westerns. There was, however, a difference in philosophy between the two companies. Essanay, driven by Anderson's vision of the scenic outdoor West, made simple melodramatic Westerns, based mostly on character and scenic backgrounds. Selig, on the other hand, tended to feature spectacular outdoor battle scenes between whites and Indians.

Though Selig and Essanay were the largest film manufacturers in the early 1900s, they were by no means the only ones, and other companies were filming outdoor Westerns. Not all of them, however, were successful. For example, the Oklahoma Mutoscene Company. In 1908 they made *The Bank Robbery* on location in Oklahoma. The film was directed by William Tilghman, who had been a lawman and was town marshal of Dodge City from 1884 to 1886. One of the stars was authentic train robber Al Jennings, a real outlaw who had just been released from prison. Though the film was made where Jennings had performed his robberies, the background and setting were considered by audiences to be too realistic and they rejected the film. By this time they had embraced Broncho Billy and preferred flamboyant film stars.

The Motion Picture Patents Company

Another important factor in the choice of the West Coast for location filming of Westerns in the early 1900s was based on legal issues, rather than on artistic visions and the drive for realism.

Though Thomas Edison did not invent the moving picture, he tried to dominate the film industry through patents. In 1908 Edison, wanting to ward off competition, organized a group of motion picture production and distribution companies to form the Motion Picture Patents Company (also known as the Patents Trust or the Edison Trust) in New York to try to monopolize the production of motion pictures. The Trust claimed that only members could produce, distribute, and exhibit motion pictures, and threatened others with lawsuits for patent violations.

Edison tried to control the industry by forcing non-member film companies to buy a license to produce, distribute, or exhibit motion pictures in the United States. Edison wanted them to acknowledge that he had invented the motion picture and to agree to make movies only with his permission. Licensees agreed to pay Edison royalties to avoid the threat of copyright infringement and lawsuits. The Trust also demanded a license from each nickelodeon of $2 a week.[46] The Trust was even able to persuade Kodak to sell raw film stock only to companies that were members of the group. Another part of the group strategy was that they did not give special recognition to actors as stars, as they did not want actors to become popular as individuals (as did Broncho Billy) and thus demand higher wages.

Essanay became an Edison licensee, along with Kalem, Lubin, Selig, Vitagraph, and the French companies Pathé and Méliès. The powerful Biograph Company held out and refused to become part of the Trust.

Some of the smaller independent companies tried to find ways to make pictures without being sued, but most packed up and left New York. They went to Florida, Texas, Louisiana, New Mexico, and California to avoid prosecution. California was preferred as Los Angeles had better weather for filming, and was close enough to the Mexican border to avoid pursuit and intimidation by the Trust's lawyers and private detectives if necessary. Edison's private detectives traveled as far as Chicago, and even to Colorado, where they reputedly sometimes destroyed non-licensee's cameras and film.[47]

The actions of the Patents Trust were to have far-reaching effects on the infant motion picture industry, as several major movie producers moved away from New York to Chicago to escape licensing fees and the Trust's detectives, trying to find places where the Trust's patents were harder to enforce. Eventually this became a contributing factor in movie companies locating in Los Angeles.

Though motion picture directors and producers moved far out West to be away from the snooping private detectives of the Trust, they quickly found that weather on the West Coast was actually far more suitable for filming than that of New York or Chicago. The abundant sunshine of Southern California allowed filming all year and crews did not have to stop for the cold of the Midwest winters. Los Angeles was reputed to have 350 days of sunshine a year.

Independent producers who escaped to the West also started to promote specific actors as a way of attracting repeat audiences to their films to see a favorite star. In this way, featured stars such as Douglas Fairbanks, Charlie Chaplin, and others gained more control over their pictures and received higher salaries.

In spite of pressure, Universal and other independent companies continued to fight the Motion Picture Patents Company. Finally the Trust was declared to be restrictive and the federal government disbanded it under antitrust action in 1918.

CHAPTER THREE

The 1910s
Growth of the Silent Film Industry

In the early 1900s and 1910s motion pictures replaced dime novels, stage plays, and Wild West shows as the leading presenters of images of the West. Mass culture has always used the history of the American West for profit, and film producers tried to make their particular image of the West be the most compelling in order to ensure the largest audience and maximum profit.

Movie distributors originally did not have a specific category for Western films, but with growing popularity by 1907 exhibitors had a separate classification for "Westerns," along with other categories for comedies, dramas, mysteries, and romances.[1] The Western became a specialized film genre and was the first distinctively American contribution to the cinema. By 1910 Westerns made up 21 percent (213 out of 1001) of all pictures released in the United States.[2]

The 1910s and 1920s saw unprecedented growth in the film industry, both in technology, artistic technique, and business dealings. The period from 1910 to the early 1960s grew to be the era of the Hollywood Studio System, also known as the Golden Age of Hollywood, a time when a few major studios dominated the entire film industry. The studio system developed into a tightly-controlled environment where the major studios produced films with the efficiency of a well-run factory. Powerful studio heads controlled the entire production system, including locking their top stars into long-term contracts.

As an apparent contradiction, though Westerns as a genre were extremely popular, by 1911 exhibitors started lobbying for a change in the movie representation of the West, and claimed that audiences were tiring of constantly-repeated sensationalized crime, hold-ups, murders, and shootings. And indeed many of the contemporary movie posters looked like dime novel covers.

Exhibitors felt that the current productions were attracting too many young men when they wanted instead to appeal to middle-class women, the ones who typically controlled the family finances. The goal of theater owners was to attract the more affluent viewers to their movie theaters and to increase their profits by appealing to respectable middle-class adults and families. As films played at all hours, additional profit could be realized from the custom that women could go unescorted to the movies during the day. Theater owners felt that the plots of the current Westerns were driving this audience away.

Opinions on how to achieve this goal ranged from downplaying the criminal activity and lurid violence in movies in order to appeal more to middle-class values, to introducing more romantic elements and heroic figures into Westerns in order to emphasize moral lessons in the stories. Still other opinions came from patrons who wanted movies to become more of a return to the Wild West shows, with Western movies providing a romanticized view of the West and featuring performers who could appeal to their preference for heroic protagonists. Some critics felt that the association of Westerns with dime novels, stage melodramas, and cheap sensational journalism was working-class entertainment and that Westerns mostly appealed to a rough crowd. Other critics complained that there were just too many Westerns altogether.[3]

Part of the controversy had as its basis the fact that many of the themes and plots of movies were adapted from the sensationalist media. Violence, chase scenes, criminal activity, and simplistic morals had become the characteristics of the genre.

Indeed, the plots of these Westerns were popular with working-class boys and young men in large cities, thus creating guaranteed large audiences for exhibitors. This popularity created the dilemma of how to still produce profitable Westerns, but

Iconic Images of the Movie West #3: Old Tucson Studios, Arizona. **Old Tucson Studios was originally built in 1939 as an exact replica of Old Tucson in the 1860s for the movie** *Arizona* **(1940), then was used for countless Western movies and television shows. Movies filmed at and near the studio are readily recognized by the sharp, prominent profile of Golden Gate Mountain on the skyline, and seen in the background of many of the Western movies filmed at Old Tucson Studios. Note also the presence of the two iconic saguaro cacti of the Sonoran Desert at the far left.**

at the same time downplay the sensationalistic aspects. Business interests continued to commercialize the Western past, but the new trend was to introduce more romanticism and more idealized Western characters.

The Western as a genre was, at the same time, also competing with European imports. By 1910 approximately half of the films released in New York were made by companies based in Europe, thus giving the American film manufacturers a financial reason for concern.[4] However, though the European manufacturers, primarily the French, German, Italian, and British, made Westerns, they were often full of factual errors, such as the use of flat English riding saddles instead of the taller Western saddle with its distinctive horn and deeper seat. Another way for American filmmakers to fight back against these foreign-made films was to use the spectacular scenery of the plains, deserts, and mountain landscapes of the real American West to provide authenticity for American-made Westerns.

By the 1910s the major American film companies had film crews constantly out on location in the West, searching for realism, authentic ambience, and natural marvels. At the time, many areas of the West consisted of a vast and wild territory, isolated and not easily accessible.

Though the first American Westerns had been filmed in New Jersey, New York, and Connecticut, featuring lush woodlands, lakes, and streams, Westerns filmed in the East did not have the authentic feel of the West and critics referred to those films as having "Jersey scenery." After about 1911 most Westerns were filmed on America's West Coast, and the prevailing film scenery and landscape evolved into the deserts, grasslands, and prairies of California.

Filmmakers gradually ventured beyond Los Angeles into the rest of the West to add authentic landscapes and striking visual images. In 1912 they discovered Arizona and New Mexico. Lubin Manufacturing Company, for example, set up a small movie studio in Tucson and filmed in the scenic desert landscape that surrounded the city. Lubin made more than a hundred movies in the desert Southwest between 1912 and 1915.[5] In this way, the Sonoran Desert with its characteristic saguaro cactus started to become identified as one of the distinctive types of scenery associated with the Western landscape. Selig also sent a crew to film in Tucson in 1912 and 1913. This association with the West became so strong that saguaros were used in some scenes of the cartoon feature *Rango* (2011) to depict the iconic West of the Westerns.

The Lubin crew later moved to Prescott, Arizona, about 180 miles northwest of Tucson, and filmed in the surrounding pine forests and valleys.

As more and more Westerns were filmed in California, the countryside around Los Angeles came to be regarded as the new classic image of the West. The Southern California landscape at the time still consisted primarily of wide-open spaces dotted with desolate and barren rocky areas, open grassy hillsides with stands of oak trees, rustic ranches, winding canyons, and rocky cliffs. These were ideal locations for filming Western action sequences involving chases, escapes, ambushes, stagecoach pursuits, and cattle drives. In the process, filmmakers created a mythical geography consisting of the most photogenic elements. The film industry reshaped the landscape, took it out of context, and put it in a new context depending on their needs.

In 1910 Essanay made 46 westerns; in 1912 they made 74.[6] As Westerns gained in popularity, other manufacturers saw the benefits of the West Coast and started to film in California. Biograph began filming in California in 1910 because D.W. Griffith felt the outdoor scenery provided authenticity for his Westerns.[7] Between 1911 and 1913 almost all of the major movie companies opened facilities in Los Angeles.

Technical Challenges for the 1910s

"Exteriors" were scenes filmed in the outdoors, shot either on location, on a back lot at a studio, or on a studio ranch. "Interiors" were scenes shot on a studio stage.

Because raw film stock at the time had a very slow speed, filming required the use of large amounts of light to ensure adequate exposure, thus exterior scenes were shot in the outdoors in bright sunlight.[8] Studios and sets used for filming interior scenes, and scenes filmed indoors that were supposed to be exteriors, were filmed in studios that had windows forming the walls, or had no roof, just an open top to let in as much natural sunlight as possible. In this way the pleasant weather of the West Coast and Southwest could achieve adequate light levels for film exposure, which made it attractive for filming. The almost constant sunshine and good weather of Southern California allowed filming all year round, even in winter.

Carbon arc spotlights and mercury vapor lights were sometimes used to boost light levels, but artificial electrical lighting was expensive to purchase and to use. Lights for movie use, called Klieg lights, were available from a theatrical lighting company founded in 1896 by the Kliegl Brothers, who had invented a very bright electric arc light. Motion picture studio lights are still generically nicknamed "klieg lights" after them.

In addition to the low light sensitivity of motion picture film, the contrast of the final image on the film was generally poor and tended to wash out fine detail. To overcome this, early film actors used heavy make-up that consisted of white face powder, bright red lipstick, and a distinctive outline of black mascara around the eyes. This created a high degree of contrast in order to delineate the actor's facial features and compensate for the low contrast of the film stock used at the time. This type of makeup was used for comic effect in ¡*Three Amigos!* (1986), a satire of Western films and their stars set in 1916. The film also satirized some of the overly-melodramatic acting that was in vogue at the time. Even the name Goldsmith Pictures was a humorous jab at the industry.

Broncho Billy Fades Away

Broncho Billy Anderson made a steady stream of Broncho Billy films between 1910 and 1915. Representative titles were *Broncho Billy and the Baby*, *Broncho Billy's Bible*, *Broncho Billy's Oath*, and *Broncho Billy's Last Spree*, with plots that emphasized the traditional values of home, family, and church. By 1911 Anderson had started to de-emphasize crime in his plots and featured white men almost exclusively as his central characters. Part of the reason he did this was an attempt to appeal to exhibitors and make his films attractive to middle-class white women.

As Anderson started to focus more on character than on spectacle, he altered his plots to make his Broncho Billy character the central feature of his films, rather than the scenery. As a result, it made sense for him to stop being nomadic, roaming all over the West looking for new locations, and to centralize his production facilities at one site. Accordingly, in 1912 Anderson built a permanent studio for Essanay in Niles, California. The facility included an indoor studio, a supporting carpentry shop, stables for horses, and garages for cars.[9] In this way Anderson could still be close to Niles Canyon, which he liked for filming because of its wild and scenic look. He used the Niles location repeatedly, thus the hills and canyons of Northern California became one of the iconic images of how the West should look that endured for many years.

By 1915, however, the general popularity of Broncho Billy was going into decline and by 1916 Anderson figured his Broncho Billy career was effectively over. Anderson was tired of making one- and two-reel Westerns, and both he and his audiences were tiring of the Broncho Billy character and the similarity of the repeated plots. Exhibitors wanted four- and five-reel feature films, but Spoor felt that what he was doing was profitable and wanted to continue with two reels. Anderson told him he wanted to sell out and Spoor agreed.[10] In January of 1916 Anderson ended the series, and he and Spoor dissolved their partnership. After Anderson left, Spoor closed the Niles facilities, along with the Essanay factory and studio in Edendale, and centralized all of the company's operations in Chicago.

Anderson intended to continue in films; however, he had a clause in his contract with Spoor that he could not make competing movies for the next two years. After this length of time, resuming his movie career never happened and Anderson left the motion picture business for good. His financial success in the movies allowed him to return to his original dream of being involved with theatrical productions.

Thomas Ince and Inceville

By late November of 1909 Fred Balshofer and New York Motion Picture Company had permanently moved their Bison subsidiary to California, where they could make pictures year-round under sunny weather, either outdoors or with open-roofed sets and studios. Balshofer planned to lengthen New York Motion Picture Company films to two reels and portray the actual life and experiences of real settlers, such as cattlemen and gold prospectors, in the West. To accomplish this, in 1911 he hired a man named Thomas Ince.

Thomas Harper Ince was a former actor with a background in legitimate theater and stage management who arrived in Hollywood in 1911, following a year of filmmaking in New York and Cuba. Ince had previously directed pictures at Biograph, and at Carl Laemmle's Independent Moving Picture Company (IMP). Ince left IMP and was hired by New York Motion Picture Company's Bison subsidiary in California, primarily to make Balshofer's new type of Western.

The second part of the plan was to hire suitable actors. To do this Balshofer made a deal with the Miller Brothers. The *Miller Brothers' 101 Ranch Wild West Show* had been performing successfully at rodeo grounds, stadiums, and exhibition halls around the country. The show included trick shooters, wranglers, ropers, wild horse riders, Indian warriors, clowns, acrobats, and bull riders.[11]

The relationship between the Wild West shows and motion pictures went back to the beginning of the movies. In 1894 W.K.L. Dickson had filmed performers from Buffalo Bill's shows in Edison's Black Maria studio in West Orange, New Jersey. Selig and others had used Wild West show performers both for stunts and as actors in films. In 1909 Selig had made pictures with Miller Brothers performers that incorporated their riding skills, shooting acts, rope tricks, and other performances from the show into simple melodramas. Many of the actions scene in these early movies were based on Wild West show staging.

The opportunity arose for the Millers to enter the motion picture business when they decided to winter their performers and stock in Los Angeles, instead of returning to their ranch in Oklahoma. The show had ended the performing season in Pomona, just east of Los Angeles, and the stock and equipment were being stored for the winter on the grounds of the Los Angeles Gun Club. Some of the performers and workers stayed at the St. Marks Hotel in Venice, a small community by the ocean just south of Santa Monica, others leased oceanfront cottages on the Venice beach. This type of arrangement was not unusual and, at the same time, the Al Barnes Wild Animal Circus was also wintering in Venice.[12]

Several independent filmmakers had approached the Millers to use the Millers' stock and performers in their movies, but in 1911 the Miller Brothers made a deal with Fred Balshofer to lease most of the show for $2,500 a week. The contract gave him and New York Motion Picture Company access to 75 cowboys, 25 cowgirls, and 35 Ponca Indians from Oklahoma, along with supporting oxen, buffalo, horses, stagecoaches, and wagons.[13] Livestock, feed, and other supplies were provided from the 101 Ranch headquarters in Oklahoma.

New York Motion Picture Company had previously filmed on a picturesque tract of land north of Santa Monica in Santa Ynez Canyon at the intersection of the Pacific Coast Highway and Sunset Boulevard. The land was attractive and isolated, though still relatively accessible from Los Angeles and contained some of the most scenic landscape in Southern California.

In 1911 Balshofer leased a large tract of this land in the rugged Santa Monica Mountains to film Western dramas that included Indian attacks on settlers, wagon trains, and stagecoaches. The property was made up of parcels of land from the Pacific Electric Railway, the Santa Monica Mountain Park Company, and Santa Monica Water and Power Company. Balshofer obtained 18,000 acres of scenic landscape for the exclusive use of his Bison Company.[14]

After Ince joined Balshofer in 1911, a town named Inceville grew up at the mouth of the canyon, on a bluff overlooking the ocean. Ince, sometimes called the "Father of the Western," built open air stages, a Western town set, a ranch set, and other Western buildings for outdoor location filming. Under Ince's management, the land around Inceville became an elaborate outdoor studio, complete with an electric power plant and a telephone system. The workforce grew so large that the ranch grew its own vegetables and raised its own cattle for food. It was officially called the Miller 101 Bison Ranch Studio, but became more popularly known as Inceville, after Ince.[15]

Ince hired Indians, built an Indian village with teepees, and went into large-scale

Inceville, at the mouth of Santa Ynez canyon in the Santa Monica Mountains, grew to be an elaborate film town that contained a Western town, an Indian village, a ranch, and all the other sets required for filming Westerns, along with the required support services. As seen in this photograph taken in 1919, the entire canyon became an elaborate outdoor set. The sign to the left of the center shows that the photograph was taken after Inceville had been renamed the Triangle Ranch (Glenn Kinnaman Colorado and Western History Collection).

production of Indian pictures. He was soon filming Westerns such as *War on the Plains* (1911), which featured the cowboys and Indians from the 101 Ranch show. Like other film companies (and Wild West shows) at the time, the 101 Ranch crew at Inceville sometimes performed in front of a painted movie backdrop while filming to give the impression of a different landscape.

By February of 1912 Ince had produced four Westerns. Ince's strength was as an organizer and supervisor. At first he acted as screenwriter, producer, director, and actor. Soon, however, the rate of production was more than he could handle alone. He directed the first few films himself, then he hired other directors and delegated production to others while he retained creative control.[16] One of Ince's directors was Francis (Frank) Ford, director John Ford's older brother.[17] Ince had multiple directors working on different films at the same time, but kept tight control over them. To do this, he developed a system of motion picture production that was based around the concept of a factory assembly line.

Balshofer's new Westerns were produced under the trade name "101 Bison," for the combination of 101 Ranch and Bison Moving Picture Company, and featured stories created around the show's performers. Filming on location outdoors in Santa Ynez Canyon gave the pictures a feel of realism and authenticity. Many of the Ince's plots were a bit thin, but viewers didn't notice that in all the spectacle.

Ince was a superb organizer and developed efficient methods for shooting Westerns. To achieve this, he developed standardized production methods that used a written script to break down many of the production details into routine tasks. He was the first filmmaker to insist that his directors use a detailed shooting script that contained the complete dialog and a description of the sets, rather than the previous method of letting them make up the story and choose locations as they went along.

Ince's directors were given the script several weeks before the start of filming, so that they could assemble the costumes, pick the locations, and locate the props. Thus, when filming started, the producer and director were familiar with what they had to do. Ince was the first to bring these modern industrial practices to filmmaking. Another innovation was that Ince hired writers with journalism backgrounds to create new screenplays for Bison's plots, instead of purchasing the rights or outright pirating of ideas from previous books or stage plays.

Ince now had the system he needed to film Westerns on a production-line basis. The stars of his films were driven 25 miles from Los Angeles in chauffeured cars. The supporting actors traveled by bus from Venice. The extras who played American Indians had their own village in the canyon, and many of the cowboys lived on the ranch in tents and cabins.

Bison hired Sioux, Cheyenne, Pawnee, Osage, Comanche, and other Native Americans to portray generic Indians. Similar to the representation of Indians in Buffalo Bill's show, the actors were all costumed and represented as if they were from a single nebulous tribe. On one occasion, to boost ticket sales, Bison's publicity agents started a rumor that the Indians at Inceville were so dangerous that security guards had to be employed to keep them from scalping the rest of the cast and crew. Another publicity rumor was that the movie producers had to constantly check to make sure that the Indians had not loaded their guns with live ammunition instead of blanks during battle scenes.[18]

The rugged Santa Ynez Canyon area, with its small side canyons and rolling grasslands, was ideal for what Ince wanted for the Western landscapes that he wished to portray. Bison filmmakers were able to use the spectacular canyon as a vast outdoor stage, and Ince used it frequently to stage wagon train and stagecoach attacks by Indians. Most of the films reached their climax with a fierce battle between the cavalry or cowboys and the Indians, and often included burning an Indian village.

Inceville was ideal for staging this type of action. The camera could film action going on at the bottom of the canyon from the rim, thus creating spectacular high-angle shots of the landscape and the entire troupe of performers, which was particularly effective for overall shots of battle scenes. The details of the action were then filmed at the bottom of the canyon.

Ince wrote film plots to make the best of the Miller troupe's capabilities, including riding stunts and other popular elements of the original Miller Brother's Wild West show. Thus he did not have to teach performers to do new tricks, as they already knew what to do. Ince tried to be authentic with costumes, and his films showed what cowboys from the 101 Ranch actually wore.

Performers from the 101 Ranch also filmed a series of Western movies in the San Francisco area. One of their favorite locations was Golden Gate Park, a 1,000-acre urban park on the coast south of the Presidio that consisted of a three-mile long scenic area full of trees and lakes.

Much of the creation of the movie image of the cowboy and cowgirl was due to the Millers' performers. The Miller cowboys continued to perform in motion pictures and the Miller's Wild West show continued sporadically into the 1920s. Though the Millers had the ranch to finance their other entertainment activities, the tough economic times of the Great Depression, falling box office receipts, rising costs at the ranch, and lowered prices for farm products took their toll and the ranch collapsed financially in the 1930s. The Millers' show went into bankruptcy and closed for good in 1931, following the deaths of two of the brothers, Joe and George. Their Oklahoma family ranch went into receivership and was sold at auction.

William S. Hart

By the mid–1910s, while the popularity of Broncho Billy movies was fading, that of William S. Hart was on the rise, and by 1917 Hart had taken over as the top cowboy film star. As a result, Hart's vision of the West and the Western landscape dominated Western films from 1916 to 1919.

William Surrey Hart was a professional stage actor who spent 30 years touring the United States in classical and contemporary plays. He started his career as a Shakespearean actor and was subsequently very good at portraying villains in Westerns with his quiet, intense style of acting.

Hart saw a Western film in Cleveland while he was touring on the stage, and decided he wanted to make Westerns himself, so he talked to former fellow-actor and old friend Thomas Ince of New York Motion Picture Company to discuss producing Westerns. The two had been roommates when they were both struggling for success on Broadway.

Ince was not enthusiastic about the idea because he felt that the popularity of Westerns were declining, and told Hart that the American public was becoming tired of the genre. But Hart was persistent, so Ince let him try anyway. Hart started making movies in 1914 at the age of 49.

Hart wanted to try a new style of Western that was later called "realism." His initial efforts were not particularly successful, but eventually the studio staff created a consistent screen persona for Hart that made him into a marketable character.[19] The central theme in many of Hart's films was the concept of a bad protagonist who is reformed and redeemed by the love of a good woman. Hart's movies preached Victorian values of godliness, self-control, sentimentality, and honor, and projected a moral sense and set of values and behavior to which he felt American people should conform. By 1916 Hart's films had captured the dominant position in Westerns.

Hart's craggy screen persona matched the landscape that he showed in his Westerns. Hart had a deep love of the West and its landscape, but he depicted a stark, grim, and unyielding vision of the West as he thought it had been. Hart dressed himself and fellow actors in what he considered to be authentic Western clothing that was drab, well-worn, and utilitarian. His movie sets and outdoor filming locations were characterized by gritty, ramshackle Western towns. His surrounding landscapes were desert-like, with only sparse grass and random clumps of brush. Critics claimed that his visual look was realistic and authentic, but is perhaps better described as harsh. He portrayed the Western landscape as raw, violent, and somber.

Hart's West was not a glamorous place, and his settings were stark and unadorned. Hart's Westerns used crude costumes, ramshackle and dilapidated town sets with drab streets and rough interiors, and an overpowering sense of ever-present heat and clouds of dust to produce the "realism" for which he was praised. Though Hart used former lawmen Bat Masterson and Wyatt Earp (who were still alive at the time) as consultants and believed himself to be authentic in his depictions of the West, some historians feel that he was not much more accurate than other filmmakers.[20] Though he wanted to make what he thought were realistic Westerns, his costumes and settings were probably no more realistic than those of Anderson or Mix.

Hart's vision of the West, just like Buffalo Bill Cody, the dime novelists, Owen Wister, Broncho Billy Anderson, and others before them, was not necessarily the real West. Film critic Jon Tuska has pointed out, "Hart's plots as plots are *not* realistic. They are keenly romantic, sentimental, melodramatic, occasionally ridiculous—but ridiculous in the spirit of Don Quixote."[21] Regardless of actual authenticity, movie audiences believed that Hart was accurate, though most of the "realism" for these early Westerns came from the pages of contemporary pulp Western magazines and earlier dime novels.

Hart's vision of the outdoor West as tumbled-down rough shacks in the middle of a bleak and dusty wilderness dominated Westerns from 1916 to 1919. His popularity, however, started to decline in the 1920s when first-run theaters started to refuse to run Hart's Westerns because he still clung to a male code of honor that audiences felt belonged in an older Victorian era.

Tom Mix Emerges

When the Miller Brothers Wild West show performed in Madison Square Garden in 1905, one of the performers was a 25-year-old cowboy named Tom Mix, performing under the stage name of Tom Mixco from Old Mexico.[22] Over the years Mix's real past became clouded by distortions and half-truths, and embellished by publicity agents. However, his contribution to the way his Westerns were filmed on location was very important.

Tom Mix became a star with a white hat, expensive cowboy boots, and fearless stunt work. Mix consistently put on popular performances in low budget Westerns that sold easily to neighborhood and small-town theaters. He created a cowboy hero who was larger than life and paved the way for the later flamboyant Hollywood show-business singing cowboys. Unlike Hart, who wore drab costumes, Mix wore fancy silk cowboy shirts, hand-made boots, and large, high-crowned white cowboy hats, complemented by a hand-tooled gun belt and holster. His movies were theatrical, showy, and fast-paced, with plenty of action, stunts, and cowboy heroics and excitement. He did many of his own stunts and daredevil feats.[23]

Tom Mix and his publicists developed a fantastic story for his background. The truth, however, seems to be blurred and much of his public biography may have been created by Mix and his press agents at Fox Studios.[24] According to them, Mix was born in log cabin near El Paso, Texas, in 1880. His father was supposedly a captain in the Seventh Cavalry and his mother a Cherokee Indian. He became a lumberjack, was nearly adopted by Buffalo Bill, and was a veteran of the Spanish-American War, the Philippine Campaign, the Boxer Rebellion, the Boer War, and he supposedly rode with Pancho Villa. He was credited with being a sheriff in Kansas, Oklahoma, and Colorado, and a Texas Ranger.[25]

As one biographer delicately expressed it, "When Mix ultimately became a big star at Fox, publicity created a biography for him far more colorful than any of his movie roles."[26] Tom Mix was actually born Thomas Hezikiah Mix in 1880 near Mix Run, Pennsylvania. When he turned 18, he dropped Hezikiah and used Edwin, his father's first name, for his middle name. Mix enlisted in the military for the Spanish-American war in 1898, hoping to fight in Cuba. Instead, he was assigned to an artillery unit guarding the Du Pont gunpowder works in Montchanin, Delaware, against a Spanish invasion of the American mainland. Movie publicists later said that he had fought alongside Roosevelt at San Juan Hill. In reality, he never left the eastern United States, and never fired a shot in combat. He was honorably discharged in 1901, then re-enlisted, hoping to fight in the Boer War in Africa. In 1902 he took leave to visit his new wife and never returned. Apparently the army never followed up, though he was officially listed as a deserter.[27] Mix did serve briefly as a deputy sheriff in Dewey, Oklahoma.[28]

Mix was good-looking with dark hair and a muscular build due to previous experience as a physical fitness trainer and boxing instructor. He met Joe and Zack Miller while he was a bartender at the Blue Belle Saloon in Guthrie, Oklahoma. They offered him a job as a cowhand at the 101 Ranch, where he learned to ride and rope well enough to compete in rodeos. He also learned many of the riding tricks that he used later in his movies. While working at the 101 Ranch's dude ranch operation he helped to entertain guests. He specialized in telling tall tales (called "windies" by the cowboys), which included his own magnified exploits.

Mix rose to prominence in the Miller's 101 show. At one point in the performance he played a rustler dragged behind his horse. He re-created this for *The Law and the Outlaw* (1913), as a stunt where his foot caught in a stirrup and he was dragged behind his horse.[29] Mix went to work for Selig Polyscope in 1910 when Selig used him as an extra and wrangler in a ranch documentary called *Ranch Life in the Great Southwest* (1910), filmed at Dewey, Oklahoma. The film showed cowboys rounding up cattle and shipping them to eastern markets. Director Francis Boggs needed someone to handle the stock and act as a safety man, so he hired Tom Mix to care for the livestock and as a general adviser.[30] Mix handled the stock, but he also asked for a part in the film and appeared briefly in a bronc-busting sequence. Mix was invited along when the unit went to Missouri to continue filming.[31]

After the film was completed, Selig hired Mix to work in California as a general stock wrangler to manage livestock and help with the animals in jungle and other wild animal features, do stunts, and provide technical advice for a series of Westerns.

Mix moved into acting and made almost a hundred one- and two-reel Westerns for Selig between 1911 and 1917.[32] He played different roles in Selig films, some as star, and some in supporting roles. Selig paid Mix $100 a week and initially sent him to make outdoor Westerns on location in Cañon City, Colorado. Selig chose Cañon City as a location because the Arkansas River, the Royal Gorge, and other breathtaking natural scenery were close by, and the town had a railroad station. Selig hired some of the local residents as extras, along with cattle herds and cowboys to herd them.

In 1911 Mix was either featured in or starred in *Kit Carson's Wooing*, *In Old California*, *The Cowboy and the Shrew*, *Saved by the Pony Express*, *Why the Sheriff Is a Bachelor*, and *A Romance of the Rio Grande*. These were all short one-reel films that were among some of the earliest filmed there on location.

In 1911 Col. Selig hired Tom Mix at $100 a week and sent him to make outdoor films on location around Cañon City, Colorado. Selig chose Cañon City because it was close to the Arkansas River, the Royal Gorge of the Arkansas, and other breathtaking natural scenery. This photograph shows the rugged grandeur and steep cliffs of the Royal Gorge, just west of the town, the type of outdoor location that appealed to Mix, who included it in a series of films he made in the area (Library of Congress).

In 1912 Mix's contract expired and he became Selig's partner, writing scripts and directing and starring in his own films. In the 1910s many Westerns were made in New Mexico by Biograph and Lubin, with much of the activity centered around Las Vegas. Selig produced one-reel Westerns in Las Vegas with Tom Mix as early as 1915.

Tom Mix introduced showmanship and a slick, polished format to his films, a type of performance later followed by other Western stars, such as Ken Maynard and Hoot Gibson. A Mix one-reel film had a budget of about $500. Of that Mix received about $150 as actor and director.[33] There were no particular scripts, so Mix devised an adventure around his riding stunts and showmanship, or started with an action sequence, such as a runaway stagecoach, then created a plot around it.

Mix continued to compete in rodeos and perform in the Miller Wild West show while he was making Western movies for Selig, and conversely film crews visited Wild West shows and ranches to collect background footage and action shots. The plots and action in all of them were very similar and all were interconnected with the same riding skills.

Mix replaced Hart's dusty authenticity and melodrama with flamboyant showmanship. He did not want realism, but preferred to perform outrageous stunts. He portrayed a sharp-shooting, fast-riding, hard-hitting cowboy, and offered flashy outdoor thrills-and-chills entertainment in ornate outfits that were more suited to circuses and rodeo parades than work as a real cowboy. Mix billed himself as America's Champion Cowboy and used his marksmanship, riding, and rodeo skills in his movies. Mix played cowboys, sheriffs, Indians, Mexicans, horse thieves, and outlaws. He belonged to the age of showmanship and role-playing, unlike Hart who strove for authenticity.

Selig Polyscope ran into serious financial problems (not of Mix's making) in 1917 and the company collapsed, eventually to be absorbed into Vitagraph, which was in turn absorbed by Warner Brothers in 1925.[34] In 1917 Mix signed a contract with William Fox, and went on to make about 60 films for Fox Studios over the next 11 years.[35] Mix realized that movies were dominating entertainment, and while audiences of thousands might attend the Wild West shows, millions might see his movies. It was an astute business move for both Mix and Fox.

Fox increased Mix's budgets to improve the production values and provided him with his own 12-acre Western back lot in Edendale. Here Mix built a western town, complete with an Indian village that became nicknamed "Mixville."

Mix's films offered unadulterated escapist entertainment. He abandoned Hart's realism and concentrated on cowboy legend. Mix's first films for Fox were similar to what he had made at Selig, such as *Hearts and Saddles*, *A Roman Cowboy*, *Six Cylinder Love*, and *A Soft Tenderfoot*. In 1918 he made six five-reel feature films for Fox, including *Cupid's Roundup*, *Six-shooter Andy*, *Mr. Logan U.S.A.*, and *Western Blood*.

Mix and his equine companion, Tony the Wonder Horse, turned out eight or nine feature films a year.[36] He filmed at authentic Western locations in Wyoming, Arizona, Utah, California, and Colorado.

Mix softened the image of the cowboy, but his movies depicted a mythical West where men spent 24 hours a day fighting and shooting it out with one another. He provided a romanticized vision of a past age with a likeable hero (namely him), who was a rugged individualist hero with no vices, such as smoking, drinking, or womanizing.

Mix felt that a good story was more important than authenticity. He developed simple plots that contained plenty of lively action, starring a moral and courageous hero battling a sneaky, underhanded villain, with dastardly schemes to be foiled, and a helpless heroine to be rescued. This combination was very popular in the 1920s. His stories contained no serious issues and nobody expected to take any of his movies too seriously. Mix maintained that this was what his audiences wanted and he provided it for them. He incorporated daredevil riding skills, furious chases, expert shooting, plenty of fist fights, and struggles with villains on top of speeding trains and automobiles. Unlike Hart, who was a deadly, no-nonsense avenger, Mix did little shooting and subdued his villains with his fists.

Mix minimized bloodshed in fights, emphasized morality over historical accuracy, amplified the role of villains, and marginalized women and Indians. His films contained a non-stop series of fist-fights, chases, riding stunts, and cliff-hangers.[37] He might be caught in a stampede of cattle or horses, trapped in a burning building, be left unconscious in a runaway wagon or car, be blown up in a mine disaster, fall from cliff, or be about to be lynched by mob.

Over his film career, Mix made over 300 silent films, and 10 talking pictures after sound arrived. *Trailin'* (1921) contains several memorable stunts, including one where Mix rode his horse across a narrow bridge spanning a river. When they were part of the way across the bridge, it unexpectedly collapsed, sending Tom and his horse into the raging current below. In another hair-raising piece of action, Mix and the heroine Sally Fortune (Eva Novak) slide down a sheer cliff to escape a posse. Yet another involved him leaping off an embankment onto a tree limb.

Stunts Enhance the Action

Movie companies visited Wild West shows to film action shots on location for their movies. Movie producers then edited these separate pieces into their plots. Show performers, for their part, wanted work during the off-season and were only too willing to do dare-devil stunts for the movies. This was a time before professional stuntmen were available and before optical special effects had been developed, therefore film crews found that cowboys from the Wild West shows were the best way to capture daredevil stunts in live shots. Conversely the performers liked to do stunts, as this provided good money for only a few hour's or a day's work. In this way, Wild West shows, rodeo performing, and movies were all interconnected. The later cowboy stars of the 1920s and 1930s, such as Buck Jones, William Boyd, Hoot Gibson, Ken Maynard, and Tim McCoy, all appeared in Wild West shows and developed their skills in the arena.

When ranching went into a decline and the Wild West shows were closing, many out-of-work cowboys headed for Hollywood because they had heard that they could make more money falling off a horse than they ever made staying on it working with cows. Stunt men were paid extra for specific individual stunts, such as participation in a rowdy saloon fight or for a particularly difficult horse fall. Employment was sporadic, but now and then a director would show up and hire some of them for a day's work. Many old cowboys hung around the Old Waterhole Saloon at Hollywood Boulevard and Cahuenga Avenue in Hollywood, a prime hangout for those who wanted to be cowboy movie stars.[38]

Complex, spectacular stunts increasingly became an important part of Westerns filmed in the outdoors, and stunt riders were encouraged by moviemakers to perform ever more daring stunts. Unfortunately the desire for increasingly spectacular stunts often resulted in cruelty to the animals involved. In 1913 three filmmakers from the Pathé studio were arrested and fined for animal cruelty when they pushed a horse over a cliff to film its fall and the animal was severely injured.[39]

The Business of Business

As the 1910s progressed, film companies came and went as they moved around the country. The motion picture industry shuffled itself, re-shuffled, and finally re-organized itself into the studio system that ushered in the golden age of filmmaking.

During these early years, the Motion Picture Patents Company did not forget its mission, even though film companies had moved to the West Coast to escape them. Incidents of intimidation by hired private detectives became so bad that some film crews hired armed guards to protect them and their equipment while they filmed. Bison had an advantage in this, because having tough cowboys around from the Miller show, armed with guns, ensured that Motion Picture Patents Company detectives did not interfere with their filming.[40]

Meanwhile, other business machinations were going on behind the scenes. Bauman and Kessel at New York Motion Picture invested in a studio named The Keystone Film Company. They hired talented comedy director Mack Sennett, who in turn hired comedienne Mabel Normand. Keystone eventually had a line-up of the best comedy stars of the time, including Roscoe "Fatty" Arbuckle, Charlie Chaplin, Gloria Swanson, Ben Turpin, and Chester Conklin. As all Bison's Westerns were being made at Inceville, Bauman moved the entire operation to California to their Edendale studio in 1912.

Out of all this came one of the few giant studios that was to survive in the motion picture industry. This was Universal, headed by Carl Laemmle. The story goes that when Laemmle was trying to think of a new name for his production company he looked out of the window and saw a Universal Pipe Fittings truck on the street and decided that was the name for him.[41]

Laemmle had originally worked for a clothing company, but was excited about the business opportunities offered by film exhibition, so he opened a nickelodeon in Chicago in 1906. He soon added another, then eventually acquired a chain of movie houses and founded his own exchange and film distribution company. He added a partner and opened his own production company in New York called Independent Moving Picture Company of America (IMP) in 1909 to make films to supply his own nickelodeons and distribution company.

In 1912 Universal Film Manufacturing Company (known simply as Universal), with Carl Laemmle as president, merged with New York Motion Picture Company, along with its Bison 101 subsidiary. Thus, after the merger, Universal gained control of both Inceville and New York Motion Picture's Edendale studio, which now included Keystone. Laemmle moved production units into Inceville to make Westerns under the 101 Bison name. In 1915 Ince left for nearby Culver City to build new studio and continued to make Westerns with Fred Balshofer under the name Broncho films.[42]

In 1915 Universal consolidated its production at a new studio built on the previous Taylor Ranch, five miles north of Hollywood, and in the early 1920s Inceville fell into disuse. The deteriorating Inceville was known for a while as Hartville, after William S. Hart purchased the property in 1916 and used it until 1918. The town continued to be used as a movie set by Robertson-Cole Pictures, though storms and brush fires made it look even more dilapidated. A final fire in 1922 completely destroyed the remaining sets.

Universal continued to make Westerns under the banner of 101 Bison, then reverted to Bison 101 after several lawsuits over the name. Universal also owned a movie ranch in the San Fernando Valley, complete with a bunkhouse for the cowboys and an Indian village. Universal was the largest producer of Westerns in the 1920s and at one time over half their production was Westerns.[43]

Another complex business arrangement started when brothers Harry and Roy Aitken purchased several nickelodeons and then opened their own studio, American Film Manufacturing in Chicago, in order to control their supply of product. They expanded the production and exhibition ends of the business as the Triangle Motion Picture Company in 1915, one of the first movie businesses to be vertically integrated. They produced pictures, distributed them, and exhibited them in their own chain of 200 theaters. They hired Ince, Mack Sennett, and D.W. Griffith to produce films. Triangle was headquartered on a triangular-shaped piece of land in Culver City, which had been laid out in the 1910s by Harry Culver. Their facility contained six

Gallup, New Mexico, was discovered as a movie location in 1915. By the 1930s Gallup was a major center for Western film production. One of the most popular areas for filming was about seven miles to the east of the town, where Red Rock Park is located today. This photograph from 1929 shows an undeveloped area of sagebrush in the foreground with red cliffs rising up behind, with the cone shape of aptly-named Pyramid Rock in the center.

glass-fronted studios to let in plenty of sunlight for film production, and they filmed on sets with open ceilings in order to gain the maximum amount of sunlight. Many of their Western films used large interior sets that represented dance halls and saloons. Triangle produced a string of prestige pictures and for three years was a dominant force in the film industry. The group broke up in 1918 due to internal management disagreements and heavy financial losses.[44]

The Studio System Evolves

By 1912 seven major studios were operating year-round on the West Coast: Selig, Essanay, New York Motion Picture, Kalem, Nestor, American, and Pathé. All specialized in Westerns. Overseas competitors suddenly realized that to produce believable Westerns they had to film on the home ground of the American studios. Accordingly, the French companies Méliès and Pathé opened production facilities in the West. Méliès located a production unit in San Antonio, Texas, and Pathé established a West Coast studio.

Pathé located their permanent studio in Edendale, less than a block away from Selig and across the street from New York Motion Picture Company. The Pathé studio soon became too small for their increased production of Western motion pictures. In order to expand operations, Pathé built a new studio in 1912 on 35 acres on top of a hill overlooking Edendale, which had by then become the center of southern California's small but growing Western film industry. This new location offered more space to make action Westerns in the outdoors.[45]

The striking scenery around Edendale could be used for backdrops to Western movies, and the relative proximity to Los Angeles made the small town a natural attraction for directors of Westerns and Indian-themed movies. But though Edendale was the hotbed of early Western film activity, most of the filming eventually moved to nearby Hollywood. In 1910 the Hollywood area was mostly covered with orange groves and boasted a population of about 5,000 people. By 1920, the population had grown to 36,000 people, and 20,000 more were moving there each year. By 1930 Hollywood had grown to nearly 250,000 people.[46]

Director Cecil B. DeMille arrived in Hollywood in 1912 after entering into partnership with vaudeville musician Jesse Lasky and his brother-in-law Samuel Goldfish (later changed to Goldwyn). DeMille supposedly traveled to Flagstaff to make a Western on location for Jesse L. Lasky Feature Play Company, which had been formed by Lasky, Goldfish, DeMille, and attorney Arthur Friend.[47] According to urban legend the train arrived while rain was pouring down in Flagstaff. The town supposedly did not look enough like DeMille's conception of the West to suit him, so he and his film company climbed back on the train and went on to Hollywood.[48] In 1914 DeMille's company produced *Squaw Man* starring Dustin Farnum, a six-reel film considered to be the first full-length motion picture produced entirely in Hollywood, in a barn on the corner of Selma Avenue and Vine Street.

Over the next few years several self-made future movie studio heads (mostly immigrant Jews with East European roots) established studios in Hollywood, including Adolph Zukor who had been a wholesale furrier, Marcus Loew who had also been a wholesale furrier, William Fox (born William Fried), Samuel Goldfish/Goldwyn who had been a glove salesman, Carl Laemmle, Louis B. Mayer who had been a scrap iron dealer, the Selzniks, the four Warner Brothers, and Jesse Lasky, who had been a vaudeville producer and showman.[49] Between them these movie moguls controlled seven major Hollywood Studios during Hollywood's golden era. They were MGM, Twentieth Century–Fox, Columbia, Paramount, Universal, RKO, and Warner Bros. Together they were often collectively referred to as the Seven Sisters, and were referred to in Hollywood as the "Dream Factories" for their imaginative entertainment.

Adolph Zukor formed Famous Players in 1912 to make feature films. In 1916 he merged Famous Players Film Company with Jesse L. Lasky Feature Play Company to form Famous Players-Lasky (FPL). FPL made deals to distribute movies from leading independent producers, including Thomas Ince. The combination later became Paramount. In 1916 Paramount's owners sold out to Zukor and he kept name. He also built Paramount's theater chain to be the largest movie circuit in the country.[50]

William Fox was the founder of Fox Films and Fox Theaters, which included the magnificent Roxy Theater in New York. Fox started in the movie business when he purchased a nickelodeon. He made it into a success and added more theaters.

Fox founded his own film exchange and then Fox Films in 1914, headquartered in New York. He started filming in California in 1915 on a rented one-acre property in Edendale with 30 employees. The facilities rapidly grew to 30 acres staffed by 500 employees. Fox's West Coast studio was in the center of Hollywood at Western Avenue and Sunset Boulevard. Other property included a ranch in Calabasas for making Westerns on location. In 1935 Fox merged with Twentieth Century Pictures, who had no outdoor lot, but made pictures at United Artists, who also handled distribution.[51]

The four Warner brothers were Harry, Jack, Sam and Albert. Warner Bros. started as film distributors and exhibitors, showing other studio's movies, then as the demand for films rose they started to make their own. Their first production was a three-reel Western titled *The Peril of the Plains* (1912), filmed in St. Louis by Sam Warner. The title of the film varied, depending on the city where it was exhibited and year it was seen. Warners initially rented space in New York, San Francisco, and Edendale. In 1919 they leased land for their first Hollywood lot on Sunset Boulevard, but continued to shoot at various locations and rented studios in Los Angeles.[52]

Warner Brothers Pictures was formally incorporated in 1923. Jack selected the scripts, hired the talent, and controlled production. Harry was the businessman and arranged financing. Sam was the technical expert, and Albert was the treasurer. Warners continued to expand, though their finances were always on shaky ground.

First National started as an amalgamation of theater chains in 1917, then became a distribution company before becoming a production studio. In 1928 First National was taken over by Warners. Part of the purchase agreement was that Warners was to keep the First National name. Warners used the logo "A First National Picture" until 1958, as the name and logo could produce higher rentals.[53]

Goldwyn Pictures, which combined the names of partners Samuel Goldfish and Edgar Selwyn, purchased Triangle's former studio facilities in October 1918, when Triangle broke up.[54] They expanded the studio facilities, which had six stages surrounded by glass for maximum light, and increased the size of the administration building. An inability to control excessive production expenditures, poor box office returns, and a lack of stars led the company on a path towards financial bankruptcy, so the board ousted Goldwyn.

MGM's parent company was Loew's Inc. Like most of the other film studio moguls, Marcus Loew started in the film business with a series of penny arcades that featured vaudeville acts, games of chance, and motion pictures. Like the others, his arcades eventually became full-scale vaudeville houses, nickelodeons, and then movie theaters. Loew built his movie empire into a large chain of high-class, high-capacity, first-run movie houses. Like other theater owners, Loew needed to constantly supply his theaters with new films, so he purchased Metro Pictures in 1919.[55]

Several other small motion picture companies tried to enter the field with their interpretation of the Wild West, but none was as successful as the Seven Sisters. Though the film studios came, went, grew, changed, and merged with one another, Westerns had come to Hollywood to stay.

Chapter Four

The 1920s
Consolidation on the Coast

By the 1920s the American film industry was firmly established in Hollywood, with 50 studios and some 50,000 employees.[1] Further consolidation of the film industry continued to take place on the West Coast, influenced by the need for new and suitable locations for filming Westerns, and by the consistent good weather and bright sunshine available for year-round outdoor location filming.

The use of location photography was considered to be so important that when Zane Grey's novel *The Vanishing American* (1925) was filmed, Grey's contract with Paramount specified that at least some of the scenes in his novels had to be filmed on location where they were supposed to have occurred. The same happened over 20 years later when Zane Grey's *Wild Horse Mesa* (1947) was filmed on location. Grey felt that the land was an important part of his plots, and the location and scenery connected the events in the novels.[2] Various of Grey's films were shot on location in Monument Valley, Utah, Montana, and Colorado.

Westerns did well at the box office. They have always been a safer financial bet than many other genres of film and almost always turned a profit. Their status, though, suffered in the early 1920s as the Western's popularity among audiences in first run theaters faded and Western films were relegated to neighborhood theaters in small-towns. Typical of the trend was the small Strand Theater in Gallup, New Mexico, which continued for years to play shoot-'em-ups to enthusiastic audiences.

The market for Westerns suffered a slump in 1926 because too many cheap Westerns were being produced. In apparent contradiction, one study of the kinds of film preferred by audiences in rural New England in 1926 showed that Westerns were the most popular of all.[3] However, Westerns in general suffered from shifting audience tastes as urban audiences turned away from the old horse operas. Studios associated them with rural and small-town audiences.

Growth of the Theater Chains

The growth of the chains of movie theaters that were owned by the studios during the 1920s was to play a major part in a shift in location filming. This growth would lead eventually, 20 years later, to the downfall of the entire Hollywood studio

Iconic Images of the Movie West #4: Lone Pine, California. **Movie Flats, near the town of Lone Pine, is closely associated with Westerns. The rugged boulders in the foreground were the location of countless chase scenes. Avid movie fans will recognize the Sierra Nevada Mountains in the background with Mt. Whitney as the distant sharp peak on the right.**

system and changes in location filming. Of particular interest was the growth of the Paramount theater chain and the theaters owned by Loew's Inc., the parent company of MGM. Both Paramount and MGM operated a chain of deluxe nationwide theaters.

Ownership in the 1920s of a chain of movie theaters by the studios stabilized the expensive and highly risky business of film production. The exhibition end of the movie business was substantial, stable, and very profitable. The United States had 20,000 movie theaters with a total weekly attendance of 55 million people that produced annual paid admissions of $700 million.[4]

The sumptuous movie theaters were aptly named "movie palaces." The Roxy Theatre, for example, which opened just off Times Square in New York in 1927 was the world's largest, most luxurious, and most spectacular movie theater. Named after theater operator Samuel L. "Roxy" Rothafel, it offered the ultimate in opulence, which gave it the nickname "the Cathedral of the Motion Picture."[5] The Roxy Theater had 5,920 seats and lavish furnishings. The building was half a block long, with a Spanish Baroque façade. The five-story-high, gold-domed circular lobby rotunda was decorated with green marble columns, wine-colored draperies, and gold-leaf wall decorations. The theater also boasted deep pile carpeting, a 110-piece orchestra pit, three massive Kimball theater organ consoles, and an ornate proscenium arch. It was staffed by 125 ushers in blue uniforms. The building had a fully-equipped nurses' station and its own electrical power plant.[6] The theater was a showcase for films through the 1950s, then was demolished in 1960.

A typical start of a movie theater chain was that of Alexander Pantages, an entrepreneur who operated penny arcades and nickelodeons. He purchased a run-down theater in Seattle, adapted it for vaudeville shows and kept it packed. He soon acquired another vaudeville palace, and another, and eventually owned 60 theaters. Like other vaudeville theater owners, Pantages gradually added movies to the vaudeville playbills.

Pantages' biggest competitor on the west Coast was the Orpheum vaudeville circuit. This became a dominant force when Joseph P. Kennedy, father of president John Kennedy, took over a chain of three dozen movie houses in New England. He then added the Balaban and Katz chains. By end of the 1920s 60 million Americans were going to movies in his 21,000 theaters.[7] Kennedy eventually also took over the Pantages theater chain.

In February of 1926 Kennedy became the head of FBO Pictures (Film Booking Offices of America), a small Hollywood studio that specialized in cheaply-made Westerns. The studio's biggest asset was Fred Thomson, the first movie cowboy to have a horse with star billing, Silver King, who traveled to work in a customized horse trailer with his name on the side. Kennedy took over the Keith-Albee-Orpheum vaudeville theater circuit in 1928 from Benjamin F. Keith and Edward F. Albee, and merged it into his movie company FBO, which became RKO (Radio Keith Orpheum). Eventually RKO became one of the major studios in Hollywood.

In September of 1928 Warner Bros. purchased Stanley Theater Corporation, which owned 250 theaters in seven states, in order to stabilize their studio finances. In October they purchased two-thirds of First National Pictures, a major film producer and distributor, then in 1929 purchased the other third. First National had been founded in 1917 by Thomas Tally and James Williams as a syndicate of theater owners who had the resources to produce films themselves.[8]

During the mid to late 1920s, the showing of Westerns declined in the large, fancy, first-run theaters, as the genre had lost its popularity with audiences. Driven by the usual business motive of profit, the owners and managers of the sumptuous movie theaters looked for audiences that would expand their business. For a film to play in these large first-run theaters, it had to appeal to middle-class women, who mostly wanted to see an appealing hero. Thus audience demands shifted from the dour William S. Hart to the matinee idols, such as Rudolph Valentino and John Barrymore, in costume dramas that were promoted to appeal to women audiences.

Movie studios continued to make Westerns in large numbers, but the low-budget "shoot-'em-up" type of Western was relegated to smaller neighborhood and second-run theaters in small towns, mostly for screenings of one or two days. Studios made Westerns to serve a niche market made up primarily of men and boys who went to these second-run theaters. Because the income from these small theaters was lower, producers had to hold the costs of these shoot-'em-ups down to keep them profitable.

Smaller budgets led to a formula approach to filming. Even by the early 1920s "series Westerns," also known as "program Westerns" or "programmers," used the same actor playing the same character in a series of movies. This was also because boys and other fans did not want their cowboy stars to vary from a basic formula of fistfights and gunplay.

Although programmers did not get critical acclaim, they were important to Hollywood's economic well-being. By 1920 most studios had a cowboy star whose films were reliable and consistent moneymakers. These cheaply-made Westerns continued into the 1930s, 1940s, and 1950s.

William S. Hart in Decline

William S. Hart's movies began to earn less money after 1920. Hart's career was in decline and Tom Mix had taken over as the star of the Westerns. Hart was still popular, but in light of Mix's flamboyant performances, exhibitors felt that Hart's movies were old-fashioned. In 1924 Hart and Ince parted ways. After that Hart wrote, produced, and directed his own pictures. He continued to live the Western lifestyle in Newhall, California, in a mansion that also had on the property a small Western movie set with corrals, horses, and cattle.

The success of *The Covered Wagon* (1923) renewed audience interest in outdoor Westerns and Paramount asked Hart to return to the screen with a series of new movies. Hart, however, would not compromise on his vision of the West and his Westerns. He saw himself as the expert on the West and he wanted complete control of production. Paramount asked him to change his approach, but Hart refused and so his contract with the studio ended. Hart's movie career was over by the mid–1920s.[9] In addition, audience tastes had changed and movie patrons of the 1920s were not interested in his version of the "authentic" West. Audiences saw his vision as belonging to the past and wanted more contemporary action like the films of Tom Mix.

Tom Mix Takes Over

By the 1920s the star system was established. The plots of Westerns mattered less than who was in them. Tom Mix, with his emphasis on excitement, stunts, outdoor action, and bravado in his films, had the largest following. He typically portrayed a hard-riding hero who never drank, smoked, or swore, and didn't have prolonged love clinches. He rarely used his guns and never killed villains, but preferred to lasso them and tie them up. He specialized in subduing them in perilous fist-fights on the top of trains, cars, and high cliffs.

Mix filmed a string of Westerns with Fox, including *The Lone Star Ranger* (1923), *Riders of the Purple Sage* (1925), *The Great K&A Train Robbery* (1926), *Outlaws of Red River* (1927), and *Son of the Golden West* (1928). Mix's films had excellent photography and used breathtaking scenic locations as Mix emphasized the importance of filming on location in the Western landscape, many of them on location in Colorado and around the West. He particularly liked to film in national parks in the West because of their spectacular scenery, as he wanted to show off the natural wonders of the West to his audiences. The film *Sky High* (1922), for example, was filmed in the rugged grandeur of the outdoors at the Grand Canyon in Arizona with a spectacular fist fight set on the rim of the canyon itself.

A good example of the spectacular location filming of Tom Mix's Western films was *The Great K&A Train Robbery* (1926), a silent film starring Mix and Dorothy Dwan.[10] *The Great K & A Train Robbery* (1926) was notable for its stunt work, primarily shot on location around Glenwood Springs, Colorado, using the Denver & Rio Grande Railroad. The film was distinguished for its excellent use of breathtaking locations, including sequences filmed in Glenwood Canyon, just east of Glenwood Springs, along the Colorado River. The Denver & Rio Grande tracks ran on the south side of the canyon, with the river flowing next to it, and U.S. Highway 6, a gravel-surfaced road at the time, running along north bank of the river. Today U.S. Highway 6 has vanished under Interstate 70, but the railroad tracks and the river still look much like they did in 1926.

The spectacular sheer cliffs of Glenwood Canyon, along the Colorado River just east of Glenwood Springs, were used by Tom Mix for filming *The Great K & A Train Robbery* (1926). The rugged canyon was used for Mix's opening stunts. Taken in the 1960s, this photograph shows U.S Highway 6 on the left, with the Denver & Rio Grande railroad tracks across the river in the bushes on the right. The building in the center is the Shoshone hydroelectric generating plant. Today, U.S. Highway 6 has vanished under Interstate 70 (Library of Congress).

This was not the first time that the beauty of spectacular Glenwood Canyon had been filmed. In 1902, Harry Buckwalter had filmed an exciting scene in the canyon on the gravel road for Selig Polyscope, for a film titled *Runaway Stage Coach* (1902).[11]

The Great K & A Train Robbery (1926), was a light-hearted adventure movie in which Mix played a special detective chasing train robbers, and was used as a showcase for Mix's stunts and choice of magnificent outdoor background scenery. Westerns with a railroading background were popular with audiences in the days of silent movies, so Mix wrote trains into his film scripts as much as possible, and incorporated as many fights, chases, and stunts involving trains as he could.

Mix took his family and 55 cast and crew members to Colorado in two Pullman train cars along with two special baggage cars.[12] Local residents were recruited as extras, and other locals from the town gathered every day for three weeks to watch Mix and his famous horse, Tony, in action. Much of the exciting stunt work took place on a train traveling through the spectacular background and steep confines of Glenwood Canyon, with the rapids of the Colorado River churning and foaming in the background.[13]

Riding and shooting skills were essential for a movie like this, and Mix's rodeo and Wild West background was ideal for the stunts he had to do. As the film opens, Mix is hanging on a rope that stretches into the distance up the side of a steep gorge, ending just under the bandits' campsite on top of the canyon rim. The sequence includes a closeup that shows that it really is Mix hanging on a rope just under the rim of the canyon. When one of the bandits sees him, Mix escapes by sliding down the rope, the lower end of which is tied to the saddle-horn of his horse Tony at the bottom of the canyon. Smoothly transitioning into the saddle, he and Tony gallop off.

Outdoor stunts abounded in the film. Mix sees the heroine Madge (Dorothy Dwan) careening away down the road on a runaway speeding buckboard and rescues her, and after galloping behind a passing train, hands her up onto the rear platform and climbs aboard. After talking to other actors inside a coach, he jumps off the moving train onto the ground, just as quickly jumps up onto the undercarriage of one of the coaches, then just as quickly jumps off again and mounts Tony. As he rides alongside the train, he lassos and rescues a tramp, DeLuxe Harry (Harry Grippe), whose hammock slung underneath the train breaks.

As Mix chases the bandits in various sequences in the film, he rides Tony off a balcony into an ornamental pool (shot back at the studio), jumps on top of a moving train from a rockfall, and pulls himself off the top of the moving train to end up swinging himself to safety on a railroad mechanism that the train passes under. After a good old-fashioned fist-fighting brawl in the bandits' secret underground cave (complete with a mysterious underwater entrance from the river), he captures all of them, turns them over to a posse, and ends up with the girl.

The Great K&A Train Robbery (1926) was one of Mix's best films, made when he was at the peak of his career and it made a large profit for the studio. Mix's Western films were so popular that they helped to finance and support less profitable "image" pictures for Fox. These were movies that were made for the prestige of the studio, but had low financial returns. By 1925 Mix was one of the most popular stars of the time, earning $17,500 a week, which made him the highest paid star in Hollywood at the time.[14]

The public loved the fantasy world of Hollywood stars. To match his income, Mix lived an extravagant, gaudy lifestyle. He owned a yacht, the Diamond S Ranch in Prescott, Arizona, and lived in a mansion in Beverly Hills with a seven-car garage and a huge sign on the lawn with his initials that were lit up at night. On screen Mix did not drink, swear, or use unnecessary violence. His clean-living, non-drinking image helped lead to the later clean-cut heroes of Gene Autry and Roy Rogers. In real life, Mix smoked, drank liquor, and was married five times.[15]

As cowboy stars were very popular in the 1920s, Mix moved further away from Western realism and created the cowboy hero. He turned the simple cowboy into a myth, with costumes, stunts, and showmanship. He admitted openly that his screen character was not intended to parallel that of the authentic Westerners. Mix evolved the impractical and uneconomical cowboy "uniform" that became more flamboyant as the decade progressed, and dominated the image through the years of Gene Autry and Roy Rogers.

Mix was a showman and his costume reflected the circus approach. He started wearing huge white hats and fancy clothes that bore no relationship to what real cowboys wore. He popularized gaudy Western shirts with "smile" pockets (breast shirt pockets shaped like a smile), with arrow points at both ends. He had multi-button cuffs, and had as many as five buttons on each wrist in *The Texas Bad Man* (1932). Mix wore striped pants tucked into fancy boots that had intricate designs on them, and introduced gloves because his hands were soft. They also provided protection during fights and stunts. Subsequent stars imitated him.

Mix realized what his audiences wanted and he provided it. The public wanted escapist entertainment, spectacular scenery, and a good story rather than authenticity. So Mix offered a romantic vision of the past and played a rugged individual who was moral and courageous, and brought villains to justice.

Mix's movies had a standardized plot line and fans protested if he deviated from it. His plots were instilled with morals that were clean and wholesome. He showed that truth and justice triumphed in his mythical West. He defeated the villains using fists, horse chases, shooting, riding stunts, fancy roping, lassoing, knife-throwing, and fights on top of trains. Trains, automobiles, motorcycles, and airplanes provided accessories for many of his stunts. Women were portrayed as pure, helpless, and innocent as Mix rescued them from the villain. To serve as a model for youth, Mix promoted perseverance, humility, and hard work.

Tom Mix made over a hundred movies for Fox Films. Many theater owners called Mix "the rent man" because Mix's name on the marquee would pack the house and helped ensure that they met their overhead every month. On average, each Mix movie was booked by 7,000 theaters, not including repeat engagements. In January of 1925 Mix and Fox negotiated a $2 million, three-and-a-half-year contract, which made him the highest salaried actor in Hollywood at the time.[16]

Eventually Mix had a falling-out with Fox, with rumors at the time that Mix was becoming too expensive for the studio and difficult to work with.[17] Reportedly fame had made him meaner and more egotistical, and he drank heavily.[18] Mix's contract was not renewed in 1928 despite the fact that Mix's films were generating huge profits for the studio and even though he was the most popular and best-earning cowboy star in Hollywood at the time. After Mix left Fox, he made several sound Westerns at Universal, including *Hidden Gold* (1932), but his career was in decline.

On October 12, 1940, Mix was driving fast, 18 miles south of Florence, Arizona, on State Highway 79. He missed a detour sign for a bridge that had washed out and was under road repair. His custom-built Cord Roadster, with a pair of longhorns mounted on the radiator, left the road when the speeding car failed to make a curve. The result was that the car plowed into a dry wash (now named Tom Mix Wash) and turned over. A metal suitcase from the back seat rammed forward and broke his neck. True to his flamboyant end, Mix was buried in Forest Lawn Memorial Park in Los Angeles, in a silver-plated coffin with his initials on it. Today the Tom Mix Memorial Monument in Arizona is a rest area on the side of the road, with picnic benches and a barbeque pit. A small stone monument with a cut-out figure of a horse with an empty saddle overlooks it.

The First Epic Westerns

By 1923 the public's obsession with Westerns had died down, with the genre at its lowest point in popularity in the previous 10 years. But public tastes in entertainment are fickle and the Western came back into favor again after 1923, and rose to a new peak in 1926. The reason was *The Covered Wagon* (1923), a film that was memorable for its superb Western vistas of the unspoiled American landscape.

The Covered Wagon (1923) was the first epic Western filmed on location. The story was about an emigrant caravan of pioneers headed west on the Oregon Trail during the time of the settlement of the Northwest. The film was memorable for several outdoor sequences, among them vast panoramic scenes of the long wagon train winding across the plains, a thrilling buffalo hunt, and an exciting river-crossing sequence shot with multiple cameras.

Audiences loved the sweeping vistas and grandeur of the scenery, filmed almost entirely on location, mostly on the border between Utah and Nevada, under conditions that resembled those experienced by the pioneers themselves. This type of location filming was a departure from the standard procedure of the time of supervised shooting in a studio. The crew had to endure wind, flood waters, heat, and dust at the location for eight weeks. Even an unexpected blizzard was written into the script.

Most of the filming took place on the Baker Ranch in the Snake Valley in Nevada. The buffalo hunting sequence was filmed at Antelope Island in the Great Salt Lake, using the large herd owned by the Buffalo Livestock Company. For the wagon crossing scene, the crew built a dam and created their own lake, though the dam burst at one point and flooded the filming camp.

The production logistics on location were as massive as the film itself. *The Covered Wagon* (1923) required almost 1,000 extras and 750 Indians, with 500 tents used to house everybody. Five hundred wagons were rented or borrowed. The negative cost (the expense of producing the film negative, before marketing and distribution costs) was $782,000; however, by 1932 the film had earned $3.8 million.[19]

The second Western outdoor epic that produced a resurgence in audience interest in Westerns was *The Iron Horse* (1924), an early silent film from director John Ford that was intended to be Fox's answer to Paramount's *The Covered Wagon* (1923). *The Iron Horse* (1924) told the story of the building of the transcontinental railroad line that culminated in the joining of the Union Pacific and Central Pacific railroads at Promontory Point in Utah on May 10, 1869. Similar to *The Covered Wagon* (1923), *The Iron Horse* (1924) was nearly all filmed on location in the Nevada desert at Dodge Flats, near Wadsworth, Nevada, with little or no work back at the studio. The scenes with cattle were filmed in Mexico. Like *The Covered Wagon* (1923), the production logistics on location were staggering. Fox claimed that the studio had employed 3,000 railroad workmen, 1,000 Chinese laborers, 8,000 Indians, and 2,800 horses. The massive production involved 5,000 extras and used a train with 56 coaches for transportation. During filming, the entire company lived under conditions similar to those of the original railroad workers.

The general settings and props were historically correct for both *The Covered Wagon* (1923) and *The Iron Horse* (1924), through the plots were not. These Westerns offered historical pictures full of action and with spectacular scenery, but producers added a romance narrative and proven box office stars. Nevertheless these two films gave theater audiences a spectacular look at the unspoiled American landscape.

To provide authenticity for *The Iron Horse* (1924), the crew built two complete town sets in the barren Nevada desert to stand in for North Platte, Nebraska, and Cheyenne, Wyoming, two of the railroad towns founded when the real railroad was built. These sets were constructed near tracks of the real Southern Pacific Railroad. This use of location photography gave the film a feeling of documentary reality that could not have been achieved by filming in the studio. For example, the use of cabin interiors with action taking place outside the windows. Some of the scenes were not totally realistic, such as the use of a backdrop of a canyon that was obviously a painted flat, but their use was minimal.

The Growing Studio System

During the 1920s Los Angeles and Hollywood continued to grow in importance as the hub of the film industry. By 1925 William Fox realized that the center of film production was never coming back to New York, so he upgraded his Hollywood studios. He built a large Spanish-style administration building with a red tile roof, and three of the largest sound stages in the world, each the size of a baseball field. The studio lot even had a small hospital with a full-time surgeon, and a schoolhouse for 50 child actors. Another plus was a 20,000-volume research library.

Louis B. Mayer, the child of penniless Jewish-Russian parents, formed Louis B. Mayer Film Company in the 1920s and became an independent producer, working in a 32-acre studio on Mission Road. Marcus Loew had previously purchased Metro Pictures in 1919. In 1924 he purchased Mayer's company and Goldwyn Studios. When he obtained them, both had been in poor financial shape and ridden with debt. Loew merged Metro Pictures, Goldwyn Studios, and Mayer's film company and renamed the entire operation Metro-Goldwyn-Mayer Studios, with Mayer as vice-president of operations.[20]

The Introduction of Sound

In spite of all this shuffling, re-shuffling, and expansion in Hollywood, the end of the decade produced a major bump in the road for the studios. This was the arrival of talking pictures in the late 1920s, which had an immediate negative effect on the location filming of Westerns and on the production of Westerns in general. As a result, few Westerns were produced in 1928 and 1929 because of the technical difficulties of recording sound on location. Luckily, these problems were eventually resolved and contributed to the box office success of *In Old Arizona* (1929) and *The Virginian* (1931).

Adding sound to pictures had been explored by Thomas Edison as early as 1895 with a system called the Kinetophone, in which sound was recorded on wax cylinders synchronized with a movie projector. Several early systems for creating talking pictures appeared between 1904 and 1911, with such names as Phonofilm, Chronophone, Cameraphone, Cineophone, Cinephonograph, and Vivaphone, but none of them were successful and they all failed within a year or two of their introduction. The quality of the sound was poor, the equipment was expensive and difficult to operate, and synchronization between the visual image and the accompanying sound was often inconsistent.

One early approach was developed in 1913 when Edison introduced a revised version of the Kinetophone, even though it had various technical problems.[21] A fire at the Edison factory in New Jersey, however, ended further experimentation with that particular system. Nevertheless, engineers and electrical equipment manufacturers continued to tinker with sound technology. Fox invested heavily in sound, pursuing a sound-on-film process that he called Movietone.

The most promising step forward for sound films occurred in 1925 when Warners acquired an experimental sound-on-disc system called Vitaphone, developed by the Vitagraph Studios in Brooklyn, New York.[22] American Vitagraph (*vita* for life and *graph* for pictures) Company had been founded in 1897 by James Stuart Blackton, Albert Smith, and William Rock at the very beginning of the motion picture industry. Their company was important enough that it was a member of the Motion Picture Patents Company. By 1907 it was the most prolific American film production company, but by 1914 the company was in decline and deeply in debt.[23]

Warners purchased Vitagraph in 1925 as an attempt to become a major force in the industry by purchasing a larger, more established company. In return, Warners gained the Vitagraph facility in Brooklyn and another in Hollywood, plus a substantial distribution network. Ironically, the Brooklyn studio location was problematic for filming talking pictures as a noisy railroad spur was located just outside the building.

After acquiring Vitagraph, Warners produced several short sound films and tested them in two theaters wired for the Vitaphone sound-on-disc system. The concept was not well received by audiences, so Warners decided to continue making their films without dialog, but to add music, sound effects, and songs. Warners first feature film released with this new concept and the Vitaphone sound system was *Don Juan* (1926). This was not a talking picture, but it had a musical score and sound effects synchronized to the images. Though limited in auditory scope, the film was incredibly popular with audiences and was sold out for months.

Though *Don Juan* (1926) was well received, only a limited number of theaters that had been equipped for Warners' sound-on-disc system had the ability to show it. The more serious problem was that, though music and sound effects had been added to the film, the result for the audience was not much different than other films of the period that produced this type of accompanying sound live while the film was being shown. Warners realized that their next production had to be different in order to make it a real success.

In 1927 the major problem of sound was that the filming set had to be soundproof with no extraneous noise. Two of the major difficulties were that the large and noisy cameras had to be soundproofed to dampen the sound of the motors, and somehow the buzzing noise of the klieg lights required for filming indoors had to be suppressed. To achieve this, early sound movies were filmed on special interior sound stages that muffled extraneous operating sounds around the set. The Vitaphone camera was enclosed in a soundproof booth so that the whirring of the camera motors would not

Opening night at one of Warners' lavish movie palaces for *Don Juan* (1926), which was the first commercially-viable feature film that added music, sound effects, and songs with Warners' Vitaphone sound-on-disc system. Though the Vitaphone system was soon replaced by Fox's Movietone system, Warners paved the way for the total switchover of movies to sound.

be recorded. The sound booths that enclosed the movie cameras were appropriately nicknamed "sweat boxes." Air-conditioning had not yet been developed, so cameramen could only stay in the hot booth for a few minutes before emerging covered in sweat.

Another problem was maintaining a consistent level of sounds and speech, which varied according to the angle and distance of the actors from the microphone. Somehow concealed locations had to be found for the microphones while still allowing a clear pickup of the actors' voices.

Furthermore the camera and recording disc had to be synchronized.[24] Sound tracks could not be mixed, and editing the recorded sound was not possible, because the technical methods for dubbing and sound transfer had not yet been developed. Thus performers had to act while they were speaking their lines. Furthermore, singers had to be photographed and recorded simultaneously. They had to act and sing at the same time, while a studio orchestra played their accompanying music on the side of the set so that the entire performance could be captured on the recording disc simultaneously.

In spite of these technical challenges, Warners chose to film *The Jazz Singer* (1927) for their next project. They built a bunker made from concrete in the middle of a filming stage to isolate any noise from the camera and struggled to overcome the other technical challenges. *The Jazz Singer* (1927) premiered in New York City's Times Square on October 6, 1927. It was a sensation, and within a year more than 400 theaters had been wired for Vitaphone sound.[25]

By 1927 three viable competing sound systems had been developed. Warner's Vitaphone system was a sound-on-disc system with a record player synchronized to the film projector. The second was Fox's Movitone system, which recorded a soundtrack on the edge of the film during filming. The third was Radio Corporation of America's (RCA) Photophone system, which was also sound-on-film. The Movietone and Photophone systems were very similar and could be played interchangeably on the same projector with only minor modifications.

Essentially then two rival technologies emerged. The Vitaphone system recorded the sound onto a disc like a phonograph record, and synchronized it with the action in the film. The Fox's Movietone system converted sound to light waves and recorded them optically on the edge of the film, embedding them in a narrow strip next to the picture frame.

The Vitaphone technology had been easier to create, as it used existing technology that had been developed for the phonograph. The big problem with the Vitaphone system, however, was maintaining synchronization of the sound with the projected image. Unfortunately, once the sound was recorded onto a disc, it could not be changed or edited. If the film broke and had to be spliced, the sound went out of synchronization with the picture as the sound was now a few frames slower than the spliced visual image. If the sound was transferred selectively onto another disc to correct this, the result was a large loss of sound quality.

A further problem in maintaining perfect sound and picture synchronization was that editing often occurred after a picture was finished. One reason might be due to censorship, which was up to local film review boards in different markets whose tastes and edits varied from town to town. If a section of film was deemed objectionable and cut out, the sound disc could not be correspondingly edited. Another editing problem was that some theaters preferred a shortened version of a film in order to play in a predetermined time slot, and producers and distributors had previously edited films to meet those requirements. But if the image was changed for any reason, the sound would not match. A further issue was that the phonograph recording discs used were made from shellac, a brittle type of black plastic, and were thus fragile and liable to break during shipment or use.

The Movietone system was a more complex technical challenge, but it maintained perfect synchronization because the sound was recorded on the film. Fox pursued this sound-on-film process as it could be synchronized and edited along with the picture. Synchronization was achieved between the recorded sound and the photographed image during the original filming by use of a clapboard. This was a wooden board on which was written the name of the film, the scene being photographed, and the number of the take. A hinged arm was hit smartly against the top of the board while it was being photographed in order to produce a sharp sound that was used to synchronize the sound track with the visual image during editing.

Technically speaking, there was sometimes a minor issue with Movietone sound editing as the optical sound reproducing head was located slightly beyond the projection gate for the projected image on the projector. But the problem was minor compared to sound-on-disc. For these reasons, Movietone became the technology of choice. Though Warners had invested heavily in the development of sound-on-disc, none of the other film companies were interested in using the Vitaphone system.

Warners has traditionally been given the major credit for the innovation of sound in movies. They were indeed the first to develop and commercialize a practical theater system, but in the end they also lost the race to introduce sound to the movies. William Fox should receive additional credit for persisting in developing an alternative system that worked better and was ultimately adopted by the other studios.[26] Eventually even Warners converted to the competing sound-on-film process.

After the success of *The Jazz Singer* (1927), by mid–1928 the major studios realized that they had to modify their filming stages for sound, and chaos swept through Hollywood as they rushed to convert. Sound equipment was expensive and awkward. Because early microphones were large and could not be moved, all the action had to revolve around the microphone location. Concealing the microphone so that it was not seen by the camera, but successfully picked up sound clearly and distinctly, became a major problem.

As a further problem, movie cameras were confined to their soundproof booths to prevent operating noise from being picked up by the microphones used to capture the actors' speech and were not able to move around freely. As a result, filming technique became static and the actors resembled players on a theater stage, as opposed to the previous fluid motion of earlier movie-making.

The introduction of sound had not been without its difficulties, but when sound arrived, it took over with a rush. By February of 1930 approximately 95 percent of the films produced by Hollywood studios included sound and, by July of 1930, nearly all the nation's first run theaters had been wired for sound. The changeover at theaters in small towns took longer because of the cost of the equipment for conversion to sound.

But by 1935 both production and exhibition in the United States had been completely converted to sound.[27]

Sound in Westerns

When talking pictures arrived in 1927, engineers claimed that it would be very difficult, if not impossible, to film sound pictures in the outdoors. The impact on Westerns was that the major studios felt that filming with sound was totally unsuitable for location filming. And they were indeed correct in that Westerns had additional practical problems that went along with sound for a movie made on location, beyond just the noise from the camera during filming. Early sound cameras were big and bulky because of sound proofing. This made tracking shots, where the camera moved with the action, very difficult. In addition, the noise produced by a speeding camera car or truck when filming a running insert, where the camera moved at high speed alongside a galloping rider or group of horsemen, made these exciting scenes virtually impossible.

Another unforeseen, but not uncommon, difficulty encountered in early talking pictures was when an actor's voice failed to measure up to audience expectations. Many actors from silent movies couldn't make the transition to the talkies because their voices were not suitable for their roles, perhaps because they had heavy accents or squeaky voices, and didn't sound like heroes. In addition, many actors had been trained for classical stage work, which often gave their voices a ponderous quality that did not sound natural.

One unexpected cultural problem was that love-making was considered to be private, not something to be flaunted in speech on the screen. So the audience response to some of the love scenes in early sound movies was often laughter. Perversely, some patrons preferred silent movies because they found them more relaxing to watch.

The original perception by both studios and audiences was that sound had to be used to make films with lots of talking. Plenty of dialog was therefore added to exploit the novelty of sound. A scene that did not contain much talking might be followed closely by a static scene full of dialog, just to make a "talking picture." The added result was that the forward momentum of the plot in early sound films often stopped while the characters stood around and talked for no particular reason other than to provide sound. This was not acceptable to audiences who watched Westerns, as they preferred lots of outdoor action and not much talking.

During the first year or two of sound movies, it did not seem to be worth the effort to solve these technical problems just for Westerns, so most studios stopped producing them. However, gradually these logistical difficulties were overcome.

A major turning point came in 1929 when director Raoul Walsh from Fox Studios successfully filmed the first outdoor talking feature film, *In Old Arizona* (1928), on location in the outdoors. The film was partly shot in Bryce Canyon and Zion National Parks in Utah, and the Mojave Desert in California.

By achieving success, Walsh pioneered the use of sound in the first major sound Western. He solved one of the most complex problems of sound by hiding micro-

The ghost town of Grafton in Utah was used for *In Old Arizona* (1928) to take advantage of the spectacular cliffs of Zion National Park seen here in the background. The movie was so successful that the next year a sequel, *The Arizona Kid* (1930), was shot entirely on location. Other movies filmed in the tiny town were *Ramrod* (1947) and *Butch Cassidy and the Sundance Kid* (1969). The building shown here was built by a settler named Alonzo Russell in 1862 and occupied by him until 1910.

phones under bushes and trees to pick up the sounds of gunshots and galloping hooves. The soundtrack featured ringing bells, the pounding of horses' hooves, a train whistle, the singing of birds, and the crackle of frying bacon.

In Old Arizona (1928), the story of a Mexican bandit called the Cisco Kid, was such a smash hit that it restored Westerns as a popular genre. It was the biggest box office hit of year, and star Warner Baxter won an Academy Award for Best Actor as the Cisco Kid. The film was so popular that in 1929 Fox decided to commit totally to sound films, and the studio made no more silent movies. Fox was the first major studio to make this decision.

The introduction of sound altered the way in which pictures were made. In the silent era, three or four films could be made simultaneously in different corners of the same studio stage, all of them lit by the sun through huge windows and skylights. With the coming of talking pictures, separate sound-isolated sets had to be used for each film production. As a result, the glass-enclosed filming stages at MGM were replaced by 30 separate ones built with concrete for sound isolation. Similarly, the First National studio had been built with no provisions for coming of sound. None of the four original stages was soundproofed, so they all had to be rebuilt for sound filming.

Westerns, which were all action, should not have been bothered by some of the logistical problems associated with sound films. Fans of Westerns did not always want the realism of Hart, but did want the sound of galloping hooves, the staccato noises of six-guns, and the meaty impact of a fist on the bad guy's chin. But the issues of sound recording were a problem because Westerns were typically filmed in the great outdoors as audiences expected. Though dialog was added to Westerns to exploit the novelty of sound, early sound Westerns did not contain much actual conversation, but used sound in other ways, such as the noises of stampeding cattle, horses whinnying, gunshots, and the yells of cowboy.

Wider Screens

The success of *In Old Arizona* (1928) spurred a renewed interest in making large-scale sound Westerns. Then the novelty of sound wore off and audiences started to decline again.

To try to recapture their audiences, Hollywood studios experimented with various types of wide-screen presentations between 1926 and 1932; however, these technical attempts were premature and development efforts died away. *The Big Trail* (1930) was filmed simultaneously with standard 35mm movie film and Fox's Grandeur process (also known as Grandeur 70), a wide screen process that used 70mm film. The larger format was not a commercial success as only two theaters, the Roxy Theatre in New York City and Grauman's Chinese Theater in Los Angeles were equipped with the special projectors required to show it. The Grandeur process disappeared after 1931.

A Cloud on the Horizon

By the end of the first decade of the 1900s, film distributors and nickelodeon operators had needed to increase their supply of films to supply an expanding need by theater owners, and at the same time sought to increase their profits. As a result, several movie distributors and exhibitors had entered the film production end of the business to ensure an adequate supply for their own theaters. The result was that the major film studios increasingly controlled large chains of theaters as well as operating distribution channels to supply other theaters. The federal government saw this as monopoly of trade and as early as 1915 threatened to break up these monopolies by moving to act against some of the early established movie companies, including Selig, Essanay, and Vitagraph.[28]

In the late 1920s about 5,000 of the existing 15,000 or so theaters in the United States had the most seats and were owned or controlled by the largest movie studios. On the production side, eight major studios produced almost all the movies. Fox and MGM alone accounted for almost 40 percent of U.S. film production.[29] In light of this, the Federal Trade Commission claimed that ownership of movie theaters by producers and distributors was unfair competition for competing producers and competing distributors, and was a detriment to the public.

As early as 1925 the government had investigated the filmmaking practices of

Famous Players-Lasky with a view towards anti-trust action. In July of 1927, the Federal Trade Commission threatened legal action against Paramount, ordering the company to cease acquisition of theaters and stop block booking practices.[30] Block booking and blind booking was a business practice in which an exhibitor had to contract to rent a complete "block" of movies from the studio's output in order to be able to rent the premier films that they wanted. Some of the block might consist of lesser movies that might not be what their patrons wanted to see. But in this way the studio was guaranteed a market for all their pictures, good or bad.

The Federal Trade Commission re-opened its ongoing investigation into restrictive trade practices in the film industry in October of 1927, fueled in part by complaints from independent producers and distributors. On September 28, 1928, the U.S. Justice Department filed an antitrust lawsuit against nine major U.S. studios and exhibitors, alleging a conspiracy to restrain trade.

Threats of anti-trust litigation ground along slowly towards the end of the 1920s; however, when the Great Depression hit the country hard, including Hollywood, the government temporarily withdrew its anti-trust actions. This anti-trust sentiment and its legal actions did not however go away, but lay dormant in the background and did not have any real effect until 1948, when it was to have a large impact on the production of movies. This action was eventually instrumental in the downfall of the established studio system and was responsible for much of Western location filming moving overseas in the 1960s.

CHAPTER FIVE

The 1930s
The Rise of the B-Westerns

In the early 1930s, the production of Westerns declined due to changing public tastes, the economic effects of the Great Depression, the introduction of talking films, and the end of the era of the great Wild West shows. The big studios did not abandon making Westerns, but a lack of investment capital created a rapid fall in their production between 1931 and 1935. Universal cut back its output of Western considerably in the 1930s and moved into a cycle of horror films. Fox cut back after Tom Mix left the studio.

As the roaring 1920s ended, America faced the worst economic depression of the century, which lasted from the stock market crash in 1929 until the country entered World War II in 1941. Under the tough economic conditions of the Depression, the public wanted and needed the escape of an afternoon spent at the movie theater more than ever. Watching the hero ride off into the Western sunset with the girl provided one of the best escapes from reality, even though the April 1929 issue of *Photoplay* magazine had commented that Western movies, along with the Western novel and Western short story, had lost their popularity.

Seven major studios offered viewing audiences a glamorous world of make-believe. MGM, Warners, Twentieth Century–Fox, Universal, RKO, Columbia, and Paramount mass-produced films for public entertainment. Their actors and actresses were put under contract and molded into "movie stars." Major studios owned their own chains of movie theaters across the country and every week produced a feature film for their theaters. The afternoon's movie entertainment was rounded out with a comedy short, a newsreel, a cartoon, and previews of coming attractions.

Though the introduction of sound had kept audience numbers and profits fairly steady, audience attendance fell as the novelty of talking pictures wore off. Fox's earnings, for example, fell from $10 million in 1930 to a loss of $4 million in 1931. The studio lost nearly $11 million in 1931 and 1932 which pushed it to the brink of disaster and led to a takeover of Fox by AT&T and Chase National Bank in 1930.[1]

The Western, as a genre, did not do well and went into a period of decline during the early Depression years and many of the cowboy stars found themselves out of a job. Theater audiences continued to dwindle as the Depression deepened. With high unemployment rates, the average worker did not have the money for luxuries, a category that included going to the movies.

As well as the effects of the Depression, the sharp decline in the production of

Westerns in 1930 and 1931 was also partly due to the introduction of sound and its problems, which halted the location filming of Westerns until the problems of recording sound in the outdoors had been overcome. It wasn't until later in the 1930s that filming left the confines of the sound stages and went back on location in the outdoors. But even when it did, shooting sound pictures on location became more complex and costly, causing the major studios and producers to leave the Western genre to the smaller independent movie companies. The demand for Westerns was still out there, but it was dominated by a niche small-town audience that was predominantly made up of young males who loved cowboy and Indian pictures.

The period from 1932 to 1934 was a low point in the production of Westerns in Hollywood. For most of the years between 1926 and 1967, Westerns made up 25 percent of all the movies being made.[2] In 1925, a total of 227 Westerns were made. In 1926, the output was 199 Westerns. This figure fell to 108 produced in 1932 and to only 65 in 1933.[3] In 1933 the declining market for Westerns cut production 50 percent to 75 percent in Hollywood. The Great Depression, with its corresponding money shortage and instability in the economy, resulted in a lack of willingness of banks to invest in movies, the immediate effect of which was to limit the number of prestige films produced, a category that included costly shooting of Westerns on location.

Iconic Images of the Movie West #5: Monument Valley, Utah. **Director John Ford claimed that this vast, empty desert valley was his favorite place to make movies. Due to his films, it became one of the iconic representations of the movie West. This view shows the two weathered rock formations known as the Mittens, Left Mitten and Right Mitten, which are considered by the Navajo to be the hands of a Holy Person. Ford used the dirt road in the foreground so much that it was nicknamed "Hollywood Boulevard."**

Though a new cycle of epic Westerns had started in 1928, it was very short-lived. At the end of the 1920s, *In Old Arizona* (1928) and *The Virginian* (1929) had been successes, but the biggest Westerns of 1930 and 1931, Fox's *The Big Trail* (1930), *Billy the Kid* (1930), *Cimarron* (1931), and DeMille's remake of *The Squaw Man* (1931) did poorly at the box office. They were not commercial successes and failed to make back their production costs.

What went wrong has never been completely explained. *The Big Trail* (1930) should have succeeded. It was filmed against the splendor of the Western outdoor scenery outside Yuma, Arizona, and St. George, Utah. The location filming included sweeping panoramas of horse-drawn wagons crossing the rolling hills, a buffalo herd, the river crossing scene, and the scenes where the wagons were lowered on ropes down sheer cliffs. The desert scenes were filmed in Yuma, Arizona; the opening Mississippi riverboat scenes in Sacramento; the canyon scenes were shot near St. George, Utah, and at the Grand Tetons in Wyoming. Other spectacular locations were the California Sierra Nevada Mountains for the snow scenes and Sequoia National Park for the concluding scenes in the redwood forests. Because *The Big Trail* (1930), in particular, was a major box office disaster and *Cimarron* (1931) failed at the box office (even though it won the Academy Award for best picture), the major studios were reluctant to invest their efforts and money in similar expensive productions filmed in the outdoors.

Because of these failures, it was not until 1936 that the major studios returned to making Westerns on location as large-scale, prestige productions. *The Plainsman* (1936), filmed in Montana, *Union Pacific* (1939), and *North West Mounted Police* (1940) all did well at the box office and helped to re-establish the Western outdoor genre as a major attraction. By then the popular glamour musicals and the screwball comedies of the mid–1930s were declining in popularity, and by 1937 audience tastes turned back to outdoor films with an emphasis on action.

The demand for prestige Westerns surged again at the end of the decade with *Stagecoach* (1939) and Fox's *Jesse James* (1939). The latter was so successful that it triggered a series of Western productions based on similar notorious outlaw gangs, such as *The Return of Frank James* (1940), *When the Daltons Rode* (1940), *Bad Men of Missouri* (1941), *Belle Star* (1941), and *Billy the Kid* (1941), in the inevitable copycat cycle that followed a successful picture.

By the end of the silent era, the earlier American Indian as a heroic character had essentially vanished. In the epic Westerns of the 1930s, Indians became stereotyped as a faceless, nameless horde of indeterminate savages from some uncertain tribe, who swooped down on wagon trains while whooping and hollering, and whose main function was to be shot down in large numbers. This type of characterization can be seen in *The Big Trail* (1930), *Union Pacific* (1939), and *Stagecoach* (1939).

The Problems of Sound

The assumption of filmmakers that location shooting of sound Westerns would be impossible posed a serious problem for Westerns, as they had always been enjoyed for their scenic outdoor locations. Indeed, as we have seen, the early Western movie production companies relocated to California specifically to exploit the picturesque advantages of filming in authentic outdoor Western scenery.

Adding sound to movies required cameras to be heavily sound-proofed so that the noise of their whirring gears would not be present in the soundtrack. This made the cameras heavy and bulky, and made transportation and use of sound equipment at remote outdoor locations very difficult. As a result, limited dialog was present in early talking Westerns, with sound added mostly in the form of bawling cattle and gunshots. Even at best, in the later days of talking cowboy pictures after many of the technological problems had been solved, it was often difficult to record voices while actors were riding horses with the camera moving alongside, so these scenes were often dubbed back at the studio during post-production.

In February of 1929, audio engineers at MGM still remained doubtful about the possibility of making sound pictures in the outdoors, so Louis Mayer continued to make Westerns as silent films, without even music or synchronized sound effects. Some of his studio executives thought that Westerns would not succeed as talking pictures simply because of the difficulty of making talking films outside a studio set. Others thought that adding sound would in itself have a negative effect on the commercial potential of outdoor films. Mayer realized that the silent film was doomed, but agreed that Westerns with sound would be impossible for the studio to make. Other studios were cutting back or discontinuing their series Westerns, so Mayer discontinued his also.

When Warners merged with First National in 1929, they also immediately phased out Westerns. In 1930 even Carl Laemmle, president of Universal, felt that sound Westerns were too much of a financial risk and stopped making them. This, however, was a decision that he reversed three years later, after the problems of sound had been resolved.

Accompanying the basic technological difficulties of sound for the industry as a whole, another problem was that small independent film production companies could not afford to purchase equipment for recording sound, and small rural theaters could not afford to invest in the equipment for playback. As a result, most of the independent companies cut back on production on location while they waited to see what was going to happen. The successful arrival of the singing cowboy made the decision for them and required a commitment to make sound movies. When it became clear that there was no going back to the old silent days, even small production companies and small theaters had to somehow make the necessary financial investment.

To make sound films workable, there was one more major investment that all the studios had to make. Hollywood had to invest in the talents of actors with suitable speaking voices, often from New York's radio and Broadway actors, and they had to find playwrights and journalists to create speech scripts and who could write credible dialog.

The A's and the B's

In the 1920s there was no double feature at the movies. In the late 1920s, the play bill at a movie theater usually consisted of a feature film accompanied by one or two short subjects. However, the dramatic decline in box office receipts as the Depression worsened led to the introduction of the double feature as an inducement to try and attract audiences back.[4]

Starting in the 1930s, most theaters started to offer a playbill of two features, one or two cartoons, a newsreel, and previews of coming attractions. In addition, incentives to keep audiences included various other attractions, such as "dish-night" when audiences could collect a set of china, one piece every week, for attending the theater, and "bingo night" when audiences played for prizes.[5]

Due to a reluctance on the part of the major studios to finance many prestige Westerns, production diverged into what were called "A-Westerns" and "B-Westerns." The A-Western was a prestige, major production that had the full backing and promotional efforts of the studio that produced it. The B-Western was a low-budget film that played second on double-feature bills, on the lower, or "B," half of the double feature bill after the major, or "A," feature. B-Westerns were shorter than A-Western films, seldom running more than 70 minutes and usually around an hour.

The "A" films were typically booked for a percentage of the box-office receipts. "B" films, on the other hand, including B-Westerns on the lower half of the double feature, typically rented at a flat rate.

During the 1930s there were only about 50 films produced that could legitimately be called A-Westerns. Only eight A-Westerns were made in 1930 and five in 1931. No A-Westerns at all were made in 1934. The number rose to four in 1938, and increased to 14 in 1940.[6] Big-budget A-Westerns made up about 5 percent (66 out of 1,336) of all Western productions between 1930 and 1941.[7] More than 1,000 B-Westerns, however, were cranked out by the smaller studios.[8]

The plot of the epic prestige Westerns usually revolved around some major historic event in the West, such as the building of the railroad, the Pony Express, emigrant wagon trains, or the Oklahoma Land Rush. The epic Westerns were expensive to make, which limited the number that studios felt they could afford to produce. *The Covered Wagon* (1923), for example, cost $782,000 to produce, which was a risky amount for 1923, even though it eventually returned an estimated $7,630,000.[9] And the running time for these spectacles might be two hours or more. *The Iron Horse* (1924), originally ran 150 minutes. As a result, the B-Westerns, which were shorter in length and made on a tight budget, were more attractive to producers. The golden age of the B-Western occurred during the early and mid–1930s, fueled by cheap production costs, a ready audience market, and the potential for high profits.

A-Westerns of the 1930s included biographies of several of the legendary Westerners, such as *Billy the Kid* (1930), *Annie Oakley* (1935), and *The Plainsman* (1936). Characteristic of the A-Westerns of the period was *Stagecoach* (1939), which used a combination of genuine outdoor locations and shots filmed indoors on a studio set. Even though many of its outdoor dialog scenes were supposedly filmed on location, they were clearly filmed inside on a sound stage, with back projection supplemented by a few cactus props and painted backdrops to set the scene.

The B-Western

The Great Depression created an opportunity for small independent studios to produce films intended for the "B" half of a double bill. This resulted in a boom in the production of B-Westerns. Production by independents jumped from 26 in 1933, to 59 in 1934, and 106 in 1935.[10] These low-budget, routinely-produced Westerns were also called "programmers" or "program Westerns." Not as politely, they have also been derisively called oaters, cactus capers, shoot-'em-ups, horse operas, sagebrush sagas, horse flickers, and horse-manure-and-gunpowder-epics, among the more repeatable names.

Most of these B-Westerns had few high-quality production values or acting ability. The audience wanted lots of horseback chases, shoot-'em-ups, extended fights, realistic stunts, rugged scenery, and a familiar cowboy star. The B-Westerns made by Columbia typically had five or six fights per picture, and just as many chases. All this action did not leave time for much of a plot, but most viewers did not mind.

The B-Western was filled with chases, gunfights, stampedes, and fistfights in order to keep the picture moving at a fast pace. A fist-fight often took place as soon as the movie started. *Branded Men* (1931) with Ken Maynard, for example, starts the action immediately with a fist-fight for no particular reason among "the boys" standing around in the street.

One of the reasons that the major studios stayed away from making many Westerns was that B-Westerns appealed to a fairly specific audience, primarily young boys and men in rural areas. As a result of this specific market, the B-Western studios tried to keep their cowboy heroes suitable for a youth audience, so their cowboy stars did not drink, smoke, or swear in their films, and they always had a clean, neat appearance.

As the young boys in the audience didn't care much for kissing or romantic scenes, these were kept to a minimum. Heroes could be pals with the heroines, or help them, or sing to them, but could not have tender romantic scenes with them. Instead, the B-Western hero often shared the screen credit with his horse. Horses or sidekicks were often included in scenes with romance to satisfy the younger members of the audience and to divert attention from the girl. Thus the female leads were limited in their relationship to the hero. These were movies made by men about men, and the women were considered by their young audiences to be window-dressing that interfered with the flow of action.

Boys in the audience preferred their heroes to have a relationship with their horse, a younger brother, a young friend such as the character of Harry Cole (Bobs Watson) in *Dodge City* (1939) or Joey Starrett (Brandon De Wilde) in *Shane* (1953), or an older humorous sidekick, such as those portrayed by Gabby Hayes or Smiley Burnette. To appeal further to the boys and young men in the audience, many heroes were younger men who were free of the obligations of older adults. B-Westerns typically did not use American Indians in their plots. Instead the bad guys were crooked bankers, swindling land developers, and unscrupulous businessmen.

Studios promoted service by their cowboy stars in the army, which at that time was an exclusively male organization. Studios publicized and exaggerated the military careers of their B-Western cowboy stars to appeal to their male audience and emphasized how army life had shaped their manhood and character. This helped to establish that these were not just actors, but men who had legitimately honed their riding and shooting skills in the military.

As the 1930s progressed, the budgets of even the B-Westerns became increasingly tighter. The studios could get away with this economy because their audience did not want fancy additions to the simple plots or any departure from the basic structure of chases on horseback, extended fights, sensational stunt work, and rugged outdoor scenery. They wanted a familiar star in his trademark fancy cowboy costume and didn't want this formula changed.

Locations

In the B-Western the specific location where the action takes place was usually only incidental to the plot, and especially to the action. The specific geography was supposed to be the West, but exactly where in the West was nebulous, rather than being an actual location. In reality, the time and budget restrictions of B-Westerns meant that producers could not afford to film in distant locations, but mostly filmed close to their studios.

The upswing in B-Westerns resulted in the creation of movie town sets built specially for filming. Buckskin Joe was created as a combination tourist attraction and Western film set near Cañon City, Colorado. The old buildings were authentic, but were moved from other locations to create the movie town. The town has since been sold and the buildings moved, and is no longer open to the public.

With the Depression hovering over the early 1930s, most low-budget B-Westerns took advantage of the convenience of suitable locations close to Hollywood. Many films were simply shot on the back lots and Western streets of Universal, MGM, Fox, Warners, Paramount, and Republic. Others were filmed on Western ranches owned or rented by the studios, such as Iverson Ranch, RKO Ranch, Paramount Ranch, Warner Ranch, Columbia Ranch, or Monogram Ranch.

Other popular locations close to Los Angeles for filming Westerns were the Garner Ranch in the San Jacinto Mountains; Vasquez Rocks, a small scenic rocky area north of Hollywood between San Fernando and Palmdale; and Kernville, a town on the southern edge of the Sierra Nevada mountains that had wooded landscapes, large rocks, a small Western set, and the Kern River. For really cheap filming, indoor studio sets might simply be dressed with rocks made of papier-mâché (later of styrofoam) and a few fake trees, or trees and bushes in pots placed in front of a painted background.

Some low-budget Westerns, such as those of Gene Autry and Roy Rogers, used modern settings which were not either the historical or the modern West. These Westerns did not claim to represent the authentic Old West, but dealt with the economic, social, and cultural issues of the times. The plots involved contemporary issues raised by the Depression, the New Deal, the impending World War II, or some other issue close to the viewers. In *Bells of Coronado* (1950), for example, Roy Rogers tracks uranium stolen by evil saboteurs who plan to smuggle it overseas in a submarine. This type of plotting had the further advantage that the production crew could use everyday settings for the location instead of renting a Western ranch. The heroine often dressed in the contemporary fashion of the 1930s and 1940s.

As one example of these "modern" Westerns, in *The Old Barn Dance* (1938), Gene Autry is a horse dealer who uses a radio show to promote the sale of his horses. Unknown to him the show is sponsored by a crooked finance company who loans money for tractors and then deliberately forecloses on farmers who cannot pay for their purchases. The plot involves the Depression and "big, bad business" taking advantage of the little guy.

As another example, in *Round Up Time in Texas* (1937), Autry's screen brother Tex has found a diamond mine and needs horses to work the mine, so Gene transports a herd to Durban, South Africa, where the police arrest him as a criminal diamond buyer. Various adventures follow before everything is set right, including a jail escape and capture by native tribesmen. The modern setting includes airplanes, short wave radio, motorcycles, and armored cars. The African setting for what was essentially a Western movie was developed to exploit the popularity of the contemporary jungle films and even used some recycled stock footage from old Tarzan movies.

Poverty Row

B-Westerns are also thought of as Budget-Westerns. This was mostly true. They were usually cheaply made, often incorporated production errors, and usually had no time in the schedule for retakes for mistakes.

Most of the B-Westerns of the 1930s were made on black-and-white film with very low budgets by independent Hollywood studios that were poorly financed. Because many of these low-cost studios were located close together, one section of Sunset Boulevard received the name of Poverty Row. Some of the so-called Poverty Row studios who made Westerns were Puritan, Mascot, Victory, Allied, PRC (Producers Releasing Corporation), Monogram, Resolute, and Spectrum Pictures. Their Westerns were inexpensive to produce, and mostly used existing outdoor sets or settings on a studio ranch so there was no need to build elaborate sets.

The production of B-Westerns was like an assembly line. To save money, the directors filmed from sunup to sundown, keeping the action going continuously, mostly with very little rehearsal. Many of these low-budget studios recycled their plots as often as possible, used stock footage, and included long shots from earlier movies where the actors' faces were unidentifiable. Actors might have to use the clothing worn by earlier silent stars to try to match the footage. This practice was also used by some of the major studios. Paramount's remakes of Zane Grey novels in the early 1930s used location footage from earlier silent Zane Grey Westerns to give them the appearance of higher production values. Scenes were often shot at the same location to match the earlier film.[11]

To save costs, the exteriors for two B-Westerns might be filmed at same time at one location. In one series of films starring Lash Larue, the budget was so tight that all the exteriors were shot in a week in 1949, then different interior sequences were blended in (with identical chase scenes) to make different movies.[12]

Hollywood's Poverty Row included Nat Levine's Mascot Pictures, an independent production company that made inexpensive action-filled B-Westerns that were full of fast-paced, frantic activity. The studio's output was characterized by inferior production values, but its product had a fast pacing that pleased the public and the distributors. A characteristic scene in its films was a posse on horseback chasing outlaws escaping in an automobile through rocky landscapes. In 1933 Mascot rented, and later purchased, the former Mack Sennett studios in Edendale, as Levine did not want to commit his limited capital to buildings. The company was eventually absorbed by Republic.

One of Mascot's specialties was serials, which it had been making since 1927. Serial Westerns were different than series Westerns, which were movies that featured the same star, pretty much same story line, and the same running time.

Serial Westerns, also known as "movie serials" and "film serials," were shown as part of a Saturday morning matinee show for younger viewers. Serials were typically made in "chapters," or episodes, of 12 parts. Each chapter consisted of two reels (about 20 minutes) of plot, plus a trailer for the next part. Each episode of the serial ended with a "cliffhanger," a perilous situation from which the hero apparently had no escape. Typical cliffhangers were the hero engaged in a fistfight in the back of a wagon as it careened out of control towards a cliff edge, or as he was about to be run over by a train or stampeding cattle. As a result, the juvenile audience had to return to the theater on the next Saturday to see how the hero escaped from his predicament.

The use of outdoor filming locations with cars, trains, and cliffs, presented excellent opportunities for cliff-hangers, though some were overdone to try and pull the audience back for the next episode. At the end of one chapter of *The Vigilantes are*

Coming (1936), star Bob Livingston is apparently crushed by a giant piece of machinery. At the start of the next chapter, however, he has somehow miraculously jumped out of the way before being obliterated and the plot continues. Similarly, at the end of one chapter of *Winners of the West* (1940), Dick Foran appears to be run over by a train. However, at the beginning of the next chapter he somehow recovered in the nick of time and jumped off the track before the train hits him. At the end of one chapter of *The Oregon Trail* (1939), Johnny Mack Brown disappears under a herd of stampeding horses, yet at the beginning of the next episode he carries on as if nothing had happened.

A serial followed a set pattern, had a set running time, and was produced for a set audience. Mascot averaged three weeks to make a serial. The average completed serial ran about five hours over 12 episodes, and needed as much action as possible. Romance and complex plotting were toned down. The characters were stereotypes and the dialog was minimal. Serials depended on motion and speed to give a feeling of action, so scenes involving fast automobiles, speedboats, accelerating trucks, airplanes, and speeding trains were prominent to create a feeling of urgency.

The B-Western's excitement came from the action, which was reduced mostly to stock situations. The characterization and probing psychology that was featured in Westerns of two decades later was non-existent.

Plots were straightforward with plenty of action, usually as much as possible. The planned shooting schedule was short because the producer had to bring in a finished product on time and under budget. For economy, the same set and the same locations were used frequently. Further economy was achieved by using stock footage from previous films and by having a series of standing sets at the studio. Republic had so many serials and B-Westerns that used dark tunnels or a cave in the plot that the studio had a permanent standing set that was made up of caves.

B-Westerns usually didn't have much management supervision once the camera was rolling. Directors and actors needed to work fast as possible to bring in a saleable product on time and at or under budget. As they filmed so fast, there was not much time for scenic composition or other cinematic niceties.

Series Westerns were planned and produced on an assembly-line basis. So much so that studios sometimes shot two or three films at same time to justify the expense of going to an expensive location. To speed up production, two or more directors might work on the same film at the same time. One would direct the scenes with dialog, while another was working on the fights and action scenes with the second unit. As the scenes were shot so much out of sequence, the actors often had no idea what they were reacting to in individual scenes. Directors had to work so fast that often some of the material was left out in the rush to complete the film. As a result, scripts often had to be revised on the set during shooting to connect up loose ends or to explain a situation that nobody could understand.

The result was that much of the final story was left to the film editor, who had to piece together various scenes shot by different directors into a coherent story. There was no time for retakes to correct mistakes or to add extra material to explain inconsistencies in the script or scenes that might have been forgotten. By the time the film was being edited the cast and crew were working on the next new production. If the editor became desperate, sometimes narration was added to explain gaps or inconsistencies in the story. Sometimes even the editor could not to figure it out and just did the best he could.

The leader of the B-Western producers was Republic Pictures. Republic grew out of Consolidated Film Industries, a company owned by Herbert J. Yates that processed film for several independent Hollywood studios. Yates centralized film production and distributed to independent exhibitors. In March 1935, Yates merged Consolidated with two of his film clients who had unpaid processing bills, Monogram and Majestic, to form Republic Pictures, which brought Monogram's leading contract player, John Wayne, to Republic.[13]

In the spring of 1935, Republic absorbed two other Poverty Row companies, Chesterfield and Liberty, in the same manner. In 1936 Yates then merged Republic and Mascot Pictures, which was producing inexpensive action B-Westerns. In the process, Yates ended up with Mascot's North Hollywood studio. Yates remained head of the studio, and retained Nat Levine from Mascot as head of production. With Republic's merger with Mascot, their consistent box-office stars were Gene Autry and previous Monogram star John Wayne. Compared to other Poverty Row studios, Republic produced consistently better movies and had a good distribution system. Though Republic did not own its own chain of theaters, it did own exchanges in the larger cities.

There was a large difference in quality between B-Westerns made by the small independent studios and those of the major studios. Independents such as Puritan, Resolute, Spectrum, and Ambassador turned out a relatively primitive product, often with poor camera work. Their B-Western plots were based around outdoor action with plenty of fistfights, chases, and riding stunts. The independents, however, did have a major advantage when it came to production costs, and the major studios were unable to match the low costs of the Poverty Row studios. Whereas a Western epic might cost $50,000 at a major studio, an independent could make a movie for between $5,000 and $10,000. Early Gene Autry pictures made by Mascot cost about $12,000 to make.[14]

The real success for the Poverty Row studios depended on wide distribution in small-town and neighborhood theaters, in order to cater to their important audience of young men, and particularly boys under 16 years of age. As a result, by 1932, most of the major studios had ceased production of Westerns. Though B-Westerns continued to be made and were very popular during the 1930s, the major Hollywood studios remained reluctant to invest large amounts of money in A-Westerns. They couldn't afford the cost of epic Westerns and they could not match the low costs of the Poverty Row studios.

B-Western Format

Profitability of the B-Westerns depended on the ability to figure out audience likes and trends, and then crank out as many similar films as the market would bear. The Poverty Row studio system was geared towards mass production and marketing of the largest possible number of low-budget films. Unfortunately for those wanting quality viewing, the system was geared to repeat and repeat successful plots and productions. Sets were recycled, along with old footage from previous productions. The constant re-use of footage sometimes produced an obvious mismatch between old and new.

The B-Western was a parallel to the dime and pulp novels in the literary world. It was aimed at a particular audience who wanted to keep seeing the same stars in the same types of plots. These movies were intended to be financially reliable, rather than artistically innovative.

Series Westerns were fashioned around a particular recurring actor, who played the same basic character in each of their movies. Examples of this type of performer were Tom Mix, Gene Autry, Roy Rogers, and William Boyd as Hopalong Cassidy. These heroes were good guys with guns, who were aristocratic and gentlemanly like the knights of old. The hero was typically paired with a humorous sidekick, such as Smiley Burnette, Andy Devine, Gabby Hayes, Fuzzy Knight, or other similar actors who often played a grizzled old-timer. This plotting was a traditional pairing of characters that had its roots in ancient literature. Villains were always straightforward crooks who were unmasked and defeated by the hero at the end. The villains were figures of authority who were motivated by greed, such as crooked bankers and politicians, or wily ranchers swindling an heiress out of an inheritance as they conspired with local outlaw gangs.

The plots used minor variations on the same basic simple formula, and could be summed up as the good guy always won and the bad guys always lost. The audience knew exactly what to expect. But the hero had to win with good sportsmanship. The basis for a B-Western was a reasonable story, stirring music to accentuate outdoor chase scenes, some comedy relief, and lots of action with horse chases, car chases, and fist fights. All this took place against the sweep of untamed land and the vastness of the West with its desert scenery and mountains, though in reality most were filmed on the back lot or at a studio ranch.

A B-Western had to be made with a shooting schedule of days, instead of the weeks planned for the prestige productions. Production times for a B-Western ranged from only three days for the Lone Star Productions released by Monogram, to 14 to 21 days for Columbia Westerns. Due to the difficulty of staging expensive scenes, such as mass Indian attacks, stagecoach scenes, extended chase scenes, crowds, wagons going over a cliff, burning buildings, and large cattle stampedes, stock footage from previous films was frequently re-used. Poverty Row studios often even used stock music on the soundtracks to save costs.

Most series B-Westerns were marketed via block booking, which meant that an exhibitor had to buy a whole group of films, such as all the Hoot Gibson or Ken Maynard films, at the same time. The typical arrangement was a flat booking fee. The small independents often worked with regional distributors, rather than having their own distribution system and selling the product themselves.

The B-Western Stars

Broncho Billy Anderson created the first recognizable cowboy star. Following him were William S. Hart and Tom Mix. Then during the 1930s a series of B-Western stars shot to the forefront. The five biggest were Ken Maynard, Tom Mix, Buck Jones, Hoot Gibson, and Tim McCoy. All were somewhat similar. All were white men of about the same age. All had served in the military. All were excellent horsemen and had experience in Wild West shows and rodeos. Studios emphasized their Western background, or invented or embellished it, to make it seem that they were not just movie stars, but were authentic figures who had deep ties to the Wild West.

Most had indeed developed their skills on ranches and in Wild West shows. Ken Maynard had worked as a trick rider for Buffalo Bill's *Wild West* and the *Ringling Brothers Barnum & Bailey Circus*. Tom Mix had worked for the Miller Brothers in 1906, then left in 1909 to form his own show. Hoot Gibson was a working cowboy who had performed with the Dick Stanley-Bud Atkinson Wild West Show, then worked for Selig and Biograph tending horses and acting as a stunt double. Buck Jones had been a working cowboy and started caring for horses before becoming a film extra and stunt double in movies for William S. Hart, Tom Mix, and others. Art Accord was a cowboy before starring in Wild West shows and becoming a movie cowboy. Jack Hoxie was a cowboy with the 101 Ranch before starring in movies.

The real identity of B-Western stars was often merged with their screen persona. When John Wayne started making movies for Warners they wanted the audience to see that he was not just another actor in a role, but was a "real" cowboy adventurer named John Wayne. In the six Westerns he made for them during 1932 and 1933 he was always named John. This was a continuation of the practice of Buffalo Bill Cody from 50 years earlier of promoting his show business persona under his own name and gaining success by playing himself as "Buffalo Bill." B-Western stars kept the same convention by keeping their same names. This also made it difficult to provide any on-screen romance. For example stars like Gene Autry who maintained a particular screen persona couldn't have a heavy love interest as they could not marry the girl at the end of each picture. He was Gene Autry in each one and could not continually accumulate wives.

By 1929, Westerns had become standardized with fistfights and gunplay, crime solving, horseback scenes and chases, and shootouts. Audiences started to tire of this formula and wanted something new, so in 1930 Ken Maynard decided to use the new medium of sound and make a singing picture. As a result he added two songs, with three cowboys accompanying him, to the plot of *Sons of the Saddle* (1930). From this minor start, the 1930s became the era of the singing cowboy and the singing Western.

Maynard had creative control over his films and added musical numbers to several subsequent movies. *In Old Santa Fe* (1934) created a new Hollywood art form that became known as the horse opera. In Maynard's *Fiddlin' Buckaroo* (1933) even the bandits had a musical number. In *Heroes of the Range* (1936) some of the bandits joined in an impromptu performance when Maynard, playing an outlaw, had to prove his identity by singing a song. Unfortunately Nat Levine, the head of Mascot Pictures, did not like Maynard's voice, so he had it dubbed.[15]

In Old Santa Fe (1934) was notable for the uncredited screen debut of Gene Autry. Maynard left Mascot after the action serial *Mystery Mountain* (1934) due to a dispute with Levine.[16] Levine had another 12-part serial ready to go, but no leading man so he gave the part to Gene Autry.

The Phantom Empire (1935) blended cowboys with science-fiction.[17] Far beneath the surface of the earth underneath Radio Ranch, where radio star Gene Autry broadcasts every afternoon, is a strange kingdom called Murania ruled by Queen Tika. The plot involved television screens and robots, but also mixed in horses and warriors with swords and spears, along with airplanes, tear gas, and radio. Autry was mild-mannered with a soft voice, so his pictures had no bad language, no violence, and no excessive gunplay. Or anything that suggested that men and women slept in the same room. Acting excellence was not as important in these singing B-Westerns as the presentation of personality.

Musical Westerns were a change for Hollywood from the traditional B-Westerns. They still incorporated the great outdoors for ranch and chase scenes, though most were filmed on a studio ranch. Either because or as a result of this, Republic invented their own never-never land for the B-Western. The Westerns of Gene Autry, and later Roy Rogers, combined the traditional outdoor location elements of the B-Western, such as horse chases, cattle stampedes, gunfights, and saloon fights, with modern elements, such as army tanks, airplanes, trucks, fast cars, and Broadway-style night clubs with chorus girls, Western singers, and lavish entertainment in small cowtowns. By 1936 the musical content of Autry pictures had overwhelmed the traditional Western outdoor action.

The plots featured contemporary social problems, such as politics or the problems of raising cattle, but still included stagecoaches, cowboys wearing guns, and barroom fights. Tight pants, decorative boots, and shirts with piping and embroidery and smile pockets worn by the singing cowboys in the earlier manner of Tom Mix, became fancier. Some critics objected to these musical singing numbers and fancy clothes as being totally unrealistic. However, even though this was obviously not the real West or the real outdoors of the A-Western, it was the film business and these movies appealed to the fantasy-starved audiences of the Depression.

There were several commercial reasons why adding songs to films in the 1930s made sense. B-Western star Buck Jones has been quoted as saying that a lot of songs were included "to save money on horses, riders, and ammunition."[18] And, as Republic's B-Western director William Witney commented, singing numbers were cheaper to stage and film than fights and brawls that involved stunt work.[19]

Another important reason was commercial, to increase crossover promotion between films and recorded songs. Singers such as Gene Autry helped to promote sales of their songs on records by featuring them in their movies. His recordings helped to promote his films and conversely his movies helped to promote his songs with crossover promotion between films and records. Not coincidentally, Herbert J. Yates, the owner of Republic Pictures, also had acquired the Columbia and Brunswick record labels in 1934 and was the leading supplier of phonograph records to the rural market.

Stunts and Falls

Along with the great outdoors and location photography, a key feature of B-Westerns was the use of stunts that consisted of sprawling action in saloon fights and high-speed chases. The public wanted authentic manhood in their heroes, and generally believed that cowboy stars performed their own stunts. Though some actors did some stunt work, other actors were not capable of performing risky stunts. Producers would often not allow actors to perform stunts because of the risk of injury to the star. Stunt doubles, when they were used, were sworn to secrecy to maintain the manly image of the star. For example Tom Mix in his later years used stuntmen who were sworn to secrecy.[20]

Typically outdoor action scenes with the stunt crew were filmed by the second unit director, while the first unit under the main director shot the rest of the footage with the stars in a studio. Many stunt scenes were filmed as long shots so that the stunt performers could not be identified, then the two directors' results were edited together to form the complete film.

Early Western film actors mostly performed their own stunts, many of which were indeed dangerous. During filming of *The Telltale Knife* (1914), for example, Tom Mix and one of the other actors were almost drowned on location when they were unexpectedly swept into a strong current as they performed a stunt in which they rode their horses into the Arkansas River in Colorado.[21]

One of Mix's remarkable stunts involved jumping on horseback across a narrow cut in a hill, 90 feet in the air, in *Three Jumps Ahead* (1923), at a film location known as Beale's Cut. The cut, north of Los Angeles, near Newhall, was first carved out by gold trader Gen. Phineas H. Banning in 1854 to make a road for wagons to carry gold and supplies between Los Angeles and Fort Tejon in the Kern River Valley. Known also as Fremont Pass, Newhall Cut, and Newhall Pass, the original cut was only 30 feet deep. In 1864 Gen. Edward Beale deepened the cut to 90 feet, with almost vertical walls separated by only 20 feet, to lower the road grade and began charging a $2 toll fee for its use.[22]

On the other hand, some critics claimed that Mix's jump was a camera trick. Still others agreed it was real, but have credited the jump to two different stuntmen. Photographs of the jump show a ramp on the left side, which wouldn't have been needed if it was a camera trick; however, this may also be the remains of the bridge destroyed by the bad guys as Mix chased them. Anecdotal accounts from the film crew present at the time said that Mix did indeed make the jump, but used a stunt double for his wonder horse, Tony. The truth will never be known as all the existing prints of the film have been destroyed, lost, or deteriorated beyond use. But it is still remarkable.

The scene was directed by John Ford (billed as Jack Ford), who had used the cut earlier for *Straight Shooting* (1917) with Harry Carey and Hoot Gibson. The narrow cut was so spectacular that it was used briefly as a filming site in *The Iron Horse* (1924) when Davy Brandon (George O'Brien) and Jesson (Cyril Chadwick) reach the pass that is a shortcut, supposedly in the Black Hills of South Dakota. Beale's cut also appeared in a quick shot of the stagecoach going through the narrow defile in Ford's *Stagecoach* (1939).

As time went on, however, many Western movie stars were unable or unwilling to perform such dangerous stunts. Stunt doubles and professional stuntmen were therefore used to perform the more dangerous daredevil feats, such as falling off a horse or turning over a wagon.

The more important reason, however, was essentially practical. If the star of a movie was injured during a stunt, filming could be halted for weeks while a broken

Tom Mix was able to perform his spectacular stunts, such as his alleged jump across Beale's Cut northwest of Newhall, because he had legitimately been a successful rodeo star and stunt performer for *Miller Brothers' 101 Ranch Wild West Show* before breaking into Western movies. He continued as a popular performer and star in rodeos and horse shows, such as this one where he was captured on a glass negative atop his rearing horse in May of 1925 (Library of Congress).

arm or leg healed. If the star was injured and production was shut down, fixed costs of thousands of dollars a day to pay the rest of the cast and crew would continue to mount. Put bluntly, an injured stunt man could be replaced without halting filming, whereas the star could not.

Sometime dummies were substituted for actors during stunts, such as when a character was supposed to fall off a high cliff. As only one example, in *The Great Train Robbery* (1903) a dummy took the place of the fireman who was thrown off the moving train by one of the villains. As stunt techniques were developed, later stuntmen performed these falls, such as when one of the gang was thrown off the moving train in the Outlaws segment of *How the West Was Won* (1962). The stunt was carefully choreographed to prevent injury and so that the stunt man's fall was cushioned by a fake saguaro cactus.

Among the more spectacular stunts performed in B-Westerns were horse falls and body-drag shots, where the stuntman was dragged by his horse. As might be expected, stunt performers suffered broken arms, dislocated shoulders and hips, concussions, sprain, fractures, and cracked ribs.

In spite of careful planning, stunts could also go wrong. *Gun Gospel* (1927), filmed in Montana, included one stunt where Ken Maynard was supposed to jump off a 60-foot cliff into a lake on his horse Tarzan and swim to shore. When filming started, the stunt went wrong. The horse slipped on the board used to make a runway, turned over in mid-air, and landed on top of Maynard, and they both almost drowned.[23] Even more hair-raising was the stunt in *The Dark Command* (1940) when stuntman Yakima Canutt drove a wagon with the horses still attached to it off a cliff into a pool of water.

Yakima Canutt was one of the most famous of the movie stuntmen and second unit directors. Enos Edward Canutt was born in Colfax, Washington, near Yakima. He was a ranch hand, a performer in Wild West shows, and was a championship rodeo rider. He received his name when newspapers called him "the Cowboy from Yakima." Canutt started as an actor in silent films, went on to play villains in early sound pictures, and then concentrated on stunts. Being a previous actor help him to stage stunt action in a believable manner. He became the top stuntman at Mascot (later Republic) and Monogram, where he was the usual stuntman for John Wayne and helped Wayne with horsemanship and stunt brawling.[24]

Riders of the Dawn (1937) contained a chase across salt flats outside Victorville, California, where Canutt did his famous stagecoach stunt where he dropped between the horses, hung onto the tongue of the stage, then let go and allowed the stage to pass over him. He then grabbed a rope at the rear of the stage, pulled himself up, and climbed back on top of the stage. This became one of his signature pieces of film business.[25]

One of the popular stunts in B-Westerns was horse falls, where the horse appeared to be shot and fell, and the rider was thrown off into the dirt. Horse falls became a large part of outdoor chase scenes. One of the early methods of staging horse falls was with what was called the "Running W." An early version was first used by Broncho Billy Anderson to stage horse falls.[26] A length of one-eighth-inch steel cable connected in a rough W-shape to hobbles on the horse's front legs and were attached to a ring held by the rider. When the rider reached the desired camera position at full gallop and wanted the horse to fall, he pulled abruptly on the ring (also called the "toe tapper") to pull the horse's front legs from under him, and tripped the animal. The rider was, of course, thrown off in a spectacular head-first dive, aiming to make a relatively soft landing in a patch of ground that had been dug up and prepared beforehand to soften the fall. The horse, unfortunately, often broke its neck in the fall.

Another technique used to create spectacular horse falls was the "Stationary W," also known as the "Deadman's Fall." This was a trip device made from 80 or a hundred yards of piano wire that was anchored at one end to a buried post and attached at the other end to hobbles on the horse's legs. When the galloping horse reached the limit of the wire, it tripped and did head-first fall, catapulting the rider over its head as it fell.[27]

Stunt men tried to make a soft landing in water or a patch of dirt, but nonetheless serious injuries occurred to both horses and stunt riders. In *Jesse James* (1939) a horse was blindfolded and run at a full gallop into a tripwire that catapulted it 70 feet off a cliff edge, twisting and turning over backwards into the water below, where it landed on its neck and was killed by the impact.[28] So many horses broke their necks or were otherwise injured during spectacular somersaults and had to be destroyed that the practice of tripping horses was stopped in 1940 under pressure from the American Humane Society. Now stuntmen create falls and other visually-exciting horse stunts with horses that have been specially trained to perform a particular trick. Canutt was an innovator who trained horses to fall without being injured. Avid fans of Westerns will notice that when a modern stuntman is "shot" off a horse, the horse falls, the rider pitches off forward, then the horse gets up and trots away unharmed.

Later filming incorporated more safety for animals. In *Silver Spurs* (1943), Roy Rogers (or actually his stunt double) drove a wagon over a rocky bluff into a river, but viewers will note that the horses had been unhitched before going over the cliff.

The most dramatic and exciting of all movie shots was the tracking shot or "running insert," where the camera was mounted on a camera car or truck and raced at high speed alongside a galloping rider or group of horsemen. This fast motion gave Western movies a breathless pace as the landscape sped by in the background. Running inserts had to be filmed in the outdoors where there was enough room for the action and the camera car. Movie makers, however, had to be on guard to preserve the illusion. In one shot during a thrilling running insert in *Showdown* (1963) with Audie Murphy, the gravel road in the foreground contains tire tracks left by the camera truck as it was filming Murphy galloping along on his horse. The same appears in *Jesse James* (1939), where tire tracks and an accompanying cloud of dust from the camera car can be seen at the bottom of the screen during a chase scene.

Another exciting addition to outdoor Westerns was the so-called "pit shot," where the camera (and sometime a cameraman) was placed in a hole in the ground while the action literally passed over them. This might be a herd of stampeding cattle, a running band of horses, a stagecoach or wagon, or even a speeding train. This was used to great effect by director John Ford in *The Iron Horse* (1924), where the train passes over the camera.

Our Western Hero and the Impact of Stagecoach

The biggest of the B-Westerns stars to emerge in the 1930s, and one who went on to star in Western movies for the next 40 or so years was John Wayne. Wayne in his big hat, boots, and bib-front or "fireman's" shirt, with a flap attached by a row of buttons down each side of the front, is the personification of Western heroism.

Wayne's birth certificate lists him as Marion Robert Morrison, born in 1907 in Winterset, Iowa. His mother changed his name to Marion Michael Morrison, so that his younger brother could be called Robert. His name in the 1925 Glendale High School yearbook was Marion Mitchell Morrison. Wayne received his name of "Duke" from his dog. He was Big Duke, the dog was Little Duke.[29]

Wayne went to the University of Southern California on a football scholarship. He started at Fox as a prop man, moving furniture and props from set to set. He got small parts in films, then went on to act in serials at Mascot, and eventually made Westerns for Lone Star Productions, a subsidiary of Monogram Pictures.

Wayne made 16 Westerns for Monogram. Wayne even played a singing cowboy. In *Riders of Destiny* (1933) he played "Singin' Sandy" Saunders, a secret treasury agent who literally sang a song as he walked towards the bad guy for a shootout. As part of the role he had to sing and play a guitar. The director was not pleased with his singing ability, and neither was Wayne, so the scenes were dubbed by Smith Ballew.[30] And Singin' Sandy was the last singing role for John Wayne.

Wayne had a difficult beginning. He made 60 films in 15 years during his early career, but couldn't break out into stardom. He did actually star in *The Big Trail* (1930), but it was not a commercial success, so he returned to making B-Westerns. The big break for both him and for location photography of the West was the movie *Stagecoach* (1939). Wayne's breakout role and the one that catapulted him to stardom was his role as the Ringo Kid. Though *Stagecoach* (1939) was not the first Western to be filmed in Monument Valley, it was the film that brought the valley to the attention of the movie public as an iconic image of the West.

Stagecoach (1939) was based on a short story by Ernest Haycox called *The Stage to Lordsburg*, published in *Collier's* magazine on April 10, 1937. The plot was also loosely based on the short story *"Boule de Suif"* ("Ball of Tallow") by French author Guy de Maupassant.[31] The prominent characters in the plot were a corrupt bank manager, a whiskey salesman, a prostitute with a heart of gold, a cavalry officer's pregnant wife, a Southern gambler, a drunken doctor, and a sheriff. And the Ringo Kid (John Wayne), an outlaw out to revenge the murder of his brother. Monument Valley was used as a scenic backdrop, but the drama was with the passengers of the stagecoach. The open emptiness of Monument Valley produced a contrast between the vastness of the landscape and the small size of the figures in the story.

Stagecoach (1939) was nominated for six Academy Awards: Best Picture, Best Director, Best Supporting Actor, and Photography, Art Direction, and Editing. The film was a commercial success, grossing an estimated $2.4 million. Thomas Mitchell won the Best Supporting Actor as the alcoholic doctor. Though *Stagecoach* (1939) was nominated, the Best Picture award for that year went to *Gone with the Wind* (1939).

Stagecoach (1939) received great acclaim and was a large commercial success, and has been credited, though perhaps too generously, in single-handedly reviving the resurgence of filming outdoor Western movies by the major studios in the 1940s.

Monument Valley

Of all the film locations used for Westerns, Monument Valley is arguably the one that is most often identified by moviegoers as "the West," starting with its use as a scenic filming location for *Stagecoach* (1939). Movies, television commercials, and advertising photographs have made Monument Valley one of the most recognizable places in the world. For many people, it is the symbol of *the* American West. Many tourists visit simply because of the Hollywood movies filmed there.

Monument Valley is a vast, sparsely-populated section of lonely picturesque desert that straddles the Arizona-Utah border. Covering an area of about 30 square miles (92,000 acres), the landscape is dotted with spectacular rock formations that rise as much as a thousand feet above the valley floor. These monoliths were formed from harder rocks that remained when the surrounding softer sandstone and limestone eroded away and left a series of harder, more-resistant, spectacular buttes, towering sandstone spires, and lofty pinnacles. The brilliant red color of the valley is due to the presence of iron oxide in the rocks.

Monument Valley first became symbolic of the ultimate Western landscape thanks to director John Ford. Though Monument Valley has been credited in popular movie histories as the location for *Stagecoach* (1939), Ford filmed the few outdoor location scenes that were used in the movie in only four days in 1938 and they only last collectively on screen for about 90 seconds in the final film. After brief location filming in Monument Valley, the director and crew moved back to Hollywood to film the rest of the movie on the Western street at Republic Studio, with interiors on sound stages at the Sam Goldwyn studio.[32] Monument Valley appears more prominent as a location in the final movie than it really was because almost all the scenes in or on the stagecoach that used dialog were shot with the use of back projection images of the valley, though filmed on a studio sound stage.

In lingering popular memory, the scenery of Monument Valley dominated *Stagecoach* (1939). The scenic background made people think that this was the authentic look of the Old West. And even though brief, Ford's location shoot produced stunning visual outdoor images that are still dramatic today, such as the stagecoach dashing across the floor of Monument Valley with Merrick Butte and the twin rock formations known as The Mittens in the background.

For the sequence where the stagecoach is pursued Indians, the crew went to Lucerne Lake, a dry lake bed near Victorville, California, to shoot with stuntman Yakima Canutt doing the daring stagecoach stunts. Canutt came up with the classic stunt sequence where he jumped onto the stagecoach's horses, then was "shot" and fell between the two lead horses. He let go and allowed the stage to pass over him, then pulled himself up onto the back of the coach and continued the fight. It was a very dangerous stunt, as the space between the horses (and their hooves) was only three feet. One slight miscalculation to the left or the right and Canutt would have been run over by the wheels of the stagecoach, which was traveling at about 35 miles per hour.[33]

After filming *Stagecoach* (1939), director John Ford made several other popular Westerns in Monument Valley over the following years that created a powerful image in his audiences that the scenic area of mesas and buttes that made up the valley was the real "West."

Monument Valley is part of the vast Navajo reservation that encompasses over 27,000 square miles of land, bordered on the north by the San Juan River and the Little Colorado River on the south, the Colorado River on the west, and the Continental Divide on the east. It is a vast and isolated region where 356,000 Navajo and Hopi Indians grow corn and melons, and raise sheep, goats, and horses.

When *Stagecoach* (1939) was in production the area had few paved roads and store-bought items were limited to a few scattered trading posts. In 1938 Monument Valley was not an easy location for a film crew to reach. The nearest railroad connection was about 180 miles away by road at Flagstaff, Arizona. The existing roads and bridges in the valley were primitive at best, and telephone connections were non-existent. In addition, the Great Depression had caused havoc with the fragile economy of the Navajo people.

The Navajo name for Monument Valley is *Tsé'Bii'Ndzisgaii*, the "Valley of Rocks."[34] According to Navajo legend, the towers of rock help to hold up the sky.[35] The formations known as Gray Whiskers and Sentinel pinnacles were considered by the Navajo to be the doorposts of a giant hogan, similar to the ones the Navajo lived in, that formed the interior of the valley. The twin buttes known as The Mittens were

John Ford used the exterior of the Goulding's two-story stone trading post in Monument Valley to stand in for a combination stage station and trading post in *Fort Apache* (1948). The trading post, built in 1927, also doubled as the fort headquarters in *She Wore a Yellow Ribbon* (1949), where the door seen in the film is now the entrance to Goulding's museum. The location today is just the same as it was, except that the parking lot has since been paved.

considered to be the hands of a Holy Person who was left behind in stone to remind the Navajo that they are not alone.[36]

Stagecoach (1939) was not the first movie made in Monument Valley. Author Zane Grey explored the area in 1913 and in 1922 showed it to Jesse Lasky, who was filming some of Grey's stories for Paramount. Director George B. Seitz filmed Grey's story *The Vanishing American* (1925), the first feature film produced in southeastern Utah, with Monument Valley as a backdrop.

Stagecoach (1939) was also not the last. Movies filmed in the valley in the 1940s included *Kit Carson* (1940) also directed by George Seitz, *Billy the Kid* (1941) by King Vidor, and *The Harvey Girls* (1946) by George Sidney, though the last one only used back projection of the valley for some scenes of Susan Bradley (Judy Garland) singing on the train. Monument Valley was used in the final sequence of *How the West Was Won* (1962), after the climactic battle with the outlaws on the runaway train, when Zeb Rawlings (George Peppard) drives Lillith (Debbie Reynolds) and his family to their new home in the West. The Mittens and some of the other iconic rock formations can be seen briefly in the background.

The original promoter of Western movies in Monument Valley was a man named Harry Goulding, an ex-cowboy who raised sheep and traded with the Navajos who lived in the area. Originally a sheep man himself, Goulding was also a tall man, so the local Navajos called him *Dibé Nineez*, which loosely meant "the long (tall) man with the sheep."[37]

In the early 1920s the area was part of the Paiute Indian reservation, and was known as the Paiute Strip. In 1922 the Paiute reservation moved and the residents headed north. The land moved into the public domain.

In 1923 Goulding and his wife Leone (better known by her nickname of "Mike") moved to Monument Valley, to the base of Big Rock Door Mesa, and homesteaded 640 acres. They lived in a tent on the property until 1927, when they were able to build the two-story stone trading post that still stands today. The presence of Goulding's trading post allowed the Navajo to purchase items of food and clothing they could not previously obtain.

During the first half of the 1930s, the Depression was particularly hard on Monument Valley and the Navajo Nation. In an effort to promote the beauty of Monument Valley to the movie industry and to try bring some business to the area, Goulding went to Los Angeles in 1938 with a portfolio of 24 black-and-white photographs by noted Western landscape photographer Josef Muench. In Hollywood, Goulding showed the photographs to independent producer Walter Wanger and John Ford, who were in pre-production for *Stagecoach* (1939). Ford had originally planned to make the film near Kayenta, Arizona, which at that time was a scenic location used for filming Westerns. As a result of Goulding's timely visit, however, the executives from United Artists, who were backing the film, approved filming the backgrounds in Monument Valley instead.

During the filming of *Stagecoach* (1939), 26 crew members camped at Goulding's trading post. Ford and the principal actors stayed 25 miles south of the valley in Kayenta, Arizona, at John Wetherill's inn and trading post, which provided lodging for tourists.[38] Wetherill and Harry Goulding were the only white men around for hundreds of miles.

The Gouldings eventually built a lodge to house the filmmakers who came to work in the area. Goulding ran his trading post in Monument Valley with Mike from 1925 to 1963, when they retired and moved to Arizona. Harry died in 1981, Mike in 1992.

There were several apocryphal versions of how Monument Valley was "discovered" for Western movies. One was that John Ford's nephew said that actor Harry Carey told Ford about it after Carey explored Navajo country in the 1920s. John Wayne claimed that he had found it and told Ford about it when Wayne was working on a George O'Brien film in 1929.[39] Ford claimed to have found Monument Valley on his own, either when driving across Arizona to Santa Fe, New Mexico, or when he discovered it on the location scout for *Stagecoach* (1939).[40] At another time he claimed he had never been there before filming *Stagecoach*. Ford didn't give Goulding credit for introducing him to the valley; however, Ford's stories about discovering Monument Valley are murky and probably Goulding's version is the correct one.

The Cloud Hangs On

The cloud hanging over Hollywood continued to loom larger in the late 1930s. In 1938 the federal government re-instituted their legal actions against Hollywood's major studios, charging that the combined ownership of production, distribution, and movie theaters constituted an illegal trust. As a compromise, the studios signed a consent decree in 1940, under which studios stopped acquiring new theaters and eliminated some of their more restrictive distribution policies.[41] The outbreak of World War II in 1941 stopped further governmental action, but the problem did not go away. It was to have a substantial impact on the major studios and their way of doing business after the war ended.

CHAPTER SIX

The 1940s
Solidly in the Outdoors

In the 1930s and 1940s, going to the movies was a way of life for many people as the major movie studios turned out hundreds of movies each year. The era of the singing cowboy reached its peak in the late 1930s and early 1940s with the happy melodies of Gene Autry and Roy Rogers. In the 1940s, films were an effective and popular escape from the harsh realities of the recently-ended Depression and the onset of the horrors of World War II.

More Western stars were working simultaneously in the 1930s and 1940s than in any other period. Between 1941 and 1945 approximately 50 percent (313 out of 645) of the films from the small independent studios were Westerns, as opposed to the eight major studios, where Westerns were only about 15 percent of their total output.[1]

During the war years, B-Western script writers introduced new villains and their heroes fought saboteurs, cattle barons with foreign accents, and various scoundrels with supposed ties to evil foreign powers. But, by the end of the decade, audiences were finding the plots in these series and serial Westerns to be too simplistic. The heroes were always good, the villains were all bad. After World War II ended in 1945, the movie industry turned to psychological anti–Westerns that were filled with complex, brooding, anti-social characters.

Even as the popularity of movies grew, audience tastes changed again. The 1940s became the era of the classic *film noir* movies that used unusual camera angles for vantage points, and heightened their atmospheric qualities by moody filming in black and white.

As America entered the 1940s, film production became more difficult for the studios. Many of their stars and directors enlisted and went off to fight in the war. As the 1940s advanced, production costs for serial Westerns rose and profits fell. At the end of the 1940s, the arrival of television offered viewing audiences serial Westerns in a weekly format.

A-Westerns made a comeback, though, and continued to be filmed in the 1940s. *Duel in the Sun* (1946), filmed southeast of Tucson, Arizona, at the Empire Ranch, was the second highest money-maker in 1947.

Many of the classic Westerns of the 1940s were filmed in beautiful landscapes in the wide-open empty spaces of the West. Though the California deserts and mountains around Hollywood were good locations for Westerns, some of these locations

Iconic Images of the Movie West #6: Empire Ranch, Arizona. This landscape of lush grass near Sonoita, southeast of Tucson, Arizona, was used for Westerns that needed a background of the rolling grasslands used for raising cattle. Used in 1947 for filming *Red River* (1948), this open grassland was also used for *Duel in the Sun* (1946), *Winchester '73* (1950), *3:10 to Yuma* (1957), *Gunfight at the O.K. Corral* (1957), *The Cowboys* (1972), and *Tombstone* (1993).

were used so often that audiences recognized them from film to film. Familiar elements were unmistakable rocks, canyons, mountains, and deserts.

Film fakery was also evident when a single supposed geographic location was assembled on film from various landscape elements, some of which were hundreds of miles apart. This created a single geographic film location that was a collection of separate parts edited together to create an artificial place without any basis in reality. Some of the scenes in *Escape from Fort Bravo* (1953), for example, were filmed near Gallup, New Mexico, and others in Death Valley, California, with other exterior scenes shot near Hollywood. In one sequence, the cavalry is seen riding in the red rock country of Gallup, then they gallop across the floor of Death Valley to an ambushed wagon train, and then ride back around the red-rock bluffs to appear near Gallup again. As another example, when the Earp brothers march to the final shootout in *Gunfight at the O.K. Corral* (1957), they stride down the street towards the camera on Paramount's back lot in Hollywood (standing in for the town of Tombstone), then in the next shot are walking away from the camera into the cactus-filled desert at Old Tucson Studios for the final gunfight. This mismatch of locations was a common problem in filming Westerns at different locations, but is generally only a picky point noticed by avid movie fans.

Filming in Color

The 1940s and 1950s were a period of splendor for the outdoor Western filmed on location. The increased use of color film and the introduction of other technical innovations, such as CinemaScope, VistaVision, Cinerama, and 3-D films, emphasized the vast outdoor qualities of the landscape.

The Technicolor process, developed by the Technicolor Motion Picture Corporation, was the leading color film process from 1922 to 1952. The three earliest versions of the Technicolor process involved a two-color system that exposed the film onto two strips of film by way of a beam-splitter to separate the light through red and green filters. Two of the earliest films to use the two-strip Technicolor process were Paramount's *Wanderer of the Wasteland* (1924) and *The Phantom of the Opera* (1925). Though commercially successful, the two-color process was plagued with technical problems. For Western fans, though, outdoor locations always looked better on film that used the new color processes, even the less expensive ones such as Trucolor, which was a cheap two-color process developed by Consolidated Film Industries and used extensively for Republic's Westerns. Another two-strip process was Cinecolor, developed in 1932. Its lower cost than Technicolor made it suitable for Poverty Row studios and features such as *The Phantom of Santa Fe* (1936) and Monogram's *The Gentleman from Arizona* (1939).

By 1930 Technicolor had perfected a three-color process that used a camera with a beam-splitter to expose three strips of 35mm film at the same time, one for each of the primary colors (red, green, and blue). In this way, light from the scene being filmed was separated into three different colors to expose three different negatives. These three were then printed together to create the final positive image for projection. The three-color Technicolor process became the premier process and the most popular color system because of its rich, vibrant, highly-saturated color and the ability to resist fading, unlike systems such as Trucolor.

By the late 1930s color had a large impact on the filming of Westerns, and provided a new burst of energy and opportunities for Westerns filmed on location to show off the full potential of the landscape in blazing color. Color was particularly striking for filming in the New Mexico and Utah deserts, such as in the red, rocky cliffs around Gallup and Kanab. The use of color accentuated the mountains, canyons, vast plateaus, and vermilion cliffs. A further benefit for filming was that when the same old familiar locations were used again they appeared to be different and more vibrant in color.

The first film to use the three-strip Technicolor process outdoors on location was *Trail of the Lonesome Pine* (1936), shot in Big Bear Valley and Cedar Lake, California. The use of Technicolor also helped the success of *Ramona* (1936), the first Western from Fox in three-strip Technicolor, with picturesque settings filmed near Kanab, Utah. The color production of *Drums Along the Mohawk* (1939) was filmed around Cedar City, Utah, among its pine forests, meadows, and lakes.

Prior to the 1970s, very high levels of light were required for all filming, due to the slow speed of existing movie film. The strong sun in the outdoors in the southwestern United States was ideal for filming Westerns on location as it provided brilliant light levels to compensate for the slow speed of the film. Early color film had even slower exposure speeds than black-and-white stock and required tripling the light level on the filming set to produce an adequate image on the negative.

Speed of the film for the three-color Technicolor process was ASA 5. Because of this, the major studios had their own power plants to produce the large amounts of electricity required to run all the lights required. Warners, for example, had six generators that could deliver 35,000 amps at 110 volts, or 3.85 megawatts. This was enough electricity to power a small town of about 1,200 homes.[2]

A source of power, typically in the form of large mobile generators, also had to go out on location or onto the back lot with the film crews in order to be able to power enough lights to adequately light the film on cloudy days or for night scenes. These generators were large, bulky, and cumbersome, and were typically mounted on large trucks, which were often difficult to bring to desired filming locations in remote areas of the West. After the 1970s, faster film stock and camera lenses with larger apertures were developed and reduced the need for such high levels of illumination.

Studio contracts with Technicolor required that Technicolor would provide the cameras used, along with their own technicians and a color consultant. This monopoly changed in 1950 with the introduction of Eastmancolor motion picture negative film from Eastman Kodak, which allowed color film to be shot in conventional 35mm movie cameras.[3] This led to a trend in the 1950s towards using more outdoor locations for filming Westerns as Eastmancolor, using a single negative, made transporting smaller cameras to an outdoor location easier than the heavy Technicolor cameras that required a bulky protective covering. In 1952 Eastman introduced a matching high-quality color print film.

MGM had its own proprietary color film stock that they called Metrocolor, which was a variation of Eastmancolor. Their process was cheaper than using Technicolor, which was still the industry standard, but it was also less durable.[4] To develop the large amounts of film they exposed, MGM had their own processing plant, which was one of the largest of all the studios' film facilities.

With the introduction of the Panaflex series of cameras in 1972, Panavision cameras became the preferred camera for most needs and became the industry standard. Panavision also owned all its inventory, so studios could only rent the cameras.[5]

Weather

Westerns filmed on location in color were generally shot in good weather to take advantage of the beauty of the Western scenery and to show off the landscape at its best. The story of *True Grit* (1969), for example, supposedly took place in Arkansas, but was filmed in Colorado in the fall to show off the brilliant yellow beauty of the aspen leaves in the mountains as they changed color.

Director Anthony Mann wanted his location Westerns to be more than John Ford's Monument Valley. He wanted to show mountains, waterfalls, forests, and snowy mountain peaks, rather than only deserts and red buttes. He filmed *The Naked Spur* (1953) in early summer in the mountains of Colorado near Silverton to emphasize the winter snow remaining on Engineer Mountain and the other snow-capped high peaks in the background. In *The Naked Spur* (1953) Mann used the changing landscape to mirror the main characters' internal brooding. As the movie progressed, the backgrounds became darker, and the terrain became rockier. The same was done in Mann's *Man of the West* (1958), where the landscape became increasingly barren and ominous as the plot progressed.

Weather could often be used to make a point. Part of *Cheyenne Autumn* (1964) was filmed in the real cold and snow of winter near Gunnison, Colorado, to emphasize the bitter temperatures and brutal weather that the real Cheyenne had to endure on their journey to Fort Robinson in Nebraska. Part of *The Searchers* (1956) was filmed in snow and cold to emphasize the brutalness of the search for Ethan Edward's niece. *The Great Silence* (1968) was filmed in the Dolomite Mountains of northern Italy to show the deep snows used in the plot, specifically because the location was supposed to be snow-bound Utah.

Weather when filming on location could also be a problem. Snow unexpectedly appeared during the filming of *Stagecoach* (1939). However, director John Ford was thrilled with the beauty of it and added it into the picture by altering the script to say that the stagecoach had taken the high road through Apache country.[6]

Monument Valley Revisited

Today when most people think of the West and Westerns, they are not thinking of the mountains, trees, and lakes of Colorado or Montana, but the deserts and canyon country of Arizona and Utah. Monument Valley represents only one small part of the American West, but popular Westerns filmed there have conditioned audiences to think that Utah and Arizona are what the West is supposed to look like. Because audiences feel this should be "the West," Monument Valley has even been named as the iconic background for the entire Western genre.

Pushing Monument Valley into prominence as "the Real West" was primarily the series of movies filmed there by director John Ford. Ford used this location more than any other. Ford described Monument Valley as "my favorite location. It has rivers, mountains, plains, desert, everything the land can offer. I feel at peace there. I have been all over the world, but I consider this the most complete, beautiful and peaceful place on earth."[7] In reality, all these geographical features are not found in the valley itself, but they are available reasonably close by. Ford said that he loved the isolation from studio heads, family, the telephone, and the lack of competition from other authority figures in Hollywood.[8] It has been claimed that other directors did not like to use Monument Valley, often called "Ford's Valley," out of respect for John Ford.

After *Stagecoach* (1939), John Ford continued to film in Monument Valley from time to time, producing such popular Westerns as *My Darling Clementine* (1946), *Fort Apache* (1948), *She Wore a Yellow Ribbon* (1949), *The Searchers* (1956), *Sergeant Rutledge* (1960), and *Cheyenne Autumn* (1964).[9] The initial stretch of dusty, rutted road that winds through the floor of the valley and passes in front of The Mittens rock formations was used so much by Ford that it became known as "Hollywood Boulevard."[10]

Ford's *Rio Grande* (1950), which is often erroneously credited as being filmed in Monument Valley, was actually filmed northeast of Moab, Utah, around Castle Valley, White's Ranch, and Professor Valley, where the landscape is very similar. Ford's *Wagon Master* (1950) was also shot around Moab, which at the time consisted essentially of only a motel, a gas station, a grocery store, and a drugstore.

My Darling Clementine (1946)

One of Ford's notable films shot in Monument Valley was *My Darling Clementine* (1946), a re-telling of the gunfight at the O.K. Corral between the Earp brothers, headed by Wyatt Earp, and the Clantons. Henry Fonda as Wyatt Earp, seeing Tombstone (actually Monument Valley) in *My Darling Clementine* (1946) for the first time, says, "Sure is rough-looking country."

The real Wyatt Earp was one of the legendary gunfighters of the Old West. At various times he was a farmer, a stagecoach driver, a buffalo hunter, a deputy town marshal, a saloon keeper, a gambler, a bounty hunter, and a bodyguard. Most of Earp's fame stems from the gunfight at the O.K. Corral in Tombstone and a popularized biography titled *Wyatt Earp: Frontier Marshal*, published in 1931 by author and screenwriter Stuart Lake. The gunfight became the most famous 30-second fight in the Old West.

Famed as a legendary lawman, Wyatt Earp was indeed a policeman in Wichita, Kansas, in 1874, but was a lawman for a total of only eight years. Earp met tubercular gambler Doc Holliday in Dodge City in 1876. Wyatt's older brother Virgil was town marshal in Tombstone, and the other brothers joined him there in 1880, followed by Holliday. Wyatt worked as a deputy sheriff, but hoped to make it rich as an entrepreneur and gambler. After the O.K. Corral fight, all the participants were dead or wounded except Wyatt. A few weeks later Virgil was shot and wounded, and Morgan was killed by a shotgun blast.

The fight would probably have been forgotten, like most of the other violent incidents on the frontier, except for Lake's biography of Wyatt Earp. The credits for *My*

Darling Clementine (1946) claim that it was "based on a book by Stuart Lake," though most historians have questioned the accuracy of many of the "facts" in the book. Historian John Mack Farragher put it in stronger terms when he said, "the book was an imaginative hoax, a fabrication mixed with just enough fact to lend it credibility."[11] Nevertheless, Lake's book provided the source material for the major movies about Earp.

John Ford knew Wyatt Earp when Earp was an old man and lived in Los Angeles. Ford claimed that Earp told him about the gunfight and always maintained that he stuck close to history, but there were several glaring discrepancies in the film, intentional or otherwise. Among them, "Old Man" Clanton was actually killed in Guadalupe Canyon on August 13, 1881, while he was driving a herd of stolen cattle to Tombstone from Mexico several weeks before the fight at the O.K. Corral; there was no Clementine love interest in real life; James Earp was Wyatt's older half-brother and was not a lawman like the others, but ran a saloon; and Doc Holliday was not killed during the fight, but died in a tuberculosis sanitarium in Colorado. Ford claimed that he filmed it "exactly the way it was" in *My Darling Clementine* (1946), but in reality it was just a screen story.

In 1881, at the time of the gunfight, the real silver-mining town of Tombstone was the largest in Arizona, with a population estimated to be between 12,000 and 15,000. At the time, Tucson's population was about 7,000 and Phoenix's was 1,800.[12] The real town of Tombstone was doomed when the lower levels of the mine workings rapidly flooded in 1881 when miners probably dug into a large subterranean water source. The Grand Central and Contention mines installed steam-driven pumps; however, most of the mines were interconnected by tunnels below the ground and the pumps couldn't handle the water from all the mines. The final collapse occurred when the pumps were destroyed by fire and the mines quickly flooded again. With the silver mining shut down, residents moved away and the population dropped rapidly to about 3,000. By 1900 Tombstone was a ghost town with a population of only 646.

My Darling Clementine (1946) was not filmed at Tombstone, which is still a real town 500 miles to the south in the Sonoran Desert of southern Arizona. Director John Ford loved to film in Monument Valley so, as a result, that is where he and his film crew visualized their version of Tombstone and Ford built his main street for the movie. The Monument Valley filming location, with its buttes and mesas towering over the actors and intense blue skies overhead, presented a mythic vision of the American West. The ambience of southern Arizona, the location of the real Tombstone, was represented by a few misplaced saguaro cactuses that were imported for the movie.

At some point in popularizing the scenery of Westerns and the American desert, the giant saguaro cactus became an iconic symbol that came to identify the West. It is the most distinctive of the cactuses, and is often identified with films shot at Old Tucson Studios. The largest of the desert cactuses, the saguaro grows only in a very few hot and arid locations, and is an indicator plant of the Sonoran Desert. It basically grows only in southern and western Arizona, and the adjoining desert of northwest Mexico, and is not native to Monument Valley. Just to add movie confusion, saguaro do not even grow in the real town of Tombstone to the south.

Location filming in Monument Valley for *My Darling Clementine* (1946) was finished in 45 days. The dance sequence with Henry Fonda and Cathy Downs as Clementine at the building site for the church is now the site of the Monument Valley Visitor Center.[13]

Ford's Tombstone set in Monument Valley cost $250,000 to construct. After filming was completed, Ford donated the Western street set to the Navajo Tribal Council. The buildings sat empty for five years until 1951, when the buildings were dismantled and sold for scrap, and the remains carted away.[14]

Ford's Cavalry Trilogy

Two films of Ford's so called "Cavalry Trilogy," *Fort Apache* (1948) and *She Wore a Yellow Ribbon* (1949) were filmed in Monument Valley. The third, *Rio Grande* (1950), was filmed northeast of Moab, Utah. All three were based on stories by James Warner Bellah which appeared originally in *The Saturday Evening Post*. *Fort Apache* (1948) was based on Bellah's "Massacre," *She Wore a Yellow Ribbon* (1949) on the stories "Big Hunt" and "War Party," and *Rio Grande* (1950) on "Mission with No Record." The three films were not connected narratives, but received the unintentional popular name because they all depicted life in the cavalry on the remote Western frontier.

At the beginning of *Fort Apache* (1948), when Col. Thursday (Henry Fonda) arrives to take over command of the fort, his stagecoach pulls up a dusty hill and stops briefly in front of a stage station where he goes in, meets some of the men under his command, and buys them a drink. The exterior of the combination stage station and trading post was played in a brief cameo role by the real Goulding's trading post. Subsequent interior scenes inside the building were shot on a sound stage in Hollywood.

Much of *Fort Apache* (1948), including the finale battle and massacre of Col. Thursday's command by the Indians, was filmed in Rock Door Canyon, just behind the location of today's Goulding's Lodge. At the time, Ford was able to use locations off the road (such as the area north of West Mitten) that are off-limits today. In another sequence, Captain York (John Wayne) and Sergeant Beaufort (Pedro Amendariz) ride past Totem Pole rock looking for Cochise's camp. The exterior set for the fort and its parade-ground were filmed over a period of two weeks at the Corriganville Movie Ranch, near Chatsworth, California.[15]

Fort Apache (1948) was filmed in black and white by cinematographer Archie Stout. Stout suggested to Ford that they film the exterior scenes with infra-red film, which had been introduced during World War II. He felt that this film, which was more sensitive to the infra-red end of the light spectrum, would produce a dramatic visual effect and emphasize the stark grandeur of the valley. The film made the sky seem darker, in some places rendered almost as black, while the white clouds stood out in brilliant contrast. The disadvantage was that the film was difficult to work with and the actors had to use special make-up that was very dark brown in color in order to prevent their faces and skin from looking white and washed out.[16] The final results, however, were spectacular and, even in black and white, emphasize the spectacular surroundings of the desert landscape.

In general, the Utah desert is very dry with blue skies and fluffy white clouds most of the time. During one sequence, however, in *She Wore a Yellow Ribbon* (1949), a sudden desert storm broke out with rain and lightning, and a rain squall swept over the valley while the cavalry actors were riding across the open valley to meet with Cochise. Ford and cinematographer Winton Hoch agreed to keep on shooting with the rain squall in the background, and ended up with one of best scenes of the movie. The gloom in the distance matched the mood of the sequence.[17]

By the time Ford returned to Monument Valley to film *She Wore a Yellow Ribbon* (1949), Goulding had built five small guest cabins to house the filmmakers. One was reserved for Ford, and the major stars doubled up in the others. The cabins, however, were still primitive. They had two bunks and two small wooden dressers, hard dirt floors, and kerosene heat. The shower was a five-gallon can full of cold water with holes in the bottom.[18]

Some scenes in *She Wore a Yellow Ribbon* (1949) were shot right at Goulding's Lodge. The exterior of the real Goulding's trading post doubled as the fort headquarters in the movie. The entrance seen in the film is now the entrance to Goulding's museum. The cabin with rock walls that was used as the quarters for Nathan Brittles (John Wayne) was a small building used by the Goulding's as a potato cellar, located right behind the trading post. As the camera moves back and forth between the post headquarters and the stone cabin in the movie, the view was just the same as it is today, except that the parking lot has since been paved. The scenes in the interior of the cabin were filmed on a Hollywood sound stage.

In the scene where Brittles goes to his wife's grave to talk to her, shot in a studio, one of the graves is marked "Pvt. B. DeVoto." The real Bernard DeVoto, author of a series of Pulitzer Prize–winning popular histories of the American West, was one of Ford's favorite historians of the West and Ford used the name as in-joke.

The set for the fort was built in the valley as only a front wall and gate. In some shots through the gate from the outside sharp-eyed viewers can see that there is no back wall and nothing behind it. This may have been unintentionally factually correct as most army forts of the time did not have a stockade surrounding them as is nearly always seen in Westerns, but were open on all sides.

She Wore a Yellow Ribbon (1949) was Ford's first use of three-strip Technicolor in a Western. Ford was fascinated by Frederic Remington's paintings and the artist's use of light, and tried to reproduce the feel of these paintings in the film. *She Wore a Yellow Ribbon* (1949) was nearly all shot on location in Monument Valley with only a few studio interiors used. The use of color in one sequence of lightning and storm clouds hanging over the valley behind a column of soldiers made the reddish mesas and buttes even more spectacular.

The Searchers (1956)

Even in 1955 when Ford returned again to film *The Searchers* (1956), considered by many to be one of Ford's finest movies, Monument Valley was still not an easy location to reach. The trip from Hollywood involved a train trip from Los Angeles to Flagstaff, then a long bus ride to Monument Valley.

Films, particularly Westerns, are often shot hundreds of miles from the real location where they are supposed to take place. A good example is placing the town of Tombstone for *My Darling Clementine* (1946) in Monument Valley. Similarly, Ford's *The Searchers* (1956), though set in Texas in 1868, was filmed almost entirely on location in Monument Valley. The interiors for the movie were filmed at RKO-Pathe Studios in Culver City. The final scenes of the confrontation between Ethan (John Wayne) and his niece Debbie Edwards (Natalie Wood) were filmed at Bronson Caves in Bronson Canyon near Hollywood.

Similar to the misplaced Tombstone set, the location for *The Searchers* (1956) is historically inaccurate. Though picturesque, the Jorgensen homestead and the Edwards cabin are completely out of place because there are no grazing grounds or water sources for cattle in Monument Valley, and the open location of the house would have been totally exposed to potential Indian attack.

In the opening sequence of *The Searchers* (1956), as Martha Edwards (Dorothy Jordan) goes through doorway, the camera reveals the rock formations of Gray Whiskers and Mitchell Butte, named for a prospector killed in Monument Valley in 1880. Ford also used the view from North Window for a spectacular view of the valley floor. Ethan and Sam Clayton (Ward Bond) overlook Scar's camp from John Ford Point, a promontory of rock that hangs over the valley.

John Ford Point was also used when Martin Pawley (Jeffrey Hunter) was lowered at night to the valley floor to find the Comanche camp. Pursued by Scar's braves, Ethan and Martin seek refuge in a narrow arch-shaped cave. The same location was used when Debbie runs away from Ethan at the end of the film. Today it is a dumping ground full of discarded trash and machinery from a nearby settlement.[19]

Shooting on location around Monument Valley wasn't always easy, particularly for the two young Wood sisters, who starred as Debbie Edwards at different ages. Natalie Wood, who played the grown-up Debbie, remembered that her sister Lana (age nine), who played Debbie as a youngster, heard the local Navajos singing around their campfires after dark and thought they were getting ready to attack. Natalie had to explain to her that sort of thing didn't happen any more. Natalie also remembered, "We were smack in the middle of the desert with nothing but sand for miles. During the day it got extremely hot, and we would break for a long lunch and get under shade when the sun was at its height. There were snakes and scorpions, and one day Ward Bond was bitten [stung] by a scorpion.... I was always on the lookout for scorpions after that."[20] John Ford was also stung by a scorpion while on location.[21]

During shooting, Natalie and Lana Wood (and their mother) lived upstairs over a trading post outside Flagstaff. Younger sister Lana remembered, "When you turned on the tap, the bathwater would come out as red and dirty as the desert sand. I was certain it would stain my skin."[22]

The river sequences in *The Searchers* (1956) were filmed at Mexican Hat, 20 miles northeast of Monument Valley, on Ford's favorite stretch of the San Juan River. He used it briefly for river crossing scenes in *Fort Apache* (1948), and more extensively in *The Searchers* (1956) and *Sergeant Rutledge* (1960).

Cheyenne Autumn (1964)

The last Western filmed by Ford in Monument Valley was *Cheyenne Autumn* (1964), filmed in color and 70mm Super Panavision. The reservation scenes in the first sequences were filmed in the valley by the rock formation named the Totem Pole. During the scenes of the Cheyenne trek, the actors marched several times up and down Monument Valley, even though the story was supposed to take place on the Northern Plains. The final refuge was Victory Cave, supposedly in the Dakota Territory, but filmed where Ethan Edwards (John Wayne) and Martin Pawley (Jeffrey Hunter) took shelter in *The Searchers* (1956).[23] The Indians of the real historical incident were Cheyenne, but Ford used local Navajo actors.

There were several scenes in *Cheyenne Autumn* (1964) where somber-looking Cheyenne leaders, played by Navajo Indians, responded to serious questions posed to them, but in Navajo. The actors playing interpreters in the film translated their answers back into English as the appropriate replies. As a somewhat apocryphal story, author Tony Hillerman said that more often the original spoken reply was a rude comment about another actor's or the director's physical characteristics or, as he politely put it, "some other earthy and humorous irrelevancy." Hillerman further commented that residents of the Gallup area would flock to screenings of the film when it was shown at the local drive-in to honk at the film to acknowledge the appearance of members of their family in the film as extras.[24]

Some scenes in *Cheyenne Autumn* (1964) were filmed in front of Goulding's Lodge, anecdotally because it was easier for the aging Ford, but that may an oversimplification. The outdoor winter snow scenes were filmed around Gunnison, Colorado, to simulate the harsh conditions that the real Cheyenne had to endure at Fort Robinson in Nebraska.

After Ford left the valley, other movies used the splendor of Monument Valley to stand in for various places in the West. In *The Lone Ranger* (2013), Monument Valley became Colby, Texas. Some scenes of the movie were filmed on location in Monument Valley, others were created with computer-generated special effects. At the beginning of the movie, before the bank robbery, the Lone Ranger appears in an iconic shot at John Ford Point with the splendor of Monument Valley in the background. Like other Westerns, various locations were used and some were blended together with computer generated imagery (CGI) in the final film. The sequence where the Lone Ranger and Tonto are buried in the sand, and the sequence of the cavalry charge, were filmed at Valles Caldera National Preserve, west of Los Alamos, New Mexico.

Another Western that used the iconic location of John Ford Point was *The Villain* (1979) (also known as *Cactus Jack*), a parody of old 1930s Westerns. At the beginning of the movie, Handsome Stranger (Arnold Schwarzenegger) travels through Monument Valley and rides out onto John Ford Point. The result is an effective view of a small, lone rider contrasted against the overpowering vast emptiness of the valley. Like other Westerns, *The Villain* (1979) was filmed in various locations. The beginning was filmed at Old Tucson Studios and the train scenes were blended with the Jamestown Railroad in California.

Ford's Legacy

Ford used members of the local Navajo tribe in Monument Valley for generic Indians. He had them act as Arapaho and Apache in *She Wore a Yellow Ribbon* (1949), Comanche in *The Searchers* (1956), and Cheyenne in *Cheyenne Autumn* (1964).

In late 1948 a deep snowfall virtually paralyzed Monument Valley. As an ex-navy commander, Ford was able to arrange a relief drop by military planes, named "Operation Haylift," to provide assistance with food and supplies for Navajo families and hay for their sheep and cattle.[25] Ford genuinely wanted to help the Navajo people. For example, he insisted that Navajo actors be paid standard movie wages the same as the rest of the Hollywood actors. For one movie he hired 200 Navajos at $18 a day each for 20 days, or a total of $72,000.[26]

Ford was so well respected by the Navajo tribe that he was honored by them on the Fourth of July 1955, during the filming of *The Searchers* (1956). In appreciation for all he had done for them, the Navajo tribe gave Ford a ceremonial deer hide, complete with ears, tail, and legs, and he was made an honorary member of the tribe. He was given the honorary name of *Natani Nez*, which means "tall leader."[27]

When Ford died in 1973 he had made 220 films, including documentaries and short subjects, over a period of 53 years.

Old Tucson Studios

Though Monument Valley is probably the most recognizable of the iconic locations for filming Westerns in the 1940 and 1950s, several other locations can be immediately identified by avid fans of Western movies.

One of the most identifiable locations is Old Tucson Studios, situated in the Sonoran Desert, just over Gates Pass and the mountains on the west side of Tucson, Arizona. Most recognizable to fans of Westerns is the readily-remembered landmark of the sharp, prominent shape of Golden Gate Mountain seen in the background of many of the Western movies filmed at Old Tucson Studios. (For younger audiences, the volcanic cone-shaped hills behind the Eaves Movie Ranch in New Mexico will perhaps be more recognizable.) Another clue in the background of Westerns filmed at Old Tucson is the profusion of saguaro cactuses, which grow only in the desert around Tucson and a few other places in southern Arizona, northern Mexico, and extreme southeast California.

Old Tucson Studios was originally built in 1939 as a movie set on a 320-acre plot of land leased from Pima County by Columbia as a location for the movie *Arizona* (1940). The set was built as an exact replica of Old Tucson in the 1860s, which was the setting for the book that the movie was based on. The film stars Jean Arthur as Phoebe Titus, a pioneer women who owns a freighting business and falls for Peter Muncie (William Holden). After filming was completed, the set was abandoned and the empty buildings sat deteriorating in the desert for a number of years. In 1946, the Tucson Jaycees took over the property and started to repair it, renting it out to movie companies to raise funds.

In 1959, Bob Shelton, a developer from Kansas, took over the property and turned it into a tourist attraction. He also built film production facilities in the town, including a large sound stage, and leased it as a filming location to movie companies. Old Tucson eventually grew to be a 320-acre filming location and theme park. Ironically, author Bette Stanton has claimed that Old Tucson made more money as a theme park than as a film studio.[28] Unfortunately, a major fire attributed to arson in April of 1995 caused serious damage, destroying many of the buildings, the entire Western wardrobe department, and much of the studio's extensive movie memorabilia collection.

About 40 percent of the studio was destroyed. The town was, however, rebuilt and reopened in 1997.

The location was surrounded by the Sonoran Desert, which was thick with saguaro, palo verde trees, ocotillo, and prickly pear cactus. The original movie town contained adobe buildings, wooden structures, and a Mexican mission. The town was cleverly constructed so that some buildings on the set could be easily changed to give them different appearances for different movies. One building in Old Tucson was constructed so that it could be made to appear like four different buildings, depending on which side was photographed.[29] This was a common practice at most studios and movie towns. By changing the rooflines, sidewalks, and front porches of buildings, a town street could be made to appear to be different for different productions.

Among the iconic movies filmed at Old Tucson Studios was *Rio Bravo* (1959), which filmed there from May to July 1958. Other movies partially filmed at Old Tucson were *Winchester '73* (1950), *McLintock!* (1963), *Rio Lobo* (1970), *Death of a Gunfighter* (1971), *Joe Kidd* (1972), and *¡Three Amigos!* (1986). For *Young Guns II* (1990), Old Tucson became the town of White Oaks, New Mexico, a real town associated with the Billy the Kid legend. The television series *The High Chaparral* (1966 to 1971), set in lawless Tucson in the 1870s, was filmed in and around Old Tucson Studios on a special ranch set. Another movie in which the iconic saguaro is highly visible is *The Guns of Fort Petticoat* (1957) with Audie Murphy, which was filmed around the old Mexican mission building. *McLintock!* (1963) was filmed at Old Tucson Studios and near Nogales and Tombstone.

The Mexican mission and plaza area of Old Tuscon Studios were featured in many motion pictures, often being transformed to meet the need of a particular film. In the television movie *Go West, Young Girl* (1978) the mission was transformed into a prison. In *¡Three Amigos!* (1986) the building received two new stucco towers to give the facade a new look. The front of the mission was also the background for the wedding scene and subsequent violent shootout at the beginning of *Tombstone* (1993). Unfortunately the original mission was destroyed as part of the arson fire of 1995.

Another filming facility of Old Tucson Studios is the town of Mescal, a movie set located on 2,400 acres in the desert country east of Tucson. The town was constructed in 1969 to provide a location with a different type of appearance than the main Old Tucson desert setting. The town was built by Cinema Center Films, which was filming *Monte Walsh* (1970) at Old Tucson Studios, but needed a second location that looked more like the Northern Plains. The resulting movie-set town, situated north of Interstate 10 east of Tucson on an arid plain covered with mesquite bush, was originally called Harmony. After filming was completed, the town was sold to Old Tucson Studios and was used as an auxiliary set for the main studio location. Other Westerns that used Mescal for a filming location were *The Life and Times of Judge Roy Bean* (1972), *Tombstone* (1993), and *The Quick and the Dead* (1995).

Sedona

Another popular filming location in Arizona in the 1940s and 1950s was Sedona, a small town 25 miles south of Flagstaff that is surrounded by mountains strewn with pine trees, red-rock canyons, and picturesque red sandstone cliffs. Flagstaff was used for much of the early movie filming in Arizona, with other productions filmed around Kayenta. Arizona was an ideal location and climate for making Westerns, and for a while Arizona was second only to California in the number of films made there. Then Tucson, Prescott, and Sedona in Arizona entered into the competition for location film business, along with Kanab and Moab in Utah.

The town of Sedona sits at the bottom of a bowl, surrounded by red cliffs that have been eroded by wind and rain into a series of beautiful canyons. The town was founded in 1902, named after Sedona Schnebly, the wife of the first settler in the area.

Sedona was discovered as a filming location by producer Jesse Lasky of Paramount, even though it was remote and difficult to travel to. Zane Grey convinced Lasky to film his book *Call of the Canyon* (1923) and *Riders of the Purple Sage* (1931) in their actual settings. After the success of these movies, more film crews came to film in the red-rock country. The Technicolor rendering of the brilliant red rocks in *Billy the Kid* (1941) helped to develop further interest in the area. Another boost to the red rocks and the beauty of the area came with *Johnny Guitar* (1954), a decidedly offbeat Western filmed in Republic's Trucolor process. Location filming was done in Sedona at Boynton Canyon. The red rocks also drew other Hollywood directors who filmed, among others, *Angel and the Badman* (1947), *Broken Arrow* (1950), *Flaming Feather* (1951), and *3:10 to Yuma* (1957).

Sedona underwent rapid development after World War II, and a small Western town movie set was constructed near Coffeepot Rock. Since then numerous Western movies have been filmed in the area, including *Tall in the Saddle* (1948). *Gun Fury* (1953), with Rock Hudson, was filmed in the slickrock country near Sedona with Bell Rock clearly visible in the background, along with the colorful redrock spires behind the town. It was originally filmed in the heyday of 3-D movies and, at several places in the plot, rocks and other blunt instruments were visually launched out of the screen at the audience during fight scenes.

Director Delmer Daves apparently liked Sedona as a location because he filmed *Broken Arrow* (1950), *Drum Beat* (1954), *The Last Wagon* (1956), and *3:10 to Yuma* (1957) in the area. The trailer for *Broken Arrow* (1950), with James Stewart, boldly proclaimed "Photographed in the Last Primitive Western Locales."

Kanab

The availability of scenic locations to provide dramatic background settings for movies has lured producers and directors to the West almost from the start of movie-making. Utah's Canyon Country, in particular, provided deserts, mesas, buttes, arches, and scenic spires, topped by intense blue skies with puffy white clouds, and red rocks that looked like they were on fire when they were lit by late afternoon sunlight. The plains, deserts, and mountains of the state added natural beauty and harmony to Western films and gave them a sense of importance.

Offering all these scenic features nearby, the town of Kanab in southern Utah, which was originally settled in the 1870s, became one of the major centers for location filming of Westerns from the 1930s to the 1970s.[30] The trailer for *Fury at Furnace*

Creek (1948), for example, filmed in the Kanab area, advertised proudly that it was made on location instead of on a studio set—"the artificial West of the motion picture studio," as the announcer disdainfully put it. So many Western movies were filmed in the Kanab area that the town was known in the 1930s and 1940s as "Little Hollywood." Indeed, Kanab was the filming location most often used outside Los Angeles and more Westerns were filmed around Kanab than anywhere outside Hollywood. *Life* magazine referred to the town as "Utah's Hollywood."

One of the first movies shot in Utah was Tom Mix's *Deadwood Coach* (1924), which was filmed in Kanab Canyon, just north of town. During the filming, Mix's production crew used a small transportation company run by brothers Chauncey, Whit, and Gronway Parry to transport the cast and crew to various locations. After this modest success, the Parrys decided to encourage movie companies to come to southern Utah, and Kanab became a popular filming location due to their efforts. Kanab of the 1930s, 1940s, 1950s, 1960s, and 1970s was firmly entrenched in the movie business.

The Parrys arranged full support for the studios for Western moviemaking, including livestock, horses, transportation, extras, location scouting, lodging, catering, and even covered wagons and carriages. The entire town, which consisted of 1,300 people in 1930, supported the movie business as extras, doubles, wranglers, transportation drivers, and general laborers. The Parrys provided lodging for the cast and crew at Parry Lodge, a combination tourist lodge and restaurant with a central Colonial-style white building and surrounding small cottages that they purchased in 1931. They also provided entertainment and diversions, such as dances and parties, after a day of filming. Not so well known was that Parry Lodge was the home of the Black Cat bar, which was open only to moviemakers because the Mormon town did not serve alcohol.[31]

More than a hundred movies were filmed in the Kanab area. A complete listing would be exhaustive, but a representative sampling of films and their stars made in and around Kanab were *Deadwood Coach* (1924) with Tom Mix, *Ramona* (1928) with Dolores del Rio, *In Old Arizona* (1929) with Warner Baxter, *The Big Trail* (1930) with John Wayne, *The Great Adventures of Wild Bill Hickok* (1938) with "Wild Bill" Elliott, *Roll Wagons Roll* (1939) with Tex Ritter, *Union Pacific* (1939) with Joel McCrea, *Billy the Kid* (1941) with Robert Taylor, *Western Union* (1941) with Robert Young, *Buffalo Bill* (1944) with Joel McCrea, *Sergeants 3* (1962) with Frank Sinatra and Dean Martin, *Eldorado* (1967) with John Wayne, *Rough Night in Jericho* (1967) with Dean Martin, *MacKenna's Gold* (1969) with Gregory Peck, and *The Outlaw Josey Wales* (1976) with Clint Eastwood. *Fort Dobbs* (1958) used a standing set at Kanab built for the earlier *Fort Yuma* (1955) that was rented for the production. A modern murder mystery, *The Girl in Black Stockings* (1957), was filmed at Parry Lodge and used the lodge itself as a backdrop.

MGM used the Kanab area so much in the 1940s that they built a movie set just north of town. This small Western town, built in Johnson Canyon, was used for *Westward the Women* (1951), with Robert Taylor and Denise Darcel. The set was improved by various studios over the years and it became known as the Johnson Canyon Movie Set. Some of the buildings are still standing, though the set is now basically only a decrepit ruin. In its prime, the set was used for dozens of movies and television

This movie set town in Johnson Canyon, northeast of Kanab, Utah, was used for the exteriors of many episodes of the television series *Gunsmoke*, *Have Gun—Will Travel*, and others. Though still standing, the buildings have fallen into disrepair since filming declined in the area.

series, including for the exteriors for more than 20 episodes of the television Western *Gunsmoke* from the 1950s to 1970s, and for *Have Gun—Will Travel* and *Death Valley Days*. Director William Wellman built a set in Johnson Canyon that became named Fort Wellman, after him, for *Buffalo Bill* (1944) with Joel McCrea.

Also north of town is the barn built by Walt Disney Productions for *One Little Indian* (1973), still being used to shelter horses. Though *Rough Night in Jericho* (1967) was mostly filmed on studio sets, the scene where Alex Flood (Dean Martin) ambushes Dolan (George Peppard) and the stagecoach was filmed at a location called The Gap, about five miles east of Kanab.

Frontier Movie Town, in the town of Kanab itself, contains several buildings from movies shot in the area, including the homestead from *The Outlaw Josey Wales* (1976). In the movie, the Texas location of the homestead was filmed along Kanab Creek under cottonwood trees and afterwards relocated to Frontier Movie Town. Though the homestead building looks like it is made from weathered adobe, it is actually made from fiberglass painted to look like mud bricks.

Director Howard Koch build a sprawling fort southwest of the town of Kanab for use in *Fort Bowie* (1958). This fort set was used in many movies until 1978 when a special-effects explosion in *The Apple Dumpling Gang Rides Again* (1979) made it unusable. The final spectacular explosion used hundreds of gallons of kerosene and succeeded beyond the special effects crew's wildest expectations.[32] The fort was severely damaged and never rebuilt. This pretty much signaled the end of movie making in Kanab.

Paria

Another location in southern Utah with spectacular colored rocks that was used for filming Westerns is Paria Canyon, about 35 miles east of Kanab. Among other films, the canyon and its later movie-set town appeared in parts of *Western Union* (1941), *The Desperadoes* (1943) (the first color film from Columbia Pictures), *Buffalo Bill* (1944), *Sergeants 3* (1962), *Mackenna's Gold* (1969), and *The Outlaw Josey Wales* (1976).

Early settlers founded a town named Pahreah in the canyon, looking for fertile land, a reliable source of water, and good grazing for cattle. Overgrazing by sheep and cattle rapidly killed off the grass and the town declined. By 1892, only eight families still lived there. By 1915 the post office had closed, and, by the early 1930s the Pahreah Town Site had become a ghost town.

In the 1950s and 1960s, Hollywood discovered the beauty of the canyon. A movie set was built close to the historic ghost town for *Sergeants 3* (1962), with Frank Sinatra, Dean Martin, and Sammy Davis, Jr., along with other members of Frank Sinatra's "Rat Pack," as a Western version of Rudyard Kipling's Indian story of Gunga Din.[33] After filming was completed, the set was abandoned and it started to disintegrate. It was later restored and used for scenes in *The Outlaw Josey Wales* (1976), which was the last time that it was used for a movie.

Other movies filmed near Paria included *Mackenna's Gold* (1969), which was partially filmed in Paria and Kanab Canyon as well as in Monument Valley and Bryce Canyon National Park. The setting for the canyon where the men finally find the gold was made by spray-painting part of the wall of Paria Canyon with gold-colored paint. The picturesque rock formation behind the former location of the movie set, seen in the background of movies filmed there and which towers over the now-deserted area, is called The Cockscomb. In *Duel at Diablo* (1966) The Cockscomb is prominent in the background.

The buildings of the movie set from *Sergeants 3* (1962) were partially restored in the 1980s and maintained by the U.S. Bureau of Land Management until 1999. Two of the buildings were rebuilt and moved from their original location, but they were burned down completely by vandals on August 25, 2006. The setting is maintained as a historic site, but nothing is left now but a few concrete foundations alongside the dirt road that winds through the canyon.

Grafton

Like Paria, other Utah movie locations used by filmmakers had genuine historic backgrounds. One example that has been used as a motion picture location is the small ghost town of Grafton, a few miles south of Zion National Park in southwest

Utah. Grafton was originally settled by pioneers in 1861 and is an authentic ghost town with a schoolhouse and several private homes that date from the 1860s, 1870s, and 1880s. The original settlers soon found out, though, that the sandy soil in the area was not suitable for growing crops. The last residents left in 1945.

The scenic quality of Grafton, complemented by the Virgin River and the spectacular cliffs of Zion National Park in the background, attracted director Raoul Walsh from Fox Studios to film *In Old Arizona* (1928), a story of the adventures of the Cisco Kid. The success of the movie brought Walsh back to Grafton the next year to film *The Arizona Kid* (1930), which he shot entirely on location. In 1947, director Andre de Toth partially filmed *Ramrod* (1947), a plot of cattlemen versus sheepmen, in Grafton because of the scenic background of Zion National Park. He used the little town's main street for the final shootout. Memorable also was the location filming in the Kolob Canyons area in the northwest section of Zion National Park.

Several other movies have been filmed around Grafton, often using Rockville Road, which runs between Grafton and the nearby town of Rockville. Probably the most well-known movie filmed in Grafton was *Butch Cassidy and the Sundance Kid* (1969), which used the town as one location. It was made famous by the bicycle scene with Butch (Paul Newman) and Etta Place (Katharine Ross) riding to the accompaniment of Burt Bacharach's Academy Award–winning song "Raindrops Keep Fallin' On My Head." A frame house was added for the movie as Etta Place's home. It was built on the street corner across from the historic church building, which was built in 1866 then partially restored by film crews and converted for the film into a schoolhouse.

Gallup

Though Las Vegas was quiet as a film location in the 1940s and 1950s, Gallup, New Mexico, was an active location for filming many Western movies. The town was easily reached by the famous Route 66 or by convenient railroad connections.[34]

Gallup was another genuine Old West town, founded in 1881 in the west-central part of New Mexico by the Atlantic and Pacific Railroad as a shipping point for the vast coal deposits mined nearby. The area attracted workers both to build the railroad and to mine the coal. After the coal business declined, Gallup returned to being a sleepy town with a small population. Today Gallup is an important trading town for the nearby Navajo Nation.

Gallup was discovered as a movie location in 1915 and, by the 1940s, it had become a major filming center. The first color picture to take full advantage of the Gallup scenery was *Redskin* (1929) with Richard Dix and Julie Carter, shot in an early two-color Technicolor process.

Many Westerns of the 1930s were filmed close to Hollywood for convenience and to save money in the budget-conscious days of the Depression. However, in the 1930s, Gallup was a major center for A-Western film production, with many of the Hollywood visitors staying at the picturesque El Rancho Hotel.

El Rancho was built to accommodate the stars and production crews making the Westerns that filled the movie theaters of the 1930s and 1940s. The hotel was financed

The El Rancho Hotel in Gallup, New Mexico, was built in 1937 by "Griff" Griffith, the brother of D.W. Griffith, to accommodate the stars and crews making the Westerns of the 1930s and 1940s in the area. The magnificent two-story lobby was built with a classic Western decor with a circular staircase made of split logs leading to the upstairs rooms. The walls of the upstairs gallery are lined with publicity photographs of the many Hollywood stars who stayed at the hotel while filming nearby on location.

by R.E. "Griff" Griffith, owner of a New Mexico theater chain and the brother of D.W. Griffith, after he came to Gallup to direct a film. The hotel opened on December 17, 1937. The magnificent old hotel has a two-story open lobby with a circular staircase made of split logs climbing to the upstairs rooms, and heavy beams holding up an interior balcony on the second floor. The rough-hewn entry doors and stone-lined walk-in fireplace give the lobby the impression of an exotic Western hunting lodge.

The walls of the upstairs gallery are lined with publicity photographs of the movies filmed in the area and the many Hollywood stars who stayed at the hotel from the 1930s to the 1950s while filming nearby on location. Typical was when MGM filmed *The Bad Man* (1940) with Wallace Beery and Ronald Reagan near the town, and the cast and crew stayed for several weeks at El Rancho. El Rancho was also a popular stopping place for tourists passing through on Route 66 and the railroad.

In the area surrounding Gallup, directors and producers could easily find colorful red sandstone, wind-eroded stone arches, steep canyons, narrow passes, desert sand dunes, and sculptured multi-colored rocks. Typical of the Westerns filmed around Gallup were *The Texas Rangers* (1936) with Fred MacMurray, *Sundown* (1941) with Gene Tierney and Bruce Cabot, *Colorado Territory* (1948) with Joel McCrea and

Virginia Mayo, *Streets of Laredo* (1948) with William Holden and William Bendix, *Rocky Mountain* (1950) with Errol Flynn, *Raton Pass* (1951) with Dennis Morgan, *Fort Defiance* (1951) with Joel McCrea and Forest Tucker, *Escape from Fort Bravo* (1953) with William Holden, *Fort Massacre* (1957) with Joel McCrea, and *The Hallelujah Trail* (1965) with Burt Lancaster and Lee Remick. The very end of *The Hallelujah Trail* (1965) shows the dejected (and very hung over) Indians riding slowly towards 1,583-foot-high Shiprock in the northwest corner of the state.

Similar to Monument Valley, the vast skies in early Westerns shot around Gallup photographed well on black-and-white film, even though it could not show the blue of the skies and the brilliant red colors of the rocks. *Pursued* (1947), *Colorado Territory* (1949), *Ambush* (1949), and *Rocky Mountain* (1950) showed off the local scenery to advantage. After the introduction of color film, the red sandstone formations were ideal for photographing in Technicolor.

There were several popular filming areas close to Gallup. The most popular and well-used by the studios stretched about seven miles east of town, north of the present Interstate 40, some of which incorporates today's Red Rock Park. Familiar rock formations often spotted in movies made in this area are Pyramid Rock and Church Rock. This location was the setting for *Rocky Mountain* (1950) with Errol Flynn. Kit Carson Cave, a large sandstone cave a few miles northeast of Red Rock Park, was used by Paramount for *Billy the Kid* (1925) and *Streets of Laredo* (1949).

Another popular filming location near Gallup was the area around Lupton, just over the border in Arizona. Red Lake, about 20 miles north of the town of Window Rock, Arizona, on the New Mexico-Arizona border to the west, was only accessed over rough roads which limited its use. A few miles north of Red Lake, on the Navajo reservation, filmmakers also used the tiny town of Crystal.

About 70 miles southeast of Gallup is Acoma, an Indian pueblo located on a high mesa. Acoma, also known as the Sky City, sits perched on a mesa 367 feet above the floor of Acoma Valley, built at that lofty location to provide protection from attack for its early inhabitants. Originally the only way to access the houses perched on the mesa was to climb up a pathway to the top, then the producers of the film *Redskin* (1929) asked permission to build an access road to the top to facilitate filming. This is still the only existing road up to the village.

About 15 miles southwest of Gallup at Lookout Point, Paramount built a gigantic set 237 feet high consisting of simulated Indian cliff-dwellings near Manuelito for the modern *Ace in the Hole* (1950) (alternate title *The Big Carnival*), which was set in small-town New Mexico. The set is now gone. This movie was impressive for using more than 1,500 extras; however, Gallup was also a good location because is close to the south boundary of the Navajo Nation reservation and could provide plenty of American Indians for extras.

Lone Pine and the Alabama Hills

One of the iconic Western locations, and one that should be familiar to anyone who has watched Westerns, is the area round Lone Pine, California, 175 miles north of Los Angeles, in the Owens Valley at the foot of the Sierra Nevada Mountains. Much of the surrounding area is public lands administered by the U.S. Bureau of Land Management (BLM). No movie sets exist in the area as BLM policy is that no permanent changes can be made to the landscape, and all sets and debris have to be removed after filming is complete.

Lone Pine offered filmmakers a variety of landscapes for making Westerns. A few miles from Lone Pine were the Alabama Hills, a 25,000-acre labyrinth of eroded granite rocks, complemented by spectacular mountain vistas of Mount Whitney in the background.[35] The Alabama Hills, named during the Civil War for the battleship CSS *Alabama*, appeared in over 300 hundred movies between the 1920s and 1950s. For added filming convenience, close by were sand dunes, a railroad, and just to the north was the dry bed of Owens Lake. Ghost towns were located at Dolomite and Cerro Gordo. Thanks to hundreds of films made around Lone Pine, this area became a classic image of the West. Through Hollywood movies, the desolate landscape around Lone Pine helped to shape the world's romanticized perception of the West.

Movies were made at Lone Pine as early as the 1920s. Since then, nearly 400 movies have been partially or totally shot at and around Lone Pine, particularly the B-Westerns filmed during the genre's heyday from the 1920s to the 1970s. So many cowboy stars, such as Roy Rogers, Gene Autry, Hopalong Cassidy (William Boyd), and John Wayne, galloped along the dirt roads of the rocky sage-covered landscape, that one area was named "Movie Flats."

The first film shot entirely on location near Lone Pine was *The Round-Up* (1920), a silent Western starring comedian Fatty Arbuckle in his first feature film as Sheriff Slim Hoover. Tom Mix starred in *Riders of the Purple Sage* (1925) and John Wayne appeared in *Westward Ho* (1935). A young Roy Rogers made his starring debut in the Alabama Hills in *Under Western Stars* (1938). In *The Gay Caballero* (1940), Cesar Romero played the Cisco Kid. *Spurs* (1930) with Hoot Gibson was filmed with breath-taking photography of the mountains, desert, and the cloud formations of Lone Pine in the background. In *The Tall T* (1957), Randolph Scott played a brave cowboy trying to defend kidnapped stagecoach passengers. For *Yellow Sky* (1948) with Gregory Peck, a film crew of 150 workers built a ghost town. In *Rawhide* (1951), where a group of escaped convicts take over a stage station in order to intercept a shipment of gold, the set for the stage station was built on open ground with a stunning view of the Sierra Nevada mountains in the background. *The Great Race* (1965) filmed a few scenes near Lone Pine with antique cars racing along the dirt roads of Movie Flats.

The Alabama Hills location also stood in for India, the Gobi Desert, Arabia, and for Africa in two Tarzan films. During the later science-fiction craze, it was used for two films of the *Star Trek* franchise and for *Tremors* (1990). The crew of *Django Unchained* (2012) spent three months filming in the area, much of the filming taking place at night. Movies, television shows, commercials, and still photographic shoots still take place in the area.

The Alabama Hills served as the northwest frontier of India for *Gunga Din* (1939), and at the beginning of *The Charge of the Light Brigade* (1936), with Errol Flynn and Henry Stephenson. *Gunga Din* (1939), with Cary Grant, Douglas Fairbanks, Jr., Victor McLaglen, and Sam Jaffe as the Indian water boy Gunga Din, was a classic hero adventure tale set in 19th-century India, inspired by the Rudyard Kipling poem of same name. The vista of the High Sierras in the background stood in for the Himalayas, with a movie set built to represent the village of Tantrapur. The landscape was very similar to the Khyber Pass area on the Indian northwest frontier, but sharp-eyed movie fans can clearly see the jagged peak of Mt. Whitney in the background.

Years later, Douglas Fairbanks, Jr., humorously recalled in an interview that the similarity was so great that friends of his from India were convinced that the movie was filmed on location at the Khyber Pass and that they recognized the area as they watched the movie.[36] Indeed, the likeness to India was so well portrayed that the location was also used for *The Lives of a Bengal Lancer* (1935) with Gary Cooper, and *King of the Khyber Rifles* (1953) with Tyrone Power. The scene in *Gunga Din* (1939) where the men cross the bridge to the thuggee hideout was actually only 10 feet or so off the ground, but special effects made it look like a bridge over a deep gorge. In some shots it is possible to see sagebrush and tell that it was only a few feet up in the air.

After filming on *Gunga Din* (1939) was complete, a local rancher moved the remains of the sets to the Anchor Ranch, where he constructed a Western town named Anchorville, a Spanish mission, a ranch house, and a hacienda as a large standing set for movie filming. The Western town was torn down in the 1950s and the Spanish mission in 1975.

A steep arroyo in the Alabama Hills was a favorite place for rolling wagons over the edge to produce spectacular stunt crashes. This location was used for a wagon roll-over in *How the West Was Won* (1962). The stunt had to be repeated and filmed three times to make it look right. The sequence that included the crash created severe logistical problems for the film crew as it also involved the use of 630 horses, 150 mules, and 107 wagons. The same ravine had been previously used for a similar wagon stunt in *Hell Bent for Leather* (1960), with Audie Murphy and Felicia Farr. It is also often seen in earlier B-Western movies, such as *The Big Show* (1937) with Gene Autry, where a wagon rolls over into the same ravine.

Death Valley

East of Lone Pine, on the other side of the Sierra Nevada Mountains, Death Valley was an important movie location until the 1960s, including such Westerns as *Three Godfathers* (1948), with John Wayne and Pedro Amendariz.

The barren wastes of Death Valley National Park on the California-Nevada border have always formed a favorite dramatic filming location. Portions of *Escape from Fort Bravo* (1953), *The Bravados* (1958), *The Law and Jake Wade* (1958), and *The Professionals* (1966) were filmed there. Death Valley was the location for stories in the television series *Death Valley Days*, which ran for an amazing 452 episodes on television between 1952 and 1975.

Death Valley was used as a filming location until the 1960s when additional government regulation on filming in National Parks made it increasingly difficult for filmmakers to schedule productions.

Other national parks, national monuments, and national forests in California have remained popular as filming locations. *Ride the High Country* (1962), for example, was filmed in nearby Inyo National Forest and at Frenchman's Flat, Conejo Valley, Malibu Canyon, and a town set on the MGM back lot.

Moab

Moab, Utah, in the 1950s and 1960s was a popular destination for filmmakers who were drawn to the surrounding natural scenery and the spectacular colors of the local red and vermilion rock formations. The country around Moab was another favorite filming location of director John Ford. Ford was particularly fond of Professor Valley and Castle Valley, where he filmed *Wagon Master* (1950) and the third of his cavalry trilogy, *Rio Grande* (1950). *Rio Grande* (1950) was filmed in Professor Valley, at George White's Ranch, Ida Gulch, and Onion Creek Narrows to the northeast of Moab, not in Monument Valley as some have subsequently claimed. It is an easy mistake to make as White's Ranch and Castle Valley have a landscape that is very similar to Monument Valley.[37]

The Mexican village in *Rio Grande* (1950) was built in Professor Valley. The army fort was constructed on private land at White's Ranch. The set was used later for *Battle at Apache Pass* (1952) and *Taza, Son of Cochise* (1954), but has long since been demolished.

Ford's interest in the Moab area started when he asked George White, who owned a local ranch near the Colorado River, to help him find locations for *Wagon Master* (1950). Rancher White came up with Professor Valley, Spanish Valley, the areas around Fisher Towers and Locomotive Rock, and alongside the Colorado River that flows through the area. Later expanding his support role, White started the original Moab Film Committee to coordinate lodging, livestock, and transportation for the film crews, and act as a liaison between the studios and government organizations. White supplied extras, wranglers for the stock, and miscellaneous equipment, such as wagons. The "Moab to Monument Valley Film Commission" claims to be the longest ongoing film commission in the world.[38]

A lesser-known part of the story is that Moab was appealing to the business end of the motion picture industry because the prices demanded by merchants and livestock owners for filming in Kanab had increased so much that the studios had started to look elsewhere for new locations.[39]

Other Westerns filmed around Moab in the 1950s included *Taza, Son of Cochise* (1954) filmed at White's Ranch and in Castle Valley and Professor Valley, and *Siege at Red River* (1954). *Warlock* (1959) was filmed in Professor Valley, at Dead Horse Point State Park as well as White's Ranch and Kings Bottom. In the 1960s, Westerns filmed in the area included *The Comancheros* (1961), *Cheyenne Autumn* (1963), and *Rio Conchos* (1964).

The Comancheros (1961) was filmed in Professor Valley and Fisher Valley, at nearby Dead Horse Point State Park, Kings Bottom, and Onion Creek near Moab. The Spanish settlement and villa in *The Comancheros* (1961) was built near Fisher Towers, but was burned down as part of the movie plot and the area afterwards cleaned up. Parts of *Cheyenne Autumn* (1963) were filmed at White's Ranch, Castle Valley,

Professor Valley, Fisher Canyon, Arches National Park, but with most of it filmed in Monument Valley and at nearby Mexican Hat.

Lightning Jack (1993), a comedy Western with Australian actor Paul Hogan, was filmed around Fisher Towers and other areas around Moab. *Geronimo: An American Legend* (1993) was filmed in Professor Valley, the Potash area, the Needles Overlook, and Onion Creek. "Fort San Carlos" was constructed for *Geronimo* on private property in Professor Valley and was dismantled after production was completed.

Another prominent filming location in Utah for Westerns was Snow Canyon, seven miles north of the city of St. George, in the very southwest corner of the state, near the Nevada border. The canyon itself was not large, but contained a variety of scenery. Part of *Butch Cassidy and the Sundance Kid* (1969) was filmed in Snow Canyon State Park. When director Lewis Teague wanted to depict "the West" for the beginning sequence in *Romancing the Stone* (1984), where heroine Angelina (Kymberly Herrin) is confronted by ultimate villain Grogan (Ted White), the director chose to use the rocks and sagebrush desert background of Snow Canyon State Park, which looked like parts of Monument Valley. When the accompanying music broke into the theme from *How the West Was Won* (1962), the sequence seemed like the ultimate Western, which was the director's intent.

Utah has been featured in over 800 films made for the big screen and for television. Filming began with *The Covered Wagon* (1923), *The Deadwood Coach* (1924), and *The Vanishing* (1925), all of which were filmed in the southern part of the state. Filmmakers here could capture the grandeur and majesty of the outdoors that could not be duplicated on a back lot in Hollywood.

Las Vegas

New Mexico has figured prominently in the location filming of Westerns almost since the beginning of the movies. The town of Las Vegas, New Mexico, and its surrounding area offered mountains to the west, grassy plains with two lakes to the east, a variety of architecture ranging from New Mexico Territorial style to Victorian houses that were ideal for filming Westerns, and even a local historic castle.

Las Vegas was a real and authentic Western frontier town that was visited at one time or another by outlaw legends such as Doc Holliday and Billy the Kid. In the 1880s, Las Vegas was the largest town between Independence, Missouri, and San Francisco. The town boasted saloons and bordellos, drunkenness and lawlessness, and real shoot-outs and lynchings.

When Mexico gained its independence from Spain in 1821, Las Vegas became a major stopping point on the Santa Fe Trail, the New Mexico trade route that ran west from Missouri and ended in Santa Fe. The trail also connected with *El Camino Real* (The Royal Road), the trade route that ran south to Mexico City.

Starting in 1879 the town of Las Vegas was the railroad division headquarters for New Mexico for the Atchison, Topeka, and Santa Fe Railroad. When the division headquarters moved to Albuquerque in 1907, Las Vegas started to fade.

Director, actor, screenwriter, and cinematographer Romaine Fielding (filmmakers had to be versatile in those days) shot 10 silent films in Las Vegas in 1913 and 1914 for the Lubin Company. When Fielding (born William Grant Blandin) was working in Las Vegas, he rented what is now the Plaza Hotel downtown for his headquarters to house his cast and crew. He renamed it the Hotel Romaine and a painted faded imprint of the name can still be seen in white paint on the brickwork on the southwest side of the building.

Two of the movies Fielding made in and around Las Vegas were *Hiawanda's Cross* (1913) and *The Rattlesnake* (1913), filmed near the Montezuma Hotel, five miles north of town. Others were *The Sheepherder* (1913), *The Toll of Fear* (1913), and *The Golden God* (1914, but not released). As Lubin's work had a large economic impact on the town, city officials tried to attract more film business.

In 1915 Selig sent Tom Mix with a film crew to Las Vegas where they filmed an estimated 20 Westerns. Titles included *The Rancher's Daughter*, *The Race for a Gold Mine*, *The Pony Girl and the Cowboy*, *Stage Coach*, *A Western Masquerade*, and *Sage Brush Tom*.[40] After Mix left town, filming in Las Vegas essentially dried up until 1968 and the filming of *Easy Rider* (1969), a contemporary movie about drifting bikers.

Other Westerns using Las Vegas for location filming were *Wyatt Earp* (1994) (where Earp courted his sweetheart at the red stone cottage across from the southwest corner of Lincoln Park), the television mini-series *Buffalo Girls* (1995), and *True Grit* (2010).

The modern Western *No Country for Old Men* (2007) filmed several sequences in and around Las Vegas. One was at the downtown Victorian-style Plaza Hotel where Carson Wells (Woody Harrelson) is shot by ruthless assassin Anton Chigurh (Javier Bardem). The night sequence where Chigurh pursues Llewelyn Moss (Josh Brolin) and the two enter into a street shootout was filmed alongside the hotel. The Plaza Hotel, which is three stories tall with a brick façade, was originally built in 1882. In its day it was one of the fanciest hotels in the southwest, and has recently been restored to its former magnificence. The guest rooms at the front that overlook the historic Plaza Park have 14-foot ceilings with 12-foot-tall windows.

The Mexico border crossing point in *No Country for Old Men* (2007) was built on the University Avenue overpass for Interstate 25, much to the confusion of passing travelers. The Desert Sands Motel where Llewelyn Moss was gunned down was supposed to be in Texas, but was filmed in Albuquerque on Central Avenue.

Longmire, a modern Western crime television series (2012–2017), was set in the fictional town of Durant, Wyoming, where Walt Longmire (Robert Taylor) is the local sheriff. The series was filmed in New Mexico, with location work mostly around Las Vegas and interiors shot at studios in Albuquerque. Viewers may have found it a bit disconcerting to see adobe houses in supposed Wyoming, and views of Taos, New Mexico, in an occasional background. The Absaroka County sheriff's office was set in the Veeder Building on the west side of historic Plaza Park in Las Vegas, and as of this writing the door is still emblazoned with a gold star and the legend "Absaroka County Wyoming."

Valles Caldera

Scenes filmed at Longmire's ranch in the series were filmed in the Cabin District of the Ranch Headquarters in Valles Caldera National Preserve, just west of Los

Valles Caldera National Preserve, west of Los Alamos, New Mexico, is a scenic flat valley surrounded by low hills. It has been used for Westerns such as *Shoot Out* (1971), *Seraphim Falls* (2006), and *The Lone Ranger* (2013). This is the view in front of Walt's ranch porch in the Cabin District in the television series *Longmire*. The parking area has been used for dialog scenes between most of the principals.

Alamos, New Mexico, a little-known scenic movie location that occasionally shows up in Westerns.

The caldera was featured in *Shoot Out* (1971), with Gregory Peck and Patricia Quinn, filmed at a set built by the movie company at the north edge of History Grove in the valley. The cavalry charge sequence in the *Lone Ranger* (2013) was also filmed at History Grove. Part of *Seraphim Falls* (2006) was filmed on the north side of South Mountain, with the set removed after filming was complete.

Empire Ranch

The rolling oak-covered hills and desert grasslands around the small towns of Patagonia, Sonoita, and Elgin, southeast of Tucson in Arizona, have appeared in many well-known Western movies and television series. The area contained wide open spaces that looked like, and could have been, the open cattle range country of Texas, Oklahoma, or New Mexico. This landscape was ideal for scenes requiring a location that looked like a large ranch. One film that used this area to advantage was the musical *Oklahoma* (1955), with Gordon McRae and Shirley Jones, which was filmed in CinemaScope to take advantage of the grandeur of the wide-open grasslands.

The original Empire Ranch was established by Englishmen Walter Vail and Herbert Hislop in 1876 as a 160-acre cattle ranch. The property gradually increased in size until it became one of the largest cattle ranches in the region, covering over a million acres and stretching over several adjacent counties. The land was acquired by the Bureau of Land Management in 1988 for preservation, protection, and conservation as the Las Cienegas National Conservation Area. The surrounding Mustang, Whetstone, and Santa Rita mountains have served as the recognizable backdrop to numerous Hollywood Westerns.

One of the first films made at the Empire Ranch was *Red River* (1948) with John Wayne and Montgomery Clift. Another was *Duel in the Sun* (1946) with Gregory Peck and Jennifer Jones. The set for the Spanish Bit Ranch was built on a hill nine miles north of Sonoita. Others of the many films made here were parts of *Winchester '73* (1950) with James Stewart and Dan Duryea, *War Arrow* (1953) with Jeff Chandler and Maureen O'Hara, *Broken Lance* (1954) with Spencer Tracy and Richard Widmark, *3:10 to Yuma* (1957) with Glenn Ford and Van Heflin, *Gunfight at the O.K. Corral* (1957) with Burt Lancaster and Kirk Douglas, *Gunman's Walk* (1958) with Van Heflin and Tab Hunter, *The Big Country* (1958) with Gregory Peck and Jean Simmons, *Last Train from Gun Hill* (1959) with Kirk Douglas and Anthony Quinn, *Hombre* (1967) with Paul Newman, *Hour of the Gun* (1967) with James Garner and Jason Robards, *Return of the Gunfighter* (1967) with Robert Taylor and Chad Everett, *Monte Walsh* (1970) with Lee Marvin and Jack Palance, *The Cowboys* (1972) with John Wayne and Bruce Dern, *Posse* (1975) with Kirk Douglas and Bruce Dern, *The Outlaw Josie Wales* (1976) with Clint Eastwood, and *Tom Horn* (1980) with Steve McQueen. In *Last Train from Gun Hill* (1959), when Marshal Matt Morgan (Kirk Douglas) goes to visit his friend Craig Belden (Anthony Quinn) at Belden's ranch, the characteristic shape of the Mustang Mountains can be seen on the horizon in the background.

Red River (1948) filmed for two months near Elgin, with logistics for the production that were almost overwhelming. Director Howard Hawks spent $150,000 to build a camp to house 400 people. Nine thousand cattle were transported by nine trucks for the cattle drive sequences, supported by five water wagons, with an additional 20 trucks and three buses for the crew and equipment. The feed bill for the livestock alone was $20,000.[41]

Several "outdoor" scenes for the movie were filmed later in Hollywood on a sound stage. To recreate the desert exterior, 20 tons of sand and rocks were transported from Arizona to Hollywood to dress a huge set that measured 110 feet by 120 feet.[42]

Several episodes from the television series *Gunsmoke* (1955–1975) and *Bonanza* (1959–1973) were filmed in the area. So was the remake of *Posse* (1993) with Mario Van Peebles and Stephen Baldwin, and a remake of *Red River* (1988) with James Arness and Bruce Boxleitner.

The Fateful Decision

While filmmakers were happily filming Westerns in the outdoors, a blow fell on the motion picture industry at the end of the 1940s that eventually led to the decline of the studio system and the rise of independent production. It was the resolution of a cloud that had been hanging over the industry since the 1910s.

In 1947 and 1948 three circumstances toppled the movie industry from its peak of economic success. The first was a series of congressional hearings into alleged communist activities in the motion picture industry. The result was that several prominent actors, screenwriters, and directors were banned from working in Hollywood. The second blow was a Supreme Court ruling that forced the studios to sell their movie theaters. The third was television. These events combined to cause the motion picture industry to change from an industry dominated by the big studios that controlled most of the stars into a collection of independent producers and theaters.[43]

After World War II ended in 1945, the Justice Department renewed its antitrust suits against the major studios. In 1948 the first of the Justice Department's lawsuits against the major studios, *U.S. vs. Paramount Pictures, Inc., et al.*, went to the Supreme Court. At the time Paramount owned and operated 1,239 theaters.[44] In May of 1948 the Supreme Court handed down the decision that control of the production, distribution, and exhibition of motion pictures by film studios constituted an illegal monopoly, and ordered Paramount to divest itself of its theater holdings.[45]

As a result of this decision, Paramount was forced to sell off its theater chain. Over the next 11 years the other major studios would receive the same treatment and were forced to sell all their theaters. Twentieth Century–Fox owned 517 theaters (National Theaters), and Warner Bros. owned 507 (Stanley Warner Theaters). Between them, five major studios owned 77 percent of the first-run movie houses in the 25 largest metropolitan areas of the country.

The divestiture was completed in 1959 with the separation of MGM from its parent company, Loew's Theaters. Some of the smaller studios, such as Universal and Columbia, did not find the decision to be as much of a burden as they did not own large theater chains.[46]

As a result of these actions, the studios lost control of the first-run movie houses and theater chains, and independent producers now had easier access to the country's best theaters. This effectively crippled the established Hollywood studio system because it took away the guaranteed outlet for studio-made films. The studios now had to compete in the open marketplace for theaters willing to show their products. This reduced the dominance of the large studios and opened up movie production to independent film producers. As a result, during the 1950s, independent filmmakers started to make and distribute movies outside the conventional studio system, which led to more filming on location away from Hollywood. One added unforeseen benefit was more authentic-appearing productions than was obtained by shooting indoors on a sound stage or on a back lot.

The lack of a guaranteed revenue stream for the studios that resulted from the Supreme Court decision forced the studio system to cut back on budgets, which included their use of location filming. Other drastic economy moves for the dream factory included selling off studio-owned properties, back lots, and movie ranches.

At the same time, some of the stars who had completed their seven-year contracts at the studios refused to sign new ones. These actors became independent agents, with the hopes of making more money and exercising more control over their careers, rather than being part of a stable of salaried studio stars.

The third factor that hit the studios hard at the same time was a serious decline in box office attendance due to television. Partially fueled by returning serviceman returning from the war starting families and a post-war move to the new suburbs, many people preferred to spend their time off work in their homes with their families in front of the small screen, rather than making a special trip to see a movie. Television was more convenient than hiring a babysitter for the kids and driving into the city to a theater. And it was free for new families on a tight budget.

CHAPTER SEVEN

The 1950s
Realistic Locations

The 1940s and the 1950s could be called the "Golden Age of the Western." But, as the 1940s became the 1950s, the B-Western was in decline. In the early 1950s the horse opera was on the wane in movie theaters and most B-Western movie stars moved over to television. By the mid–1950s many small-town theaters had closed and, because cowboy films with Gene Autry, Roy Rogers, and others were available free on television, B-Western production faded away. Because of a lack of demand, Universal Pictures stopped making B-Westerns in 1946, Republic ceased in 1955, and Columbia in 1956.[1] Paramount stopped B-Westerns in 1941 and United Artists released their last one in 1950. MGM hadn't made a B-Western since 1929.

The simplistic action plots of most B-Westerns did not seem relevant to contemporary audiences after the horrors of the reality of World War II, and national fears in a time overshadowed by the Cold War and the threat of nuclear holocaust. Singing cowboy pictures lost their appeal for audiences and science-fiction was on the rise with movies for the Atomic Age featuring invasions from outer space and giant mutant bugs created by aberrant nuclear radiation.

Another factor in the decline of B-Westerns was that the cost of making them rose sharply after the end of World War II. A movie that could have been made for $20,000 now cost perhaps three times as much. An ambitious outdoor A-Western feature film in color might cost $150,000 or more.

Even as the B-Western faded, the decade started with the continued use of outdoor filming at scenic locations around the West. In the early 1950s the major studios still controlled the motion picture industry and A-Westerns were still popular enough that many were made. A peak was reached in 1958 when 54 feature Western films were produced. The popular Western stars of the time were the likes of Gary Cooper, John Wayne, James Stewart, and Randolph Scott.

As a result, a new type of Western started to emerge in the early 1950s. This consisted of 80-minute Technicolor Westerns filmed on location with established stars such as Randolph Scott, Audie Murphy, Rory Calhoun, and Sterling Hayden. They were produced by major studios such as Warners, Columbia, Paramount, and Universal. Among the best were *Santa Fe* (1951) with Randolph Scott, *Shotgun* (1955) with Sterling Hayden, *Wichita* (1955) with Joel McCrea, and *Drums Across the River* (1954) with Audie Murphy. These films were lower in ambition and budget than the major A-Westerns, but they had good scripts and good production values. They were

Iconic Images of the Movie West #7: Gallup, New Mexico. **The red sandstone cliffs east of Gallup, in today's Red Rock Park, have appeared in many Westerns. This typical location shows sheer, rugged cliffs, blue skies with a few scenic clouds, and open space in the foreground for movie action, such as the cavalry riding around in** *Escape from Fort Bravo* **(1953) and** *The Hallelujah Trail* **(1965).**

often the supporting feature on a double bill, but contained slick, fast-paced action, and were well-received by the public.

In the 1950s new directors departed from the previous styles of Howard Hawks, John Ford, and Henry King. One of the new breed was Anthony Mann, who made *The Tin Star* (1957), *Man of the West* (1958), and a series of well-made films on location with James Stewart, including *Winchester '73* (1950), *Bend of the River* (1952), *The Naked Spur* (1953), *The Far Country* (1954), and *The Man from Laramie* (1955). *Bend of the River* (1952) used the Columbia River for location filming, and Mt. Hood in the Cascade Mountains of Oregon as a spectacular backdrop to the ending of the film. *The Far Country* (1954), which was set in the time of the Klondike gold rush of 1898 in Canada, was filmed in Jasper National Park in Alberta, Canada.

These films, made primarily on location, were not part of the film industry's prestige Westerns, but were good moneymakers. In addition, Mann's films transformed James Stewart's screen persona from a gentle domestic figure of the 1930s and 1940s into a violent, driven protagonist. The plots used violent punishment as a test for the hero who, after a series of setbacks, found that he could be reconciled with society.

The Great Outdoor Beckons

By the late 1950s A-Westerns were filmed mostly on location in the West, rather than on a studio back lot. Although other film genres were often filmed on sound stages, big-budget Westerns tended to be filmed outdoors, as the open landscape was more suitable for action shots and spectacular scenery.

The 1950s was a time of strong production of A-Westerns and the continued use of realistic outdoor filming locations, though some of the Westerns from the 1950s, such as *High Noon* (1952), *At Gunpoint!* (1955), *Star in the Dust* (1956), and the original *3:10 to Yuma* (1957), had a different feel to them than today's movies. These movies, made in the style of the 1950s, seem static and talky in today's terms, with not as much outdoor action or location work.

Many colorful locations for Westerns were available close to Hollywood, which again changed the audience perception of the "real" West. But at the same time filmmakers discovered and used other magnificent locations in the West that could not be found or duplicated close to Hollywood. This included the use of popular movie "towns" in other states, such as Old Tucson Studios in Arizona.

In the 1940s and 1950s filming Westerns in the Rocky Mountains and the Pacific Northwest was popular. These locations offered spectacular scenery, with snow-covered mountains, lakes, forests, and rivers. The area around Jackson Hole in Wyoming was used for *The Big Sky* (1952) and *Shane* (1953). Oregon was used for *Canyon Passage* (1946), *Bend of the River* (1952), and *The Indian Fighter* (1955).

Texas had always been used for Westerns and filming there was invigorated in the 1950s. Western filming locations included Brackettville, a small town 120 miles southwest of San Antonio, with *Arrowhead* (1953), *The Last Command* (1955), and *The Alamo* (1960). John Wayne chose the large ranch of James "Happy" Shahan, the mayor of Brackettville, as the location for the giant set he constructed for *The Alamo* (1960). When filming was completed, the set remained as an authentic recreation of the Alamo and was turned into a tourist attraction called Alamo Village. Some tourists reportedly preferred it to the real Alamo in downtown San Antonio.[2] Alamo Village closed to the public in 2009 after the owners died.

In the 1950s and 1960s more shooting was done on location than the back lot. Independent producers and directors used original outdoor locations to make their films seem more authentic. Some filmmakers, however, still chose to shoot exterior scenes on a sound stage. Director Cecil B. DeMille tended to shoot his exteriors on a sound stage, even when filming Westerns. He felt that in this way the quality and placement of the lighting could be more carefully controlled. But a sound stage did not have the look or feel of outdoor location shooting. Outdoor enthusiasts felt that William Wellman's *The Ox-Bow Incident* (1942), for example, suffered from being filmed on a sound stage. Though other genres were successfully filmed on studio sets, Westerns always appeared more vibrant when filmed on location in the outdoors.

Special Effects Advance

The use of special effects was an important part of making movies and was commonly used in Westerns. Special effects were frequently used to film a location scene that was too dangerous to film with live actors, such as a horse and rider jumping across a chasm or actors fighting on a swinging bridge high above a deep canyon.

The term "special effects" covers a wide range of illusions. Special effects could create the illusion of large-scale destruction, such as the burning of an entire town, or the derailing and crash of a railroad locomotive. Another use was to place actors in scenery when they were not really there. Because dialog was easier to film in the studio, spoken lines were often filmed on an indoor set with an image of the outdoors projected on a translucent screen behind the actors. This, for example, was done extensively during the filming of *Stagecoach* (1939). The actors spoke their lines in a mock-up of a stagecoach on an indoor set at Samuel Goldwyn Studio while moving images of Monument Valley were projected onto a screen behind them. The combined images created the impression that the stagecoach and actors were speeding across the floor of Monument Valley.

A common use for special effects photography was to avoid dangerous situations for the actors. This was used in *The War Wagon* (1967), when Taw Jackson (John Wayne) and Billy Hyatt (Robert Walker) pack a bridge with nitroglycerine in order to blow it up and cut off a pursuing posse of stagecoach guards. Though they appeared to be dangling on support beams over a deep gorge, through movie magic the two were only a few feet off the ground and the image of the gorge was added later through process photography. The same technique was used in *Mackenna's Gold* (1969) when Marshal Sam Mackenna (Gregory Peck) and the villainous gang led by Colorado (Omar Sharif) are crossing the swing bridge over a canyon on the way to find the lost gold. The deep chasm beneath them was added as a matte painting.

Backdrop Paintings and Glass Shots

One of the first special effects in movies was to film a supposed outdoor location scene in a studio in front of a large backdrop that was a painting of the outdoors. To the unsophisticated movies audiences of the time, this created the illusion of having been filmed in the outdoors. Buffalo Bill used the same technique in his *Wild West* when his cowboys performed in an arena in front of a huge painted canvas background.

Special effects in the early 1900s also used what were called "glass shots," in which part of the desired scene, such as a ranch, background mountains, or beautiful clouds, was painted on a piece of glass which was then placed in front of the camera lens. The painted glass was photographed at the same time as the action being filmed and thus created a combined image. This could, for example, be used to make an actor appear to be jumping his horse over a deep chasm. The chasm would be painted on the bottom of the glass plate placed in front of the camera, and the top of the glass was left clear so that the actions of the actor could be photographed as he galloped across a flat meadow then, at the appropriate point, made his horse jump into the air.

Matte Paintings

Special effects were used to combine actors with a scene that was a painting to produce a composite shot that created the appearance of reality when it was not feasible to film the real setting. If a location was impractical for filming because of cost, safety, or other reasons, filmmakers turned to matte paintings. The use of matte paintings was an advance in filming that was used to give the illusion of changing the location that the actors were in. The matte painting technique combined a high-quality painting in the background with live action by the actors in the foreground. The scene had to be carefully planned to make the painting and the action blend together with the correct perspective and matching lighting, and not show any obvious defects, such a placing an actor in the wrong part of the shot. Most matte painting shots were very short in duration so that the viewer did not detect the deception.

The "matte" was a mask that covered part of the camera view in order to leave part of the image on the film unexposed while the actors acted out their scene. Then, back at the studio, the film was rewound, the area of the lens where the actors acted was masked off, and the previously masked-off part of the film was exposed to photograph a painting of the desired background. In the final shot this double-exposure of the film combined the actors with the painted background. Precise alignment of the camera lens, painting, and film was required in order to achieve a believable and natural-looking result.

In *Sergeants 3* (1962), for example, the rope bridge over the bottomless gorge that Sergeant Deal (Dean Martin) and Jonah (Sammy Davis, Jr.) cross to go to the "high country" to find the ghost dancers was filmed in some rocks just west of the town set of Paria. The bridge was only about 15 feet off the ground and was combined with a matte painting to create the illusion of a deep ravine. This technique was called a stationary matte.

As another example of the usefulness of matte paintings, movie dialog was often recorded more clearly if a scene was filmed on a sound stage, rather than recorded outdoors. Thus a director might prefer to film actors riding horses and conversing on a sound stage in an indoor studio, rather than out on location. The special effects department would later add a matte painting background that made the actors appear to be out on the trail or galloping through the desert. Another example of using a matte painting in a Western might be to show actors on horses traveling over a treacherous mountain pathway with a yawning drop-off beside them. This might be too dangerous or difficult to film on location, so a matte painting would be used.

The process became more complicated when, rather than just adding a simple background, it was necessary to combine two or more separately photographed moving scenes into one final picture. This was done with a process called a traveling matte.

In essence, the camera created an image that contained a black, moving silhouette of the actors' motion. Several techniques were used to create these black silhouettes for a traveling matte, but the most common one involved the use of a blue-screen process, which allowed the creation of a corresponding traveling matte while the scene was being photographed. In this technique, the actors performed their scene in the studio in front of a blue screen. A particular shade of blue was used that was rarely found on actors' faces or clothing. When re-photographed through an orange (the complementary color of blue) filter onto high-contrast film, the blue screen in the background turned to black, but the foreground action was not altered. This image was then reversed to create a white background with a black silhouette of the desired action. When this was combined in an optical printer it was possible to place the images together. These silhouettes were used as moving mattes that allowed images to be combined without visually interfering with other images on the final negative.

What made all this possible was the development of the optical printer. An optical printer was a combination projector and camera that re-photographed an exposed piece of film. By re-winding and re-exposing the master negative to each image separately before it was developed, the optical printer allowed several separately photographed images to be combined onto one piece of film. The printer had to operate in a very precise fashion to allow accurate registration of all the images into one final composite negative. Such scenes had to be carefully planned and photographed to make the various separate elements blend together flawlessly.

Optical printers were also used for various other tasks, including dissolves, fade-ins and fade-outs, and superimposing titles and credits. Readers wanting more than these brief descriptions can consult several good books on film technique.

Rear Projection

Two other types of system were commonly used to combine actors in a studio with an outdoor location. These were rear projection and front projection. Rear projection, which started to receive extensive use in the 1930s, used a previously-filmed outside background scene (either static or moving) that was projected onto a translucent screen behind the actors as they acted out their scene in the foreground on a studio set. Thus an actor appeared to be outdoors, while he or she was really being filmed in a studio. At MGM, actors walked and talked in front of a giant back projection screen on Stage 14, the Process Stage.[3]

The rear projection process had several limitations. One was that it often created visible "hot-spots" on the screen, where the light from the projector was brighter in some places than others. Another problem was that the speed of the camera had to be precisely synchronized with the film in the projector to prevent visible flickering in the combined images.

Rear projection declined in favor as a technique after improved movie film made the projected backgrounds look washed out and unreal. As a result, in the 1950s and 1960s, front projection started to be used. Front projection combined the actor's scene with a projected image that was reflected into the camera lens through a semi-reflective mirror (beam-splitter) placed in front of it, so that the actors appeared to be in the projected image. Some filmmakers felt that the front-projection system produced a sharper and more evenly lighted image than rear projection.[4]

In both the rear and front projection systems the camera and the projector for the background were synchronized to ensure that there was no interfering flicker in the final image. Both techniques could be used to combine more than one image by using several projectors or by running the film several times through the camera or an optical printer to combine the different images onto the final negative.

Today these types of scenes are shot using a fluorescent-green screen behind the actors and the scenes blended together with a computer. Like the earlier blue-screen process, this particular color is rarely found on actors' faces and it is easily recognized by the computer.

Although this all sounds complicated, special effects are routinely found in almost all movies, whether they are Westerns or not. As one example in a Western, in *3:10 to Yuma* (2007) stagecoach guard Cyrus McElroy (Peter Fonda) shot at a bundle of dynamite attached to one of the bandits' saddles. The resulting massive explosion that eliminated the dynamite, rider, and horse was produced by combining pieces of film containing the horse and a separate explosion to make it look like the rider was blown up. Similar optical techniques were used to intensify the explosion in the scene at the railroad tunnels when it looked as if the entire tunnel blew up after the riders raced through.

Big-Screen Technology

Another piece of movie technology was used to make the screen bigger. In 1953, Twentieth Century–Fox introduced CinemaScope to try to entice people back to the movies after television started to steal theater audiences away. The studio reasoned that a wide-screen process had a tremendous advantage for outdoor scenery over the conventional narrower screen size.

The CinemaScope wide-screen process was originally developed in France by Henri Chrétien, but was perfected and copyrighted by Fox. The process used a special design of camera lens to optically compress the width of a scene when it was put on film, and then another corresponding lens on the projector that expanded the width back to its normal proportions on the screen.

To compete with CinemaScope, in 1954 Paramount introduced a similar concept called VistaVision. This wide-screen process exposed the standard 35mm movie film on its side to create a bigger image, which resulted in better picture quality on a wider screen during projection. However, the disadvantage was that Vistavision required a special projector, and most movie theaters were reluctant to make the additional investment for new equipment. Only about 20 theaters made the modifications to show the full-sized film. CinemaScope, as opposed to the VistaVision process, did not require a special projector for screening a film. For this reason VistaVision was not a commercial success.

The Searchers (1956) was one of the few films made in Paramount's VistaVision widescreen process, complemented by full color to show off the magnificent exterior locations filmed in Monument Valley. Paramount made its last VistaVision film, the Western *One-Eyed Jacks*, in 1961.[5]

Other attempts at increasing the size of the projected picture included Ultra Panavision and the Todd-AO process, which used 65mm film instead of standard 35mm film to create a wide-screen effect.

The biggest of the wide-screen processes was Cinerama, which used three separate synchronized cameras to create a wrap-around experience when projected onto a giant curved screen that was 105 feet long by 35 feet high. The idea was to make the screen so big that the viewer would feel that he or she was immersed in the action. Later Cinerama processes used 70mm film and special lenses to try to create the same effect without the technical problems of three synchronized cameras and projectors.

The debut of Cinerama was a travel feature film first exhibited in 1952. Feature Western films, such as *How the West Was Won* (1962), *The Hallelujah Trail* (1965), and *Custer of the West* (1967), followed in the 1960s.

In another attempt to try to re-capture audiences that were defecting to television, studios added three-dimensional (3-D) viewing, which was used for Westerns such as *Hondo* (1953), *The Charge at Feather River* (1953), *Devil's Canyon* (1953), and *Taza, Son of Cochise* (1954). For shock value these were filmed with the 3-D visual effect of arrows, fists, knives, and galloping horses appearing to leap straight out of the screen at the audience. This gimmick, however, did not have much success in retaining theater audiences and the technology faded away.

Some Problems of Outdoor Filming

Though filmmakers used outdoor locations for Westerns because that was what audiences wanted and expected, filming outdoors was not always easy and was often plagued with problems.

One recurrent problem was the noise of the wind in the outdoors. Wind that blew during filming could create havoc with the microphones used for speech recording, causing a raspy sound that overwhelmed the actors' voices as the wind blew across the microphone diaphragm. In many instances the speech had to be re-recorded in a studio after filming. Sharp-eyed viewers will notice in some movies that trees and bushes in the background of a scene wave and bend in the prevailing wind, but the actors' voices are perfectly clear with no hint of wind noise.

Another problem was the undesired pickup of extraneous noise along with the actors' speech. This often came from nearby sources such as cars, trains, machinery, planes flying overhead, and similar types of ambient noise in the filming environment. Again, the speech often had to be dubbed in the studio to remove the noises. Sound stages at Warners had two-foot thick walls, padded and soundproofed, to prevent this problem when filming interior scenes.[6]

Another problem was that sound recorded outside did not always "sound right" to audiences. Director George Stevens, for example, was not happy with the sound of the gunshots used for *Shane* (1953). After some experimentation, the crew finally fired into a trash can to get what Stevens considered to be the right sound for the shots.[7] A similar issue arose during the production of the television series *Highway Patrol*. The sound crew went outdoors to a canyon near Los Angeles and tried different methods of recording gunshots before they settled on what they thought was the "correct" sound.

Another problem related to filming on location is that scenes in movies are normally shot out of sequence, thus continuity from scene to scene is very important. For example, imagine a scene shot at an outdoor location in which an actor walks through a door into a ranch house from the outside. If the next shot is from the inside, showing him coming onto a studio set on the other side of the door, everything will have to be carefully matched to the outdoor scene. The two scenes may be shot weeks apart, but the actor has to be wearing the same clothes in the same state of wear, be carrying the same props, and have the same makeup and hair length in order for the two shots to match. The problem is particularly apparent in fight scenes where torn clothing, make-up bruises, and movie blood have to match in all the shots.

Planning a movie shoot in the outdoors also involves matching various locations, lighting conditions, lighting for night shots, and the vagaries of the weather at outdoor locations in the West, which varies from spring to fall, and may include rain, snow, cloudy days, or brilliant sunshine. A typical problem might be starting to film a movie when the trees are just budding out in the spring, and then matching this to shots filmed later in the summer when they are fully leafed out. When stock footage was commonly used in B-Westerns, often the desert scenes from location filming didn't match up with shots filmed on the wooded back lot, but the two were spliced together anyway.

Lighting in the outdoors is always a problem. Outdoor weather can be difficult because of changing light and weather conditions in the mountains or the desert. As filmmaker Tom Reilly succinctly put it, "shoot in flat light," in other words with total cloud cover without shadows, so that the editor can easily match the shots.[8] But that is often easier said than done in outdoor locations. Shadows change over the course of a day, and shots have to match as the sun moves from sunup to sundown, or suddenly disappears behind a cloud.

Other problems include coordinating the schedules of actors with other commitments, and the cost of rental of a location or a movie ranch. Film companies do not want to have down-time because each extra day on location might cost $150,000 to maintain the cast and crew, even if they are sitting idle. Contingency plans have to be made for Westerns shot outdoors to move to a backup interior location if the weather turns bad. Filming on a sound stage allows control of light and weather, but the results usually look fake.

A problem peculiar to filming location Westerns often arose when a large number of Indian actors were required for battle scenes or other large outdoor gatherings. In *They Died with Their Boots On* (1941), a biography of Gen. George Armstrong Custer, the rousing climax of the film was the Battle of the Little Bighorn, which took place on June 25, 1876. The real battle took place in Montana, but the movie version was filmed about 40 miles north of Los Angeles in a wide valley that resembled the plains on the border between Wyoming and Montana. The problem was that director Raoul Walsh couldn't find enough Indians in Hollywood to play the Sioux warriors who were in the real battle. So he filled the ranks with Filipino extras.

Conversely, when director Dick Powell made *The Conqueror* (1956)—one of John Wayne's few non–Westerns—near St. George, Utah, the studio hired 300 Indians from a nearby reservation to play the parts of Mongol warriors.[9] When 35 Chinese extras were required for *The Iron Horse* (1924) for the track-laying scenes, not enough could be found, so the director used Indians to act as Chinese laborers.[10] Director John Ford routinely used Navajos for whatever the script called for, whether the Indians were Apache, Kiowa, Comanche, or Cheyenne.[11] In *Cheyenne Autumn* (1964) Ricardo Montalban and Gilbert Roland (both born in Mexico) played the Cheyenne chiefs; however, the rest of the Cheyenne tribe was played by Navajo Indians.

Movie Ranches

A movie ranch was a Western ranch that was fully or partially dedicated to the creation and production of motion pictures and television productions. Most of the larger studios owned their own movie ranches where they made outdoor movies on location, and Westerns in particular. Movie ranches were also used for other productions that needed large, undeveloped settings for outdoor scenes, such as battle scenes for war films or for medieval spectaculars.

Movie ranches first came into use for location filming in Southern California during the 1920s with the rising popularity of Westerns, when the major movie studios started to purchase large tracts of open land near Hollywood. The studios invested in undeveloped rural land, in many instances existing ranches, located close to Hollywood. In most cases, the ranches were located in the Simi Hills in the foothills in the western San Fernando Valley, the Santa Monica Mountains, or the canyon country of the greater Los Angeles area.

These studio ranches were all within about a 30-mile range of the studios in Hollywood. This distance had a particular significance. To achieve greater reality for outdoor filming, in particular Westerns, many studio productions were filmed on location in California, Arizona, and Nevada, away from the studios. Because of the distances involved, the payment of travel expenses for film crews and the rest of the production staff created a dispute between workers and the studios. The settlement was that the studios agreed to pay union workers additional compensation if they worked out of town. The definition of "out of town" referred specifically to a distance of greater than 30 miles from the home studio, thus most of the ranches were located within the 30-mile limit to save on added expenses.

By the late 1930s most studios had a ranch of at least 20 acres or more, and most contained permanent Western streets and sets for filming. The RKO ranch was in Reseda. Paramount's ranch was in Agoura. MGM's was in Thousand Oaks. Twentieth Century–Fox located in the Santa Monica Mountains in Malibu Canyon. Disney owned a ranch near Santa Clarita, though the studio also had a Western street on their back lot in Burbank. Some movie ranches, such as Iverson Ranch and Corriganville, were not owned by any particular studio and could be rented by anyone for filming.

Some of the better-known movie ranches were Gene Autry's Movie Ranch at Newhall (formerly the Monogram Ranch), Iverson's Ranch, Ray Corrigan's ranch, Jack Ingram's, and Pioneertown. All these had permanent sets that were typically needed for outdoor filming of Westerns, such as a sheriff's office, a saloon, stables, and a blacksmith's shop.

As a result of the suburban development and resulting urban outwards sprawl around Los Angeles that followed the end of World War II in 1945, rising property values and property taxes, and the crippling financial effects of the divestiture of movie theater chains by the studios, most of these movie ranches were eventually sold and subdivided for housing development. A few survived as regional parks and a few are still used for filming. In the meantime, location shooting using movie ranches gradually moved to other states, such as New Mexico and Arizona.

Below is a partial listing of some of the classic Southern California movie ranches, along with some of the other, newer locations in other states.

Apacheland Studio

In late 1950s location filming was popular in the Superstition Mountain area, east of Phoenix in central Arizona, using facilities at existing ranches for filming Westerns. One such movie filmed in this time period was *Gunfight at the O.K. Corral* (1957) with Burt Lancaster and Kirk Douglas, which showed the area known today as Gold Canyon, with the Superstition Mountains towering over the movie version of the Clanton ranch.

After the initial modest success of filming in the area, Victor Panek and J.K. Hutchens discussed the idea of building a studio in the Superstition Mountains. They looked for a suitable site and found what they wanted in Gold Canyon. They started construction of a Western town called the Apacheland Studio on February 12, 1959, with the plan to make it the "Western Movie Capitol of the World." Apacheland was open for use by production companies in June of 1960.

The first television Western filmed there was an episode of *Have Gun—Will Travel*, filmed in November 1960. Many of Hollywood's best known Western actors, including Audie Murphy, Jason Robards, Stella Stevens, and Ronald Reagan, were filmed in movies at Apacheland. Westerns included *The Purple Hills* (1961), *Charro!* (1969), and *The Ballad of Cable Hogue* (1970). Among the television productions filmed there were episodes of *Death Valley Days* and *Have Gun—Will Travel*. The last full-length movie to be filmed at Apacheland was an HBO television movie titled *Blind Justice* (1994), with Armand Assante and Elisabeth Shue.

Apacheland was devastated by two major fires. The cause of the first fire was unknown, but it destroyed most of the movie ranch on May 26, 1969. Only seven buildings survived, but the town was soon rebuilt. A second fire destroyed most of Apacheland on February 14, 2004, and the ranch permanently closed its doors to the public on October 16, 2004.

Bell Moving Picture Ranch

The Bell Moving Picture Ranch, later renamed the Bell Location Ranch, was located in the Simi Hills on the western edge of the San Fernando Valley, above the site of the Spahn Movie Ranch and Santa Susana Pass State Historic Park.

Among the many movies filmed at Bell Ranch were *Love Me Tender* (1956) with Elvis Presley and Debra Paget, *Gunsight Ridge* (1957) starring Joel McCrea, *Gun Fever* (1958) with Mark Stevens, *Escort West* (1959) with Victor Mature, and *Hombre* (1967) with Paul Newman. The ending sequence in *Love Me Tender* (1956), which was Presley's first movie, was filmed on a rugged slope known as "Rocky Hill." *Escort West* (1959) filmed at the same location.

Many television Westerns were filmed at the ranch, including episodes of *Gunsmoke*, *Zorro*, *The Big Valley*, and *Have Gun—Will Travel*. An episode of the original *Star Trek* series, "A Private Little War" (1968), was partly shot at Bell Ranch's Box Canyon, which stood in for an alien world.

Big Sky Movie Ranch

Big Sky Ranch, widely used for the filming of Western television and film productions, was located in the Simi Valley, west of Los Angeles. Television episodes and productions filmed there included *Rawhide, Gunsmoke, Bonanza,* and *Little House on the Prairie.* A fire in 2003 destroyed most of the standing sets that had been used in many movies, including a replica of the farm house from *Little House on the Prairie,* and sets used in the television series *Gunsmoke.*

Bonanza Creek Ranch

Many Westerns have been filmed at movie ranches in New Mexico, particularly around Santa Fe. Three Western towns and settings, the Bonanza Creek Ranch, J.W. Eaves Movie Ranch, and the Cook Ranch, were located on the high desert south of Santa Fe in the Galisteo Basin. Among other Westerns, the Bonanza Creek Ranch was used for *The Man from Laramie* (1955), the Eaves Movie Ranch for *The Cheyenne Social Club* (1970), and the Cook Ranch for *Silverado* (1985).

The first movie filmed at the Bonanza Creek Ranch (then called the Jarrett Ranch) was *The Man from Laramie* (1955), nominally set in Wyoming, followed later by *Cowboy* (1958) with Glenn Ford and Jack Lemmon. Other films partially filmed at the ranch were *Butch Cassidy and the Sundance Kid* (1969) and *Young Guns* (1988).

Western filmmakers came to the West for its scenic qualities and often incorporated natural features of the landscape whenever they could. This is Camel Rock, an odd-shaped rock formation that looks like its namesake, just off U.S. Highway 285 north of Santa Fe. It was used in *Cowboy* (1958) during a short sequence where the cattle herd is being driven to Chicago.

The sequence in *Cowboy* (1958) where the cattle herd passes picturesque Camel Rock was filmed just off U.S. Highway 285, north of Santa Fe.

A partial list of other films made in and around Santa Fe includes *The Texas Rangers* (1936), *The Cowboys* (1972), *Lonesome Dove* (1989), *Wyatt Earp* (1994), *Seraphim Falls* (2006), *No Country for Old Men* (2007), *3:10 to Yuma* (2007), *True Grit* (2010), and *Cowboys and Aliens* (2011). *Cowboys and Aliens* (2011) was an uneasy mix of science-fiction and cowboy movies, with aliens from outer space taking the place of the conventional bad guys. Part of the movie was filmed at the Zia Pueblo near Santa Fe, which provided an unusual landscape that was suitable for the plot.

The New Mexico Film Office is good example of why independent studios choose to film their productions in New Mexico. It was created in 1968 by Governor David Cargo in an attempt to draw more film business into the state. In 2002 Governor Gary Johnson signed additional legislation that provided tax rebates and other incentives to filmmakers. In 2003 Governor Bill Richardson expanded the incentives from 15 percent with a 25 percent rebate on production costs and interest-free loans to qualifying productions, thereby helping to increase the number of film productions. In 2013 Governor Susana Martinez signed a bill providing more subsidies (including increasing the rebate to 30 percent) for films shot in the state. By 2014 New Mexico was estimated to have been used for 663 film productions.[12]

Local movie studios opened as part of the way to attract film companies to New Mexico. Santa Fe Studios was used for *A Million Ways to Die in the West* (2014) and television's *Longmire*. Garson Studios was used for *True Grit* (2010) and *Longmire*. Albuquerque Studios was used for *The Lone Ranger* (2013) and *The Last Stand* (2013). *The Lone Ranger* (2013) built Western sets for extensive filming around Albuquerque. The combination of state-of-the-art production facilities, experienced film crews, modern sound stages, and financial incentives have made New Mexico popular for filming. Another desirable feature is that New Mexico boasts 300-plus days of sunshine every year, and the high plains and desert landscapes are ideal for outdoor filming.

Though not as active as Santa Fe, Gallup, and Las Vegas, the rest of New Mexico has provided popular locations for filming Westerns. Parts of *Hang 'em High* (1968) were filmed near Las Cruces, where the old town of Mesilla looks like Old Mexico, and at White Sands National Monument. The historical town of Lincoln, which looks much like it did in the days of the outlaw Billy the Kid, was used for filming *Dirty Little Billy* (1972). *Young Guns* (1988), another recounting of the Billy the Kid story, was partially filmed at the town of Cerillos, south of Santa Fe, which was dressed for the movie as Lincoln, New Mexico. In 1958 Disney filmed a series of 10 television episodes for *The Nine Lives of Elfego Baca* (1958) there, based on a true story about self-appointed lawman Elfego Baca in the town of Frisco, New Mexico.

Parts of the filming for *Seraphim Falls* (2006), including the final fight between Pierce Brosnan and Liam Neeson in a dry lake bed at the end, took place around in the desert area around Lordsburg. Filming also took place around Taos and Santa Fe.

Buckskin Joe

Buckskin Joe was originally created in 1957 as a combination tourist attraction and permanent Western film set built about eight miles west of Cañon City, Colorado. The town had plenty of history, because the old buildings were authentic, but they were moved from other locations in Colorado onto an 805-acre site near Cañon City to create a movie town. Over the years the town set has appeared in various productions, such as *The Cowboys* (1972), and a few of the scenes from the Western comedy *The Duchess and the Dirtwater Fox* (1976). The entire town was sold to a private party in 2010 and is no longer open as a tourist attraction.

Some of the scenes from the comedy Western *Cat Ballou* (1965) were filmed at Buckskin Joe, with the ranch setting filmed in the Wet Mountain Valley near Westcliffe, Colorado, about 30 miles southwest of Cañon City, with the rugged Sangre de Cristo Mountains prominently visible in the background. The railroad scenes used the Denver & Rio Grande railroad alongside the Arkansas River near Cañon City.

In the same general area, *Saddle the Wind* (1958), was filmed at the ghost town of Rosita, also in the Wet Mountain Valley. Unlike Buckskin Joe, Rosita ("Little Rose" in Spanish) was originally an authentic historical Western town that was founded in 1861 as a result of silver mining in the area. The town, complete with a history of gunfighting and lynchings, was inhabited by about 1,200 people until 1881, when a disastrous fire burned most of the town and it was never fully rebuilt. For many years the town had the authentic look of a ghost town—which it was—until Hollywood found it and made it look even more authentic than it was when people lived there. MGM rearranged the positions of some of the old buildings, built several new buildings that were constructed to match the old ones, and added features, such as signs and hitching rails, to fit the set designer's conception of the town. Unfortunately, like other unprotected abandoned movie sets, the remaining buildings were destroyed by fire and today nothing remains of the town.

Columbia Ranch/Warner Brothers Ranch

When Columbia Pictures decided in 1934 that it needed a suitable outdoor location for filming Westerns, the studio purchased a 40-acre back lot to provide additional space for its Sunset studio location. The Columbia property was not large, but it had enough space for a small town. Often the interiors of the buildings were dressed so that filming could take place inside them and thus save the expense of building an additional interior set on a sound stage.

Among the classic Westerns that were at least partially filmed on the ranch were *High Noon* (1952), *3:10 to Yuma* (1957), and *Cat Ballou* (1965). The town of Hadleyville in *High Noon* (1952) was filmed on the Western street at the Columbia Ranch. Location filming for the movie was also done at the towns of Columbia, California, and at Jamestown.

Columbia's back lot was small compared to some of the other studios. It was so small that in *High Noon* (1952), viewers who are fast can see telephone poles in the upper left of the screen and a few buildings of Los Angeles in the right background during the crane shot that shows Marshal Will Kane (Gary Cooper) standing alone in the middle of Hadleyville just before the final shoot-out begins.[13]

In 1972 Columbia combined with Warners to become the Burbank Studios. In 1990 the ranch became the Warner Ranch. After Columbia was purchased by Sony Corporation, the back lot was cleared in 1993 and replaced by a parking lot.[14]

Corriganville

More Western movies were made in Chatsworth than anywhere else in the Los Angeles area at the movie ranches at Corriganville, the Iverson Ranch, and the Spahn Movie Ranch, all of which were located close to each other.

In 1937, Ray "Crash" Corrigan, a B-Western movie actor, invested in property around Chatsworth in California's Simi Valley. Though Corrigan started out as a rancher, he eventually developed his property into the Corriganville Movie Ranch. Most of the Monogram *Range Busters* film series, which included *Saddle Mountain Roundup* (1941) and *Bullets and Saddles* (1943), were shot there. Other movies filmed at the ranch during the 1940s were *The Trail of the Silver Spurs* (1941) and *Troubleshooters* (1942).

Parts of the vast Corriganville movie ranch were open to the public on weekends as a park, and visitors could explore the rustic Western town, a Mexican village, a Western ranch, various outlaw hide-outs and shacks, a cavalry fort, a rodeo arena, a mine, a wooded lake, and the interesting rock formations found around the ranch. Non-Western sets included a Corsican village, an English hunting lodge, and a country schoolhouse. Over time, the rock formations, bushes, and hills that formed the background to the ranch became very familiar to audiences of Westerns.

The cavalry fort was used for the parade ground sequences of *Fort Apache* (1948) and as Fort Bravo for the *Escape from Fort Bravo* (1953). The television series *The Adventures of Rin Tin Tin* used the fort set for filming from 1954 to 1959.

In 1966, most of Corriganville was purchased by actor Bob Hope for real estate development. The remaining section, about 200 acres of the original 2,000 acres, is now part of the Simi Valley Park System, open to the public as Corriganville Regional Park. Though the original movie and television buildings are long gone, concrete foundations from the previous sets are still visible.

Eaves Movie Ranch

The J.W. Eaves Movie Ranch was opened in the early 1960s on the Eaves' ranch just south of Santa Fe, New Mexico. The first production was filmed in 1962 for the CBS television series *Empire*. Over the years more than 250 productions have been filmed there, including Marlboro cigarette print advertisements. Feature Westerns included *The Cheyenne Social Club* (1970), which used a Western town built for the production, *Chisum* (1970), *A Gunfight* (1971), *The Cowboys* (1972), *Silverado* (1985), *Young Guns II* (1990), *Wyatt Earp* (1994), and *Outlaws and Angels* (2015). *Silverado* (1985) was also partly filmed at the nearby Cook Ranch, south of Santa Fe.

Many Western movie towns have fallen into disrepair as the filming of Westerns has declined. These buildings are part of the movie town at the Eaves Movie Ranch, south of Santa Fe, New Mexico. The ranch was first used for filming in 1962 for the television series *Empire*. Over the years more than 250 productions have been filmed there, including *The Cheyenne Social Club* (1970), *Chisum* (1970), *A Gunfight* (1971), *The Cowboys* (1972), *Silverado* (1985), *Young Guns II* (1990), *Tombstone* (1993), and *Wyatt Earp* (1994).

For *Tombstone* (1993), part of the town was shown as being under construction in 1881. The state of disrepair was so accurate that a film critic for *Entertainment Weekly* complained that it looked as though the town hadn't been completed before filming. But that was the point. When the remake of the *3:10 to Yuma* (2007) was in production, the producers didn't have enough money to complete the town set, so they deliberately left some of it in an incomplete condition.[15] This actually added to the effectiveness of the sequence in the town where Ben Wade (Russell Crowe) and Dan Evans (Christian Bale) are running to the train station through and past unfinished buildings.

Iverson Movie Ranch

The 500-acre Iverson Movie Ranch was owned by Karl and Augusta Iverson as a family ranch in the Simi Hills around Chatsworth, California, along the western side of Topanga Canyon Boulevard.

The ranch was used as early as 1912 for filming movies with the non–Western *Man's Genesis* (1912). Among the Western feature films shot on the ranch was *The*

Squaw Man (1914). After this, the Iverson Movie Ranch quickly became a popular outdoor location for filming Westerns, though the ranch also appeared in adventure films, war movies, comedies, and science-fiction films, including standing in for Africa, the Middle East, the South Pacific, and other exotic locations. The rocky landscape of the ranch and its narrow, winding roads were frequently used in Republic serials of the 1940s and were prominently featured in chases and shootouts throughout the golden era of the action B-Westerns in the 1930s and 1940s.

When Hollywood's focus shifted to television Westerns in the late 1940s and throughout the 1950s, the Iverson Ranch remained a popular place to film. Early television series filmed there included *The Lone Ranger*, *The Roy Rogers Show*, *The Gene Autry Show*, *The Cisco Kid*, *Buffalo Bill, Jr.*, *Zorro*, and *Tombstone Territory*. An estimated 3,500 or more productions, about evenly split between movies and television episodes, were filmed at the ranch during its peak years. The long-running television Western *The Virginian* was filmed on location at the Iverson ranch in the ranch's later period, as were episodes of *Bonanza* and *Gunsmoke*.

In the 1960s, ownership of the ranch was split between two of Karl and Augusta's sons, with Joe Iverson owning the southern half of the ranch (the Lower Iverson), and Aaron Iverson owning the northern half (the Upper Iverson). In the mid–1960s the state of California began construction on the Simi Valley Freeway, which ran east and west, roughly following the dividing line between the Upper Iverson and Lower Iverson, thus cutting the movie ranch in half.

The declining popularity of B-Westerns as important business for the ranch coincided with the arrival of the freeway, which opened in 1967. In addition, pressure to develop the area for housing signaled its end as a working movie ranch. Most of the former Iverson Ranch has now vanished under development. In 1982, Joe Iverson sold what remained of the Lower Iverson to a developer who almost immediately began subdividing the property, which became a mobile home park and condominium development. The Upper Iverson became a gated community of high-end real estate and is no longer open to the public.

Part of the ranch north of Santa Susana Pass Road, on both sides of Red Mesa Road, was preserved as parkland. This section included what was called the Garden of the Gods, a collection of rock formations that have been seen in countless old movies and television shows. Also preserved in the park was an area on the east side of Red Mesa that included the popular Lone Ranger Rock, a picturesque bluff that appeared next to the Lone Ranger's rearing horse, Silver, in the opening of each episode of *The Lone Ranger* television show.

Jack Ingram Movie Ranch

As well as at the Iverson Movie Ranch, many of the Republic, Columbia, and Monogram Westerns were made at Jack Ingram's ranch.

In 1944 Jack Ingram and his wife purchased a 160-acre ranch formerly owned by actor Charlie Chaplin in the Santa Monica Mountains above Woodland Hills, California. With a bulldozer and the help of his friends, Ingram built a Western town that consisted of two streets. Eventually the movie ranch grew to 75 buildings and three different towns. During the next 14 years many Westerns and television series were filmed there. The property included Ingram's house, which could occasionally be seen in the background of some scenes filmed at the ranch. In 1956, Ingram sold the ranch to Four Star Television Productions.

Lasky Ranch: San Fernando Valley Providencia Ranch

The Providencia Ranch was leased by Universal in 1912 before their move to Universal City. They named the property Oak Crest Ranch and used it for the production of Universal 101 Westerns. In 1918, Jesse L. Lasky Feature Play Company began leasing the property. The ranch consisted of 500 acres, with an additional 1,500 acres of adjoining government land that they were allowed to use. The ranch was also known as Providencia Flats and the Lasky Ranch. When the lease expired, Paramount purchased a location in the Agoura area, and moved all of the ranch sets to the new location. In 1929, Warner Bros purchased a portion of the ranch from Hollingsworth Realty Company. By 1950 the property, located across the Los Angeles River from the First National/Warner Bros. studios, became part of Forest Lawn Cemetery.

Lasky Ranch: Ahmanson Lasky Mesa Ranch

The Lasky Company acquired a 4,000-acre ranch in 1914 in the San Fernando Valley on which they built a large two-story Spanish house to be used in *Rose of the Rancho* (1914). The studio planned to use the entire property for what they claimed was the largest scene ever to be filmed.

In 1963, Home Savings and Loan, the parent company of Ahmanson Land Company, purchased the property and adjacent land, and the ranch became known as the Ahmanson Ranch. Washington Mutual Bank took over ownership of Home Savings and proceeded with the development plans for the ranch, however public pressure to preserve undeveloped open space was very strong and development was halted by groundwater tests that showed contamination of the aquifer with toxic substances. The State of California purchased the land for a regional park, and the former Lasky movie ranch is now part of the Upper Las Virgenes Canyon Open Space Preserve.

Monogram Ranch/Melody Ranch

The Monogram movie ranch was an independent Western filming location on 110 acres of land in lower Placerita Canyon near Newhall, California, just north of San Fernando Pass. The landscape included oak trees, chaparral hillsides, and a spruce forest. Filming took place in Placerita Canyon as early as 1926 when Tom Mix filmed Westerns in the canyon. In 1931, Monogram Pictures negotiated a five-year lease on a parcel of land in the central part of Placerita Canyon. In 1935, as a result of the merger of Monogram with Republic, the Placerita Canyon Ranch came under the control of the newly-formed Republic Pictures.

Originally known as the Placeritos Ranch, the land was more commonly referred to as the Monogram Ranch. The Western town was just east of what is now the junction of the Antelope Valley Freeway and Placerita Canyon Road.

The owner from 1936 until 1952 was Russell Hickson, who constructed the original buildings on the ranch. In 1936, when the first lease expired, the entire Western town was relocated a few miles north to Russell Hickson's Placeritos Ranch in lower Placerita Canyon. In 1937 Monogram Pictures signed a long-term lease with Hickson, with the condition as part of the terms that the ranch would be named the Monogram Ranch.

In 1953 actor Gene Autry purchased the Monogram ranch from the Hickson heirs and renamed it Melody Ranch, after his film *Melody Ranch* (1940). Autry used it for filming with his own production company, Flying A Productions, for his television series. He later rented out the facility for filming for the television series *Maverick* with James Garner, and *Gunsmoke* with James Arness.

Most of the original Western sets on the ranch were destroyed by a brush fire that swept through the area in August 1962. Fortunately a large Spanish hacienda and a complete adobe village survived on the northeast section of the ranch. However, the land was too badly burned over to be useful for filming Westerns, so Autry sold off 98 acres and the last two of Autry's movie horses named Champion lived in retirement on the remaining property.

After the Champions died in 1990, Autry put the remaining 12 acres up for sale. It was purchased by investors who re-created a movie ranch for location shooting. The new ranch consisted of a 22-acre complex of sound stages, western sets, a prop shop, and the backlots. It was known as the Melody Ranch Motion Picture Studio and Melody Ranch Studios.

Among other productions, the ranch was used for filming *Django Unchained* (2012), HBO's television series *Westworld*, the HBO television series *Deadwood* and the TV movie *Deadwood—The Movie* (2019) drawn from the series.[16]

Paramount Ranch

In 1927 Paramount Pictures purchased 2,700 acres of the Rancho Las Virgenes in the Santa Monica Mountains near Agoura Hills, to the west of Hollywood and north of Malibu. Several of the major studios owned movie ranches in the area. The Paramount Ranch was used for filming parts of such classic Westerns as *The Rough Riders* (1927), *Under the Tonto Rim* (1928), *The Virginian* (1929), *Wells Fargo* (1937), *High Noon* (1952), and *Gunfight at the O.K. Corral* (1957) as well as several television Western series.

The studio built numerous sets on the ranch, including a replica of early San Francisco and an Old West town. The ranch stood in for Tombstone and Dodge City as well as Tom Sawyer's Missouri, 13th-century China, and many other locations around the world.

Paramount owned the ranch from the 1920s to the 1950s. The Supreme Court decision of May 1948 that forced Paramount to divest itself of its theater holdings, and the subsequent changes in the movie industry in the early 1950s, meant that Paramount had to sell the land.

The ranch property changed ownership several times then came into the public domain in 1980. The National Park Service purchased 397 acres, including the studio buildings, for Paramount Ranch Park in the Santa Monica Mountains National Recreation Area. In 1980 the National Park Service purchased an additional 750 acres. The older sets were removed, but some of the buildings from the Western town were preserved for visitors to view and the sets continued to be used for filming, notably for the television series *Dr. Quinn, Medicine Woman*. The structures at Paramount Ranch were totally destroyed during the Woolsey Fire in the Santa Monica Mountains in November of 2018.

As a side note, Paramount's Western town on their back lot at the main studio was built in 1947 for *Whispering Smith* (1948) with Alan Ladd. Fans of Western movies and television series filmed in the late 1950s and 1960s on the Western street will recognize the distinctive prominent mountain in the background of the town. This became an iconic view in Paramount Western movies and was also prominent in many episodes of the television series *Bonanza*, when the series was filmed at Paramount. However, it was a fake mountain constructed from chicken wire supporting an outer shell of plaster. The "mountain" was built in 1955 to hide a new building with

Countless Westerns were made at the Paramount Movie Ranch in the Santa Monica Mountains, west of Los Angeles, starting in 1927. The streets were quiet when this photograph was taken in the 1990s, when the town was owned by the National Park Service and Western filming had all but ceased. Unfortunately these streets and structures are now gone, totally destroyed during the Woolsey Fire in the Santa Monica Mountains in November of 2018.

a very tall roof peak behind it. By the 1970s the mountain was starting to look derelict and was finally torn down.

Another permanent outdoor fixture that was at the end of one of other streets at right angles to the mountain was a huge painted backdrop of blue skies with fluffy white clouds that was used to give an open outdoor look to that particular street.

The entire Western town was demolished in 1979 for an executive parking lot.

Pioneertown

Pioneertown, located near Palm Springs in Southern California's Mojave Desert in San Bernardino County, not far from Joshua Tree National Park, was built as a Western movie town in the 1940s. The town was designed to provide housing for the actors at the same time that the buildings were used as part of the movie set. At one time the property was 32,000 acres in size.

The original developers and investors of Pioneertown were Roy Rogers, his singing group the Sons of the Pioneers, Dick Curtis (a movie villain), cowboy star Russell Hayden (who starred in the Hopalong Cassidy series of movies with William Boyd), and Frank MacDonald (a director of B-Westerns). The partnership hoped to turn the property into a popular Western movie film location similar to Chatsworth, Lone Pine, and Corriganville. The plan was to promote the location to studios who wanted authentic locations, and at the same time to cater to tourists on their way to the recreation area at Big Bear.

A number of Westerns and early television shows were filmed at Pioneertown, including *The Cisco Kid* and *Judge Roy Bean* with Edgar Buchanan. Gene Autry filmed the first season of his series *The Gene Autry Show* there before he could afford his own ranch facilities. Unfortunately, the optimistic plans did not work out as well as the owners had hoped and the property was repossessed.[17]

Red Hills Ranch

Red Hills Ranch was a movie ranch in Sonora, California, that was used for location filming for the television series *Bonanza*, *The Adventures of Brisco County, Jr.*, *Little House on the Prairie*, and other productions. An outdoor Western set built for *Back to the Future Part III* (1990), and later used for *Bad Girls* (1994), was destroyed in 1996 by a wildfire caused by a lightning strike.

Republic Pictures Ranch/Walt Disney Golden Oak Ranch

The Republic Pictures movie ranch was located off Soledad Canyon in central Placerita Canyon near Newhall, California, in the foothills of the northern San Gabriel Mountains.

The Republic Ranch became Walt Disney's Golden Oak Ranch in 1959. Disney purchased the 315-acre ranch due to concern that the other movie ranches were being sold off for housing development and were being sub-divided. Over the next five years, Disney Studios purchased additional land and enlarged the property to 890 acres.

Part of the western border of the ranch was purchased for the Antelope Valley Freeway, but the studio worked closely with the State of California when construction was planned so that the freeway didn't show up in the background of films.

RKO Ranch

The RKO Pictures ranch consisted of 89 acres of land on the outskirts of Encino, California, in the San Fernando Valley. RKO purchased the property as a location to film their epic motion picture *Cimarron* (1931), which won four Academy Awards, for Best Picture, Best Writing, Best Art Direction, and Best Make-Up. Art Director Max Ree won an Oscar for creative design of the sets constructed on the movie ranch, which consisted of a complete Western town and a three block-long modern main street built as the fictional town of Osage, Oklahoma.

In addition to the *Cimarron* set, RKO continued to create an array of diverse sets for their expanding movie ranch, including a New York brownstone street, English row houses, a slum district, a small town square, a residential neighborhood, three working train depots, a New England farm, a Western ranch, a version of Paris, a European marketplace, a Russian village, a Yukon mining camp, a Moorish casbah, a Mexican outpost, a Sahara Desert fort, and an ocean tank with a backdrop behind for the sky. They also constructed support buildings, including a carpentry shop, props storage, a greenhouse, and three large fully-equipped soundstages.

All these unique sets were bulldozed in 1954 and a subdivision called Encino Village, with modern homes, was built on the property.

Spahn Movie Ranch

The Spahn Movie Ranch was a 55-acre property with a Western town set that was located on Santa Susana Pass in the Simi Hills above Chatsworth, California. The ranch was once owned by actor William S. Hart, and was used to film many Westerns, particularly from the 1940s to the 1960s. Filming included *Duel in the Sun* (1946), and episodes of television's *Bonanza* and *The Lone Ranger*.

In 1970 a mountain wildfire destroyed the film set when the movie ranch and the residential structures caught fire and burned to the ground. The Spahn Movie Ranch is now part of the Santa Susana Pass State Historic Park.[18]

Twentieth Century–Fox Ranch

Located in the Santa Monica Mountains, the Twentieth Century–Fox Movie Ranch (also known as Century Movie Ranch and Fox Movie Ranch) was purchased in 1946. In 1956 and 1957, Twentieth Century–Fox filmed its first television series on the ranch, *My Friend Flicka*, for CBS television. The ranch was subsequently used as a location for dozens of films and television productions.

The movie ranch property was subsequently purchased and preserved in Malibu Creek State Park, which opened to the public in 1976.[19]

Warner Bros. Ranch

The Warner movie ranch was located in Agoura Hills, California, south of the Ventura Freeway in the Calabasas area.

In 1929 Harry Warner started purchasing land that would become the Warner Ranch, and leased the Providencia Ranch across the street for outdoor scenes. This had previously been the Universal Ranch, used as early as 1915 to film battle scenes for *The Birth of a Nation* (1915) by D.W. Griffith.[20] The ranch eventually grew to 2,800 acres in size.

The Warners Ranch was used for filming numerous productions from 1933 until 1960. Standing sets on the property included a sprawling Western town built for *The Oklahoma Kid* (1939), a train depot, a Mexican village, a colonial street, a fort, a ranch house, stables, and a racetrack for horses. Use of the ranch started to decline after 1956 due to financial cut-backs in Hollywood and the need for television Westerns to be filmed in a shorter time than feature films.

Warners didn't have a permanent Western street until 1956, when they built one for *Shootout at Medicine Bend* (1957).[21] Their Westerns were either made on location, or at their studio ranch in Calabasas. The interiors for Westerns were often shot on a soundstage on the back lot. The finale of *The Shootist* (1976) with John Wayne was filmed in the "Metropole Saloon" on Midwest Street on the back lot. Most of *Rio Bravo* (1959) was filmed on location at Old Tucson Studios, but interiors were shot on what was called Stage 4 at the Warners lot.[22]

Locations Near Hollywood

As well as at movies ranches, hundreds of Westerns were filmed in the hills, canyons, and deserts surrounding Los Angeles. In the early days of movies, actors and the crew often simply rode out on horseback with a camera and made up the story when they reached a suitable scenic location.

The following are some of the popular locations around the Los Angeles area that might be familiar to Western movie fans.

Agoura Ranch

This was once part of the large Russell Ranch, which was widely used for filming B-Westerns. This is now a state park north of the Ventura Freeway in Agoura.

Griffith Park

Griffith Park was close to Hollywood and contained large expanses of scenic hills, rocks, canyons, streams, and trees that were used for filming early Westerns by New York Motion Picture Company, Biograph, and other pioneering Hollywood film companies.

Located in the same area, almost at the entrance to Griffith Park, was Bronson Canyon. Bronson Canyon had steep walls, caves, and was strewn with rocks. The canyon, formed in the shape of an L and closed in by steep walls about 240 feet high, was a popular background for B-Western shoot-'em-ups. Though close to Hollywood, Bronson Caves were forbidding and remote-looking, which made them ideal as a low budget filming location for numerous film and television productions. The canyon was originally mined in 1903 by Union Rock Company as a stone quarry during the construction of the Los Angeles street car system and for paving streets.[23]

Los Angeles State and County Arboretum

It has been claimed that the Los Angeles State and County Arboretum is one of the most photographed spots in the world. The location consisted of 127 acres of exotic gardens created on the former Lucky Baldwin Ranch near Arcadia, just east of Los Angeles. Baldwin was a silver mining magnate who founded the town of Arcadia and helped introduce horse racing to southern California. Films such as the Tarzan movies, the *Road to Singapore* (1940) with Bing Crosby and Bob Hope, *The African Queen* (1951) with Humphrey Bogart, and the television series *Fantasy Island* were filmed there.[24]

The Mojave Desert

The Mojave Desert near Barstow and the nearby old mining towns, such as Victorville, was often used as a backdrop for Westerns, primarily B-Westerns and television series. The part of the Mojave Desert north of the San Fernando Valley contained flat open spaces, bare hills, and big rock formations that were ideal for filming Westerns. Much of the Western filming in the desert was concentrated near Victorville and Apple Valley, an area easily reached in the early days by actors and crews via the railroad. Local iconic vegetation included the very recognizable Joshua Tree, which was strongly identified with many of the Westerns filmed in the Mojave Desert.

Lucerne Lake, 16 miles east of Victorville, was the setting for the land rush sequence in *The Three Bad Men* (1926), filmed by John Ford. He also filmed it again in 1938 for the chase across the salt flats and the Indian attack in *Stagecoach* (1939).[25]

Red Rock Canyon State Recreation Area

Red Rock Canyon became a California state park in 1958. Red Rock Canyon consisted of 4,000 acres of rocks in the high desert, 25 miles northeast of the town of Mojave. This location was another favorite of Western moviemakers as it contained spectacular natural scenery that included rock formations that formed temples, columns, and amphitheaters. The first movie company to film in this area was Keystone. Other film companies started to use the area in the 1920s when the access by road was improved. The area was used as a movie location until the end of the 1970s.

San Bernardino Mountains

The San Bernardino Mountains were a convenient area close to Los Angeles that contained suitable locations for filming Westerns at Big Bear Lake and surrounding

Big Bear Valley, Lake Arrowhead, and Cedar Lake. Big Bear Lake, located at 6,000 feet elevation at the top of the mountains, was used as early as 1911 by the Bison Company. Other companies soon followed, attracted by the natural beauty of the area.

Vasquez Rocks County Park

The 932-acre Vasquez Rocks Natural Area Park, north of Hollywood between Santa Clarita and Palmdale, contained a maze of sandstone rocks, which made a good backdrop for chase scenes, stagecoach robberies, and Indian attacks.

Wildwood Regional Park

More than 300 Westerns were filmed in this area west of Thousand Oaks. This included the few outdoor location scenes at Tom Doniphon's (John Wayne) ranch house in *The Man Who Shot Liberty Valance* (1962), which showed the strategic positioning of a few fake saguaro cactuses on the California hillside to try to create Western authenticity. Television series filmed there included *Wagon Train*, *Gunsmoke*, and *Rawhide*. The 1,765-acre park was created in 1967 to save the last of the open space in the Thousand Oaks area. The park includes the so-called Stagecoach Bluffs, where countless Western stagecoaches were rolled off a cliff.

These Locations Today

Universal Studios in Burbank, the Monogram/Melody Ranch in Newhall, Disney's Golden Oak Ranch in Placerita Canyon, and Ranch Maria in Placerita Canyon are still used for filming. Among the movie ranches that are now gone are Inceville in Pacific Palisades, the Universal/Jesse L. Lasky Ranch in the Hollywood Hills (where Forest Lawn Memorial Park is today), Mixville in Edendale, the Warner Ranch in Calabasas, Jack Ingram Ranch in Woodland Hills, Columbia Ranch in Burbank, RKO Ranch in Encino, Republic Studios in Studio City, Bell Ranch in the Santa Susana Mountains, Spahn Ranch at Santa Susana Pass, Patterson Ranch/Big Sky Ranch in Simi Valley, and Burro Flats in East Simi Hills.

Protected as parks, at least in part, are the former Iverson Ranch in Chatsworth (where by far the greatest number of western films was made), Corriganville in the Simi Valley, Paramount Ranch in Agoura, Twentieth Century–Fox Ranch in Malibu Creek State Park, Conejo Ranch in Thousand Oaks, and Walker Ranch in Newhall/Placerita Canyon.

The Rise of Television Westerns

A major factor that affected the established studio system during the 1950s was the growth of television, the new mass medium of popular culture. When television sets became widespread in homes, movie theater attendance declined. People did not want to spend money at the movies when they could watch Westerns free on television.

Westerns were first broadcast on television in the late 1940s, and were essentially reduced versions of popular B-Westerns with established stars such as Hopalong Cassidy, The Lone Ranger, Gene Autry, and Roy Rogers, that were edited into a half-hour format. By 1950 the television screen was inundated with television versions of Westerns that had been made in the previous two decades. *The Lone Ranger* alone aired 221 episodes between 1949 and 1965. The program was primarily filmed on cramped interior sets, with old stock footage of chase scenes intercut with the interior scenes.[26]

Western television series made specifically for television started in 1949. In 1950 there were 10 on the air. By 1957, there were more than 25 Westerns on the air each week.[27] In the 1957–1958 season, 12 of the top 25 television series were Westerns, including seven of the top 10.[28] At their peak in 1959, there were 48 prime-time Western programs. By 1965, the number was down to eight weekly, as the television networks and audiences lost interest in the genre.[29] Cable television revived the Western genre in the 1980s with reruns of old Western movies and television reruns of *Bonanza*, *Gunsmoke*, and others.

In 1955 Warner Bros. Television was run by William T. Orr, Jack Warner's son-in-law. Under his capable guidance, television was flooded with a spate of Warner Brothers Westerns. The initial success of *Cheyenne* (1955–1963) led to *Sugarfoot* (1957–1961), *Maverick* (1957–1962), *Colt .45* (1957–1960), *Lawman* (1958–1962), and *Bronco* (1958–1962). In 1958 four Western television series were being filmed at the same time. The studio needed more space and Warners had to built two more Western sets to accommodate this increased production.[30]

The Western Street on the Warners back lot was heavily used for filming television shows, such as *Cheyenne, Colt .45, Sugarfoot, Maverick, Lawman,* and for *Bonanza* when it was filmed at Warners. The Warners lot was also used for feature films, such as *Shootout at Medicine Bend* (1957), *Fort Dobbs* (1958), *Guns of the Timberland* (1960), in *The Great Race* (1965) with Laramie Street as the Western town of Boracho, and in *Blazing Saddles* (1974) as Rock Ridge. A few scenes of *Firecreek* (1968) and *The Cowboys* (1972) were filmed there after main production was complete.

Television Westerns were mostly limited by time and budget constraints to filming on movie studio back lots and Western towns. In order to cut costs, production values were cheaper due to reduced budgets. The budget for a half-hour Western was typically about $30,000.[31]

As an example of the result of economy-minded strategies in filming for the small screen, television Westerns often included a lot of talky scenes and many did not have much outdoor action. To save money, the more expensive—though visually more exciting—running inserts shot from camera cars were replaced by simpler, cheaper, and less dramatic shots that simply followed the action from a stationary location by panning the camera to follow the actors. This lack of mobile camera work reduced movement to a minimum and resulted in long scenes of static dialog with not much action.

Extensive use was made of stock footage for action scenes, which resulted in the need for less filming on location. This followed the trend pioneered by Republic and Columbia B-Westerns that even started to form plots around the stock footage that they had available, resulting in even less location filming.[32] At Warners, if a location action shot was needed, then the producers often used stock footage from old Warners films. The actors on the television show were dressed in the same outfits as the original actors to match continuity. Either old costumes were pulled from storage or recreated by the wardrobe department.

Epic Western feature-length movies were filmed in Technicolor and used panoramic backgrounds and settings, and were filmed on location at scenic places in the West. These outdoor pictures included riding, horse chases, and the thrills of the Old West, with plenty of action of people falling over cliffs, crossing rivers, and driving cattle. Television reduced the grandeur of these outdoor Westerns filmed on location to the small screen. When televisions were first introduced, the screen size was indeed small and a screen size of 12 or 14 inches in diameter was considered to be large.[33] The small size of the television screen and the early days of black-and-white images were definite limitations for audiences that enjoyed expansive scenic Western outdoor locations.

Television Westerns were produced on an assembly line. Like the B-Westerns, they had to be produced weekly, fast, and on a strict budget. And each episode had to be completed on schedule to meet air-time deadlines. Television series involved very little location shooting, and most of the filming took place on the back lot of a major studio or independent movie ranch, where there was always a saloon, a church, a marshal's office, a stable, and a blacksmith shop. Television's *Rawhide*, for example, used the same town set and constantly redressed it to represent every town the drovers stopped in between Texas and Kansas.[34]

More obvious were studio sets used to simulate outdoor scenes. For example, when *Bonanza* was being produced at Paramount, the Ponderosa Ranch, the home of the Cartwright family, was filmed on a studio set for many of the scenes at the main ranch-house. The ranch house exterior, the barn, the bunkhouse, and the horse corral were built on Stage 16. The set was decorated with fake trees and papier-mâché boulders, with a few fresh real trees brought in each season.

Another example was *The Rifleman*, which filmed many outdoor town street scenes on an indoor set. This lack of location filming, often using a blank white backdrop with a couple of false trees or other plants in pots, did not look like a real exterior.

Cheaply-made television series staged both exterior and interior shots on interior sets, and the town scenes in some series that were filmed on interior sets looked very flat and sterile. A few chases might be filmed as exteriors, but many were gathered from stock footage and intercut into the series along with artificial-looking studio footage.

On the other hand, some of the requirements for a television Western series were more rigid than for theatrical release. Everything was subject to scrutiny. Each episode had to pass inspection by the sponsor, their advertising agency, and network censors. In the 1950s and 1960s, each story had to be 26 minutes long to allow for commercial breaks in a half-hour program.[35] Plot structure required a dramatic or action highlight before each commercial break to hold the viewer's attention. The production company had to produce 13 or 39 episodes a year for a series. Thirty-nine episodes ran over the winter, then a 13-episode replacement series filled in for the summer months.

CHAPTER EIGHT

The 1950s
Locations That Moved

Although railroads are not movie locations in the same sense as movie towns and studio back lots, they are nevertheless very much a part of the location filming of Westerns. Railroads and locomotives have always played an important part in the background of movies, as location filming on moving trains created a sense of action and excitement. Tom Mix, for example, loved trains, and included them and stunts on them in his movies whenever he could.

Railroads have always been an important part of movies depicting the West because they represented the nation's wave of westward expansion and the powerful forces of Manifest Destiny. As well as presenting a dynamic image of strength and splendor, the locomotive was a symbol of power, progress, and the country's industrialization. Trains have been an integral part of Westerns since *The Great Train Robbery* (1903) and its many imitators.

By 1911 major producers of Western films had started to settle permanently in southern California where year-round production was possible, away from the harsh winters of New York and New Jersey that limited outdoor film production for several months of the year. By 1920 the film industry was firmly entrenched in Hollywood.

Filmmakers soon included local trains in their movies to add suspense and drama to the plot. Locomotives and rolling stock were provided by the regular railroads around Los Angeles, such as the Southern Pacific and Union Pacific, that still had trains in regular service. From about 1920 to 1940 filmmakers used these trains and the smaller short-line local railroads that dotted the West, such as the Lake Tahoe Railroad, the Pacific Coast Railway, the Sierra Railway, and the Yosemite Valley Railway. Main line railroads continued to be used for filming into the 1950s.

Engines and trains featured in Hollywood Westerns fell into two categories. One was trains that were rented from existing railroads. This was a lucrative business for the railroads as renting out trains brought them from $3,000 to $5,000 a day.[1] The other category of railroad included those that were owned by the studios themselves. At one time all the major Hollywood studios had their own trains located on their back lot or at their studio ranch. If they did not own an entire train, they at least had a short length of track and some rolling stock, and were able to rent an engine from another studio that had one available.

Iconic Images of the Movie West #8: San Juan Mountains, Colorado. The high San Juan Mountains of Colorado have been a popular location for outdoor Westerns, often including the still snow-capped peaks of early summer, such as did *The Naked Spur* (1953), or in order to capture the radiant beauty of the aspen leaves on the Colorado mountainsides as they change from the green of summer to the gold color of fall, as in *How the West Was Won* (1962) and *True Grit* (1969). Shown here at the top of Owl Creek Pass, near Ouray, are iconic Chimney Rock with Courthouse Mountain behind it, both of which appeared in several sequences filmed in fall colors in the latter two movies.

Rental Railroads

Though not always an appealing situation for purist railfans, the same locomotives show up again and again in different movies. This was a limitation forced on the studios by having to use and re-use the limited amount of historic railroad equipment that was still available and operational. Part of the problem was that by the mid–1930s most of the engines from the Old West period were worn out and had been scrapped.

Filmmakers therefore had to use newer locomotives that had to be dressed to look old, or to use engines from short-line railroads that still had older equipment in service. To make the engines appear that they came from the Old West period, studios typically altered the locomotives to have diamond-shaped wood-burning stacks instead of straight stacks, and added oil-burning box-type headlights. These additions made the movie audience think that the engine was "old," even though most of the available locomotives were built after 1890 and the end of the real Old West period

As one example, a limitation for crews filming on the Denver & Rio Grande

(D&RG) railroad around Silverton, Colorado, was that the still-existing narrow-gauge D&RG engines were added to the railroad in 1923. Ten engines of the 470-series had been originally built by the American Locomotive Co. in New York, but only three still existed for filming. Railroad movie fans will recognize No. 473, No. 476, and No. 478.[2] Fake diamond stacks were added to these engines at one time for movie use, but were removed in 1981 to restore the engines back to their original authentic state for the tourist trade.

Denver & Rio Grande Railway

One of the railroads most often used in Westerns was the Silverton Branch of the Denver & Rio Grande Narrow Gauge Railroad, based today in the mountain town of Durango in Colorado. The Denver & Rio Grande was incorporated in Denver in 1870 to go from Denver, Colorado, to El Paso, Texas. The Durango & Silverton was a narrow-gauge steam railroad built in 1881 and 1882 by the D&RG as a working railroad to transport passengers and freight in the area.[3] The train offered some of most spectacular scenery in the West as it wound alongside and above the Animas River on its climb from Durango up to Silverton.

Like most railroads of the time, the D&RG went through various periods of bankruptcy, reorganization, and name changes. Like most other railroads of the late 1800s, the D&RG was finally abandoned and the Silverton Branch was sold in 1981 to the Durango & Silverton Narrow Gauge Railroad for use with tourist traffic.[4] Today, this remaining section of steam railroad runs as a tourist attraction in the summer from Durango north to Silverton, an authentic historical silver mining town 45 miles away in the mountains.

The D&RG railroad was first used by Paramount for *The Texas Rangers* (1936). Other notable movies were *Denver and Rio Grande* (1952), which was filmed completely on location on the Durango & Silverton line, parts of *Colorado Territory* (1949) with Joel McCrea, *A Ticket to Tomahawk* (1950), *Night Passage* (1957) with James Stewart and Audie Murphy, *The Naked Spur* (1953), the Western steam train sequence in *Around the World in Eighty Days* (1956), part of *Butch Cassidy and the Sundance Kid* (1969), and part of *Support Your Local Gunfighter* (1971).

A Ticket to Tomahawk (1950), with Dan Dailey and Anne Baxter, was filmed on the Silverton railroad and in the town of Silverton in August and September of 1949. The depot was renamed Epitaph for the movie. The plot was about a narrow-gauge railroad line in the Rocky Mountains that had to complete laying its track and make the line operational before it fell into the hands of receivers. The movie showed off much of the rugged breathtaking scenery of Colorado's San Juan Mountains.

For the film, Rio Grande Southern locomotive No. 20 was given an 1870s appearance with a diamond stack and bright red and yellow paint highlights to accent its original black color, and was renamed the *Emma Sweeny* (more formally the "Tomahawk & Western #1"). The studio prop shop also built a full-scale wooden replica of the engine for use in studio scenes and scenes filmed off the track in Silverton and Durango. As this was only a non-working model, it was "powered" by a team of 20 mules when it had to be shown in motion. This replica, slightly weathered now, is on display today in Santa Rita Park in Durango.

The Durango & Rio Grande railroad has been popular for Westerns requiring a train and spectacular mountain scenery. Notable movies were *Denver and Rio Grande* (1952), *Colorado Territory* (1949), *Night Passage* (1957), and the Western steam train sequence in *Around the World in Eighty Days* (1956). This realistic-looking replica railroad engine, named the *Emma Sweeny*, though mostly made of wood, was constructed for *A Ticket to Tomahawk* (1950) for use in off-the-track scenes, when it was pulled by a team of mules. This replica, slightly weathered, is on display today in Durango, Colorado.

The original color of the coaches was the standard green of the Pullman Company, who built them. For the movie, the engine was given a colorful paint job to match its name, and Fox painted the coaches a bright yellow color to give them an "old-time" look. The officials of the railroad liked this look and repainted their other coaches the same color, which became known as "Rio Grande Gold." After the movie was released, many vacationers wanted to ride the train they had seen in the movies, so the railroad started running special excursion trains and promoting itself as a tourist attraction.

Night Passage (1957), with James Stewart and Audie Murphy playing brothers, was partly filmed on location on the railroad and around Silverton in September and October of 1956 in order to capture the beauty of the aspen leaves on the Colorado mountainsides as they changed color from the green of summer to the gold of fall. One long sequence was filmed on the train as it wound up along a spectacular cliff-face alongside the Animas Canyon, with the river far below it. Another part was filmed at an abandoned mine near Silverton, though several scenes were intercut with film from a studio soundstage with a vast mural of the mountains in the background. One spectacular sequence occurred when a locomotive crashed through a wooden water tank that the outlaws had pushed onto the tracks to try and stop the train to rob it.

Denver and Rio Grande (1952) was filmed on the Silverton Branch in 1951 (though the title background was filmed on the D&RG tracks through Glenwood Canyon) and helped to publicize the railroad even more as a tourist attraction. As the narrator of the introduction solemnly intoned, "An epic of pioneer western railroad builders and their fight for the route through Royal Gorge."

The story of the film was loosely based on real-life incidents when survey crews from the real Denver & Rio Grande were competing with the Atchison, Topeka & Santa Fe Railroad for the right-of-way across Raton Pass from Trinidad, Colorado, south to Raton, New Mexico, and on to El Paso. Shortly afterwards, the two railroads were also in competition for the right-of-way through the Royal Gorge, west of Cañon City, Colorado, to the rich silver-mining town of Leadville. Mercenary fighters were hired by both railroads to protect their rights-of-way and to prevent the other railway from grading a railbed through the canyon. At one point an armed confrontation took place between thugs hired by the rival railroads. The final fight, however, turned out to be bloodless and was eventually settled in the courts.[5] The resulting agreement was that the D&RG stopped building over Raton Pass, and the Atchison, Topeka & Santa Fe Railroad gave up their plans to connect to Leadville.

The movie blurred the two incidents and put the armed confrontation in the Royal Gorge, but filmed it north of Durango, Colorado. In the movie, the competing railroad was named the fictional Cañon City & San Juan Railroad.

Railroad wrecks always made a spectacular addition to location filming. Train wrecks were usually done in the studio with miniatures, but a real head-on collision was staged for *Denver & Rio Grande* (1952) using two engines that were already destined for the scrap heap. One of the most spectacular parts of the entire movie was when the two collided. Two real, full-sized railroad locomotives, No. 319 and No. 345 from the D&RG, were used and were crashed head-on on July 17, 1951, in an open meadow at milepost 475. The location was 23 miles north of Durango in a small meadow that the film crew nicknamed "Scrap Iron Junction." This was the railroad stop for Tall Timber Resort, which was only accessible by train. A small movie set of an 1880 town was built alongside the existing railroad track for the movie.

The preparations for filming the crash scene took five days. Heavy wooden barricades were built to protect the five cameras that were used for simultaneous filming. Obviously this was a one-time stunt and the crash could not be repeated if anything went wrong.

The controls on the two locomotives were set so that they were both traveling towards each other at 30 miles per hour, so the combined speed when they collided was 60 miles per hour. As a final effort to ensure a spectacular collision for the cameras, 300 sticks of dynamite and 30 pounds of black powder were added. Both engines were totally wrecked in the spectacular collision. The debris from the wreck was cleaned up in September of 1951, and sent to the Colorado Fuel and Iron smelter in Pueblo to be melted down as scrap.

Part of *Butch Cassidy and the Sundance Kid* (1969) was filmed on the Silverton Branch. As part of the plot, Cassidy (Paul Newman) and his gang stop the train and then blow open the door of the locked baggage car when the conductor refuses to open it. An incident like this actually happened when the real Butch Cassidy robbed a Union Pacific train near Wilcox, Wyoming, on June 2, 1899. In the process of trying to open the baggage car, Cassidy used so much dynamite that he literally blew up the car instead of merely blowing the door open, as he had planned.

The fiasco happened when Cassidy and his gang stopped the train, surrounded the express car and told the guard, Charles Woodcock, to open the door. Woodcock refused, so the gang placed a large charge of dynamite next to the door and lit the fuse. The resulting explosion blew the top of the express car into the air, along with Woodcock. He was injured, but alive. The bandits then placed 10 pounds of dynamite on top of the safe and, as a result, blew a 10-inch hole in it. The explosion also blew about $30,000 in bank notes into the air, which the gang had to pick up from all over the ground.

For filming the movie version of the explosion, the crew built the studio baggage car that was to be blown up on a special flatcar so that they would not damage any of the railroad's historical rolling stock. The design included reinforcements at the two ends of the studio-built car to protect the engine and rest of the train during the explosion. In addition, the car itself was structurally designed so that it would blow apart easily in a modestly spectacular fashion for the film. However, just like the real Cassidy, the special effects crew used so much explosive that they also blew their car completely apart.[6] That was not the intended result, but it certainly made for historical accuracy.

Other action Westerns filmed on the railroad were *Three Young Texans* (1954) with Jeffry Hunter, and *The Maverick Queen* (1956) with Barbara Stanwyck. *The Maverick Queen* was a story about a civic leader who was also secretly the leader of an outlaw gang. Barry Sullivan played an undercover agent sent to infiltrate the gang and bring the miscreant to justice.

Cumbres & Toltec Scenic Railroad

The other movie railroad in Colorado used for filming Westerns was originally also a part of the original Denver & Rio Grande railroading empire.

In 1967 the D&RG filed an application to abandon their narrow gauge line between Alamosa, Colorado, and Farmington, New Mexico. The application was approved but, before the process of scrapping the line started, public outcry led to the states of Colorado and New Mexico jointly purchasing 64 of the most scenic miles of track over Cumbres Pass between Antonito, Colorado, and Chama, New Mexico. In 1970 the newly-incorporated Cumbres & Toltec Scenic Railroad started operation as a tourist railroad.

The Cumbres & Toltec started its film career with *The Good Guys and the Bad Guys* (1969). Universal filmed part of *Shootout* (1971) with Gregory Peck in October of 1970 to coincide with the changing colors of the aspen trees. The railroad was also used for the railroad scenes for filming *Bite the Bullet* (1975) with Gene Hackman and Ben Johnson, including several sequences at the Cumbres & Toltec railyards.

The authenticity of the Old West time period using the Cumbres & Toltec Scenic Railroad is sometimes dubious as their locomotives were built by Baldwin Locomotive Works in 1908. However, except to the purist, they still have an old-time Western railroad look.

Wood-burning engines in Westerns are often shown trailing a spectacular rolling plume of black smoke as they steam along. In reality, wood-burning locomotives at cruising speed mostly put out only a gray haze. Even coal-burning engines are relatively pollution-free when cruising on flat ground. Additional smoke for a more spectacular flair often had to be created by Hollywood special effects men. One way to achieve these dramatic clouds of black smoke was to spray oil into the engine firebox while the engine was rolling. Cold, snowy weather in winter in the mountains was another matter, and steam locomotives put out a magnificent scenic white plume as the steam from the smokestack condensed in the frigid air. More modern filming can add rolling black smoke as a computer-generated effect.

Sierra Railway

Tuolumne County in California is on the western side of the Sierra Nevada mountains, with the towns of Sonora, Columbia, and Jamestown that contain build-

Though the locomotives on the Cumbres & Toltec Scenic Railroad were built in 1908, they have been used for period Western productions, sometimes by adding diamond-shaped wood-burning smokestacks and oil-burning box-type headlights to make them appear to be older. Productions filmed on the railroad include *The Good Guys and the Bad Guys* **(1969),** *Shootout* **(1971), and** *Bite the Bullet* **(1975).**

ings that date back to the mid–1800s. Many Westerns were shot in the area of Sonora, an old 1849 Gold Rush town, because Sonora and the surrounding area had a wide variety of scenic possibilities for location filming. Prairies, lakes, rivers, forests, and a large variety of other natural scenery in the area were ideal for the purpose.

The main attraction of the area was the Sierra Railroad, the uncredited star of many Westerns, which has probably appeared in more movies than any other historic railway over the years. The Sierra Railroad, often referred to as "the Movie Railroad," was built in 1897 as a 57-mile rail connection to transport lumber from the mountains of Tuolumne County to the main rail line at Oakdale. The complex that houses the railroad engines and shops in Jamestown is more properly known as Railtown 1897 Historic Park, owned and operated by the California State Railroad Museum. The site was purchased in 1982 by the State of California to preserve the steam engines and existing railroad facilities. Several antique steam locomotives and rail cars were (and are) maintained for movie use at the railroad's mechanical shops in Jamestown.

One of the first movies filmed using the railroad was *The Red Glove* (1919), a cliff-hanging 18-chapter serial that featured a train robbery. The next year Tom Mix filmed *The Terror* (1920). In 1923 Paramount built a complete 1849 Western gold-mining town at Melones for filming part of *The Covered Wagon* (1923) and the Sierra Railroad was used to transport the crew and hundreds of extras to the site.

In the mid–1920s, a group of businessmen from Sonora realized the financial benefits of catering to filmmakers, so they formed the Sonora Motion Picture Cooperative Association to promote the area for filming. They also acted as a liaison for film companies who needed to find locations, hire extras, arrange for lodging, and find help with many of the other production necessities required by film crews.

One of the most popular filming locations was the Jamestown railyard where the railroad's movie trains were stored. Another favorite railroad filming location was the section of track between Jack's Siding and McCormick. Another section commonly seen in Westerns filmed on the railroad was a stretch of open prairie between Cooperstown and Warnerville. The opening part of *Dodge City* (1939) with Errol Flynn, was filmed on this section a little further west, around Paulsell.

Duel in the Sun (1946), with Gregory Peck and Jennifer Jones, was partly filmed on the railroad. One scene called for a train loaded with dynamite to derail and turn over on a hill. After considering wrecking a real locomotive for the filming, the producer finally decided to use a plywood mock-up instead of an actual engine.[7]

The Sierra Railroad has appeared in more than 200 movies, television productions, and commercials. Earlier movies using the railroad were *The Virginian* (1929), *Dodge City* (1939), and *My Little Chickadee* (1939). Another Western was *The Great Missouri Raid* (1951), with Macdonald Carey and Wendell Corey, detailing the exploits of Frank and Jesse James. The same year it featured in *The Texas Ranger* (1951), with George Montgomery and Gale Storm, and *The Cimarron Kid* (1951) with Audie Murphy and Beverly Tyler. Other films that used the railroad the 1950s were *High Noon* (1952) with Gary Cooper, *Kansas Pacific* (1953) with Sterling Hayden, and *Rage at Dawn* (1955) with Randolph Scott. In *The Cimarron Kid*

In this postcard view from the movie, Sierra Railroad engine #18 (numbered for the movie as #8) is pouring out black smoke at the fictitious town of Little Bend as it stops to pick up Flower Belle Lee (Mae West) so that she can meet Cuthbert Twillie (W.C. Fields) on the train in *My Little Chickadee* (1939). This Western scene was filmed in the town of Standard, a few miles east of Jamestown, California.

(1952), Bill Doolin (Audie Murphy) was involved in a gunfight that was staged in and around the railroad roundhouse at Jamestown before he made a quick getaway on his horse. In *High Noon* (1952), the train station for Hadleyville was shot on the Sierra Railroad at Warnerville, with a set constructed as a depot near the old water tank.

To avoid repainting the names of different railroads on the engines and coaches for different movies, the rolling stock used wooden boards with the names of various real and fictional railroads on them that were bolted in place on the coaches and replaced as needed.

Sierra locomotive No. 3 and the railroad were featured in exterior location shots for *The Great Race* (1965) when the comic villains were driving their automobile on the railroad tracks to the town of Grommet. The engine was also used for the "Hooterville Cannonball" engine in the television series *Petticoat Junction* (1963–1970). To avoid the expense of traveling frequently to Jamestown to film the outdoor railroad scenes, the replica engine that had been built by Twentieth Century–Fox in 1949 for *A Ticket to Tomahawk* (1950) was used for studio shots. The engine was filmed on a sound stage in Hollywood for scenes where the engine was static and was not required to move. If the plot called for the locomotive to be shown in motion, stock footage of a Sierra Railroad train was added.[8]

The old depot and movie town set burned down in a devastating fire in 1978 that was started by arsonists.

The Baltimore & Ohio Railroad

As opposed to the other railroads, the equipment from the Baltimore & Ohio Railroad Museum in Baltimore was used only a few times for Westerns because the rolling stock pre-dated the era of the typical trains needed for most Westerns. One of the major Western movies it was used for was the epic *Wells Fargo* (1937) from Paramount, where rolling stock was used to portray a train traveling between Albany and Buffalo, New York. The museum shipped a replica of an 1837 engine to Hollywood and used it on the Southern Pacific branch near Chino. It was filmed during two days of location shooting then shipped back to Baltimore.[9]

The Magma Railroad

In the desert east of Phoenix, Arizona, was a short line railroad, 28 miles long, that was built in 1915 to connect the mine of the Magma Copper Company to Superior, Arizona. The picturesque railroad and the scenic surrounding desert were popular for filming Westerns. The area featured rugged rock formations and a desert landscape that contained saguaro cactuses, one of few the places where they grow naturally. The first movie using the Magma Railroad was filmed in 1960.

The railroad had a short life as a movie railroad, but appeared in several Western films and television shows between 1960 and 1972, notably in *How the West Was Won* (1962) and in 1970 in the television movie *Powderkeg* (1971), with Rod Taylor and Dennis Cole.

Extensive filming took place in March of 1962 for "The Outlaws" segment of *How the West Was Won* (1962). The locomotive used for filming was supposed to be an 1890s engine, but was relatively modern-looking, so MGM added some features to give it an old-time look as a wood-burner. At the end of the sequence the train was supposedly derailed and wrecked in a ravine in a spectacular crash. The sequence was carefully shot so that no damage occurred to any of the railroad's equipment, but only to two flatcars that were replicas built specially for the film.

A short sequence for *Cheyenne Autumn* (1964) was shot on the Magma Railroad. The engine was modified by the film crew with a fake diamond smokestack added to make it look more like an antique locomotive. The sequence was filmed at night (actually during the day with heavy filtering to simulate a moon-lit night) to further hide any anachronistic discrepancies.

The railroad was used again for *Blood on the Arrow* (1964), with Dale Robertson and Martha Hyer. Also in 1971 for a short segment at the end of *The Life and Times of Judge Roy Bean* (1972), posing as the engine for actress Lily Langtry's (Ava Gardner) private train. When the Magma Railroad sold off their steam locomotives and converted their motive power to diesel engines, the railroad became less useful for making period Hollywood Westerns.

Mexican National Railroad

Several Hollywood Westerns have featured standard-gauge and narrow-gauge locomotives from the Mexican National Railroad. The trains were often taken from regular service without redressing and can be recognized by the "NdeM" (*Nacionales de Mexico*) lettering on the engine or tender. The railroad had many old pieces of rolling stock, so it was easy for film crews to make up an entire train. To add confusion, though, the engine used in *The Professionals* (1966), even though lettered NdeM, was not one of these trains. The locomotive used for this movie was the Great Western Railway engine No. 75, re-lettered for the movie.

By the 1960s most of the Mexican National Railroad line had been converted to diesel, but standard-gauge locomotive No. 650 was stored in the roundhouse at Durango, Mexico, specifically for use with Western films. This engine had previously been used for hauling freight, and remained in regular service until the 1960s.

Engine No. 650 was used for *The Sons of Katie Elder* (1965) in the depot scene at the beginning of the picture, for *The Wild Bunch* (1969) during the raid on the army munitions train, and in *Rio Lobo* (1970) for the Civil War train robbery sequence. For *Rio Lobo* (1970) the engine was re-located and filming took place around Cuernavaca, 40 miles south of Mexico City and about 500 miles from Durango. The engine was re-dressed to become "U.S. Military Railroad No. 17."

In *Big Jake* (1971), also starring John Wayne, the train was again used at Durango for the sequence of him returning to his home town. For *The Train Robbers* (1972), also with John Wayne, the film crew laid several thousand feet of track across an isolated stretch of desert and built a small Western Texas town named Liberty alongside it. Number 650 was re-numbered several times during the filming of the movie in order to appear as several different engines. In *Cahill U.S. Marshal* (1973), the engine appeared in a brief scene where Cahill (John Wayne) transported prisoners in a boxcar. The engine was used again in *The Great Scout and Cathouse Thursday* (1976), with Lee Marvin and Oliver Reed.

The Great Western Railway

The Great Western Railway was incorporated in 1901, consisting of a series of railroad lines around Loveland, Colorado, used for hauling sugar beets from the fields where they were grown to the Great Western Sugar Company's Colorado processing plants at Loveland, Eaton, Longmont, Windsor, and others.[10] The railway started to switch to diesel engines in 1951 and their old steam trains were sold off until only No. 51 and No. 75 (both built by Baldwin in 1907), remained. In 1964 Columbia leased Great Western Railway engine No. 51 for *Cat Ballou* (1965) to film the train robbery sequence that was filmed in the Royal Gorge in Colorado on the Denver & Rio Grande's tracks.

In 1965 Columbia needed a locomotive for *The Professionals* (1966) and a producer remembered No. 51, however, it was out of service at the time with mechanical problems. Instead they used No. 75, which played a large role in the plot of the film. It played both the Mexican engine railroad No. 903 in the Mexico location sequences (re-labeled with "NdeM"), and was the J.W. Grant No. 75 in the sequences set north of the border. The footage was filmed on Kaiser Steel's Eagle Mountain Railroad in the desert of Southern California near Indio.

After filming was complete, the engine passed into private ownership and was moved to Salt Lake City for a tourist train, but the scheme was not as successful as the owners had hoped. The engine was modified to look like an 1880s engine for film and television use with a stubby diamond smokestack and a paint scheme of red and gold.

Locomotives are not always where film crews need them and they sometimes have to be moved long distances, either by truck or by actually driving the engine along existing railroad lines. Locomotives often had to be trucked around to existing railroad tracks for location shooting, or sometimes transported by flatbed trailer even though some of these engines weighed as much as 250,000 pounds (125 tons).

The other method was to drive the engine over existing tracks. When Columbia was filming *The Professionals*, engine No. 75 that they wanted to use was located in Denver, Colorado, where the owners lived, but the filming location was near Indio, California. As a result, the engine had to be driven on existing railroad tracks from Denver to Colton, California, using a top speed of 25 miles per hour, with frequent stops for inspection and maintenance along the way. After filming was completed the engine traveled back to Denver in the same way.

This was the engine used in *Breakheart Pass* (1976), with Charles Bronson. Though the story was set in the Wahsatch Mountains of Utah during the winter of 1886, it was filmed in western Idaho on the Camas Prairie Railroad. This particular stretch of railroad line was ideal for the movie as it had tunnels and wooden trestles that played a part in the plot. The locomotive was used in the television miniseries *Centennial* (1978–1979), with the engine back-dated to the 1880s for the early scenes and then modernized for the scenes that took place 30 years later. It was also used during the spring and summer of 1979 for *Heaven's Gate* (1980), during filming of location scenes shot in Montana.

Studio Trains

Before 1937 none of the studios owned trains, although some owned a few pieces of rolling stock that they kept on their back lots for scenes that were filmed in depots. Generally the studios leased what they needed from existing railroads and used these trains on regular railroad lines for location action scenes. But renting entire trains was not always feasible or economical. Therefore, in the late 1930s, several of the major studios solved this problem by purchasing old locomotives and moving them to their studio lots onto short pieces of track. Between 1937 and 1947 six of the movie studios purchased four engines and two dozen railroad cars.

Most studios, such as MGM and Warners, had only limited lengths of track on their back lots, so location shooting of lengthy moving scenes still had to be done with rental trains that ran on long stretches of track. The most popular rental railroad for this was the Sierra Railroad, which was used frequently for large-scale scenes. When the popularity of Westerns declined in the late 1960s and early 1970s, most of the studios sold off their locomotives.

MGM

Engine No. 11, nicknamed Reno, was built in 1872 by Baldwin Locomotive Works for the Virginia & Truckee railroad, which originally served Nevada's fabulous Comstock lode in Virginia City, Nevada, one of the most important silver strikes in the

West in the 1860s.[11] The line originally went from Reno to the state capital at Carson City and on to Virginia City. MGM purchased the engine for $5,000 in 1945 for *The Harvey Girls* (1946).

The intended arrival of the locomotive was delayed because railroad traffic to support World War II was considered more important than a movie train and they were not allowed to use the standard railway network. So MGM ended up leasing Virginia & Truckee engine No. 22 from Paramount for the film.[12] This was the AT&SF engine and train that pulled into the fictional town of Sandrock, Arizona, for *The Harvey Girls* (1946), to the accompaniment of Judy Garland singing the popular song "Atchison, Topeka and Santa Fe."

As part of their railroad empire, MGM had two railroad stations, their own tracks, and a train on Lot 2. The Western street on Lot 2 was used for *Billy the Kid* (1930) and *The Squaw Man* (1931).[13] The Western street on MGM's Lot 3, which was built in 1938 for *Stand Up and Fight* (1939), a war picture, also had a section of railroad track.

Originally studio trains that were leased moved between studios on existing railroad tracks in Los Angeles. During the 1960s, however, the main-line railroads became reluctant to allow movie crews and trains to use their tracks, so more and more Westerns were filmed on MGM's "railroad system."

MGM experienced financial difficulties in the 1960s and, in 1969, management decided to sell off their props and surplus real estate in order to raise money. In May of 1970, MGM's property department auctioned off engine No.11 and it was purchased by Old Tucson Studios. It was used in *Support Your Local Gunfighter* (1971), then shipped to Tucson, where it was located on 500 feet of track.

Some of the MGM rolling stock also went to Old Tucson Studios, some to private individuals, and the rest to a State of Nevada museum. Old Tucson had only a short section of track so, for extended running scenes, their locomotive was moved by truck to one of the short lines in the area for filming. Engine No. 11 was used for *The Villain* (1979) with Kirk Douglas, and for *The Wild Wild West* (1999) with Will Smith.

Paramount

Paramount purchased their first engine, Virginia & Truckee No. 22, in 1937 and towed it to Hollywood behind a regular freight train. The studio realized that it also needed some coaches, so the same year they purchased enough to make an entire train, which was first used in *Wells Fargo* (1937).

Paramount purchased more equipment in 1938 for *Union Pacific* (1939), filmed by director Cecil B. DeMille near Ogden, Utah. Most of the scenes were filmed on the Union Pacific's Cedar City branch. The film sequence of driving the Golden Spike at the culmination of *Union Pacific* (1939), when the Union Pacific and the Central Pacific railroads finally met at Promontory Point in Utah, was filmed in the San Fernando Valley north of Los Angeles, where Paramount laid a section of rail adjacent to the existing Southern Pacific track. The original transcontinental locomotives were played by studio locomotives used formerly by the Virginia & Truckee railroad. Engine No. 22 stood in for the Central Pacific's Jupiter and Paramount's Virginia & Truckee No. 18 stood in for Union Pacific engine No. 119. Both engines steamed out to the site under their own power.[14]

Engine No. 22 was used in the Technicolor remake of *The Virginian* (1946), with Joel McCrea, for the sequence where the train steamed into "Medicine Bow, Wyoming" though through hills near Los Angeles. Other movies included a brief appearance in *How the West was Won* (1962) in the transcontinental railroad segment for the sequence of the construction camp, which was filmed on a specially-laid section of track near Rapid City, South Dakota. Then it was moved and used for the scenes of the mining town and depot scenes, which were filmed near Prescott, Arizona. The smokestack was dressed to make it look like it was a more modern engine. In July of 1969 the engine was used at the Eaves Movie Ranch in New Mexico for *The Cheyenne Social Club* (1970).

Virginia & Truckee No. 22 made its last appearance in *The Wild Wild West* (1965–1969) television series. The engine was leased by CBS television for several months in 1965 and located on a siding on the Santa Fe's San Jacinto Branch to provide stock footage that was used throughout the series.

Paramount's equipment was frequently leased out to other studios for Westerns. Paramount engines were featured in *Whispering Smith* (1948) with Alan Ladd, and were used for *The Last Train from Gun Hill* (1959) and *Sergeant Rutledge* (1960). A Paramount engine was used on the MGM lot for the railroad scenes in *The Sheepman* (1958).

Warner Brothers

In 1939 Warners acquired a locomotive that had been used to haul logs to the sawmill at Hobart Mills, near Truckee in northern California. They installed it on their back lot in Burbank on 1,400 feet of specially-laid track.

In 1951 NBC Television purchased Warners' back lot and the engine was moved to the Warner Ranch near Thousand Oaks, California, west of Los Angeles. The engine had to be moved again when the property was sold for a housing development. Then it was moved back to the Burbank lot and placed on 200 feet of track on the studio's "Laramie Street" set. Even though the length of track was short, this was not necessarily a problem as studio locomotives were filmed for some scenes with a cold boiler. The steam seen in the final film was produced by the special effects department using a steam generator, and the engine sounds were dubbed in later. Walls or canvases behind the trains were painted with outdoor scenes so that realistic-looking railroad scenes could be filmed on the back lot.

The Warners engine was used for *Cheyenne Autumn* (1964), where it was shown hauling an army troop train on "Western Street," which was dressed for the movie as Dodge City, Kansas. In 1971 Columbia and Warners merged into The Burbank Studios to avoid duplication of services and property departments. The engine was used in *The Shootist* (1976) on the studio's "Midwestern Street," dressed to be Carson City, Nevada, in 1901.

Universal

The narrow-gauge engine owned by Universal was originally used for transporting timber from the Lake Tahoe area to Virginia City, Nevada, in the 1880s. It was purchased in 1941 for *The Spoilers* (1942), which was filmed in 1942 in Tujunga Canyon in the San Fernando Valley near Los Angeles, where the studio laid a section of track and built an Alaskan mining town. The engine then remained idle on the Universal back lot until 1950 when it was used for *Winchester '73* (1950). It was used extensively for *Rails into Laramie* (1954), but by this time the bodywork had started to deteriorate and had to be rebuilt. The engine ran on 2,000 feet of track on the back lot, where there were two railroad depots, one at the Western town and one made up as an Eastern-style station.

The studio acquired several railroad cars and boxcars as well as building several of their own on purchased railroad flatcars in order to provide a complete train. This equipment was used frequently in the 1960s and 1970s for television Westerns.

Twentieth Century–Fox

Twentieth Century–Fox's locomotive was originally used for freight and passenger service with several railroads in the Midwest. It was originally leased from the Dardanelle & Russellville Railroad in Arkansas for *Jesse James* (1939), which was filmed in Pineville, Missouri, dressed to be the home town of the James Brothers at Liberty, Missouri. Location photography for the train robbery sequences was filmed near Neosho, Missouri, on the Kansas City Southern Railway, with other sequences filmed on the Sierra railroad at Jamestown.

The engine was purchased in 1954 by Fox, which had decided that they needed an old-time locomotive for various productions. In the late 1950s the engine was moved to Fox's 2,000-acre ranch near Malibu. After several ownership and location changes, the engine ended up as part of the collection of the railroad museum at Jamestown, California.

CHAPTER NINE

The 1960s and Beyond
The Shift In Power

By the end of the 1950s, Hollywood Westerns were in trouble. The last great year of the traditional studio system was 1948, the year that the Supreme Court ruled that the studios' combined ownership of production, distribution, and exhibition of movies was a monopoly. The system that the movie moguls had built their fortunes on were effectively dismantled.

Box office figures had been falling off since the end of World War II. Part of the problem was the growing competition of television, which provided free entertainment in the living room and, at the same time, theater audiences wanted more plot realism and more realistic locations in their entertainment than corny singing Westerns.

The bigger problem, though, was that with shifting audience tastes the very late 1950s became the decade of big-budget spectacles and extravagant musicals. Historical epics, such as *Ben Hur* (1959), *Spartacus* (1960), *El Cid* (1961), and *King of Kings* (1961) became very popular with audiences. And with increasing competition from television Westerns and the large number of Western series that were appearing free on television in the late 1950s, Western feature film production fell drastically.

The End of MGM

By the 1960s, all the major studios were in turmoil. The story of what happened to MGM was not unusual. Louis B. Mayer, studio founder and head of MGM, had been ousted in 1951 and replaced by Dore Schary, the new vice-president in charge of production. Schary himself was ousted in 1955 by Nicholas Schenck, chairman of MGM's parent owner Loew's, when the studio began to flounder under financial and internal management problems.

MGM began a slow collapse. In 1969 the studio was purchased by Kirk Kerkorian, a Las Vegas–based airline and hotel financier. His management team systematically dismantled the studio, and in 1970 auctioned off many of the classic props and costumes, including Judy Garland's ruby slippers from *The Wizard of Oz* (1939) for $15,000.[1] The entire Western-style wardrobe department was sold off to Old Tucson Studios, at the time making the resulting wardrobe department the largest West-

Iconic Images of the Movie West #9: Sedona, Arizona. The red rock country of Sedona was discovered in the 1920s as a colorful backdrop for Western dramas, and it continued as a popular filming location through the 1940s and 1950s, providing the background setting for nearly a hundred movies. Perversely, the beauty of the area depicted in films helped to fuel so much growth of the town in the 1950s that it became difficult for filmmakers to find pristine scenery.

ern movie clothing collection in the world.[2] MGM also owned 175 acres of studio property, and the new management's plan was to sell off the back lots for real estate development.

In October of 1972 crews started to bulldoze the sets on Lot 3, which had been used for filming many Westerns, and the lot was left as a derelict ruin covered by mountains of rubble. As a result, MGM's *Westworld* (1973) had to be filmed at Warners, because MGM had already torn down their Western street.[3]

Films that had been made on Western Street on Lot 3 included *The Harvey Girls* (1946) with the street dressed to be Sandrock, Arizona; *Annie Get Your Gun* (1950) where it was used for various locations; *Ride, Vaquero!* (1953) where it was the West in general; *Bad Day at Black Rock* (1955) for some of the exteriors; *The Law and Jake Wade* (1958), where it posed as a town in New Mexico; and for various episodes of the television series *Rawhide* (1959–1966), standing in for various cowtowns.

What was named St. Louis Street on the back lot consisted of a series of very ornate turn-of-the-century houses, including one called the Bluett House. This stately mansion was used for Lilith's (Debbie Reynolds) house in San Francisco in *How the West Was Won* (1962), and for Molly Brown's (Debbie Reynolds) house in Denver in *The Unsinkable Molly Brown* (1964).[4]

Lot 3 also had two cavalry sets, Fort Scott and Fort Canby. The Fort Canby set was used for *A Thunder of Drums* (1961), where it played Fort Canby, and for various episodes of *Rawhide*. Westerns filmed on the Fort Scott set included *Carbine Williams* (1952) and *Dirty Dingus Magee* (1970), where it was used as a cavalry fort.

The buildings on what was called Billy the Kid Street on Lot 3 were built in 1941 to portray New Mexico for *Billy the Kid* (1941) with Robert Taylor. Billy the Kid Street was also used for *The Harvey Girls* (1946) for scenes that did not require the railroad, for *Apache War Smoke* (1952) as the hacienda, *Escape from Fort Bravo* (1953) as the main street of Mescal, *The Fastest Gun Alive* (1956) as the town of Oak Creek, *The Sheepman* (1958), *The Law and Jake Wade* (1958) as a generic frontier town, and for the television series *Rawhide*. It was later used in the modern Western *The Rounders* (1965), with Glenn Ford and Henry Fonda.

In the mid–1980s Kerkorian sold the remaining studio assets to media mogul Ted Turner for $1.5 billion. Turner, who owned Turner Broadcasting System (TBS) and Turner Network Television (TNT), kept the MGM film library, then sold the MGM name, studio, and logo back to Kerkorian. In 1996 Warners merged with TBS and took over control of the massive MGM film library. The remaining real estate and assets were sold off. In 1981 MGM acquired United Artists for $400 million. In November 2010, the remains of MGM filed for bankruptcy.[5]

And so the decline in Hollywood went on. RKO ceased to exist in 1957, replaced by Disney as a major studio. Most of the Twentieth Century–Fox lot was bulldozed beginning in 1961 to create Century City, a 176-acre shopping and business complex. The MGM back lots were demolished and sold off. The Columbia lot on Sunset Blvd was sold off. Universal transformed their back lot into a theme park. Paramount was purchased by Gulf & Western in 1966. Warners continued on, though with diminished production.

The Studio System Transforms

In the wake of the collapse of the traditional studio system, in the mid–1950s a growing number of directors and film stars started to produce their own film projects. One advantage of this new independent system was that the stars and directors obtained tax breaks by working for themselves, while at the same time maintaining more control over their films. They used the traditional studios primarily for financing, the rental of sound stages, and then distribution of the final film. This trend accelerated the already weakening influence of the studio system.

This transformation had been foreshadowed in a low-key way as early as 1919 when William S. Hart was part of the original discussions that led to the creation of United Artists. The company was formed by Mary Pickford, her husband star Doug Fairbanks, director D.W. Griffith, and actor Charlie Chaplin, in order to give them more creative control over their movies. Hart, however, dropped out after he found out that they planned to finance their own productions.[6]

During the golden age of movies, from the 1930s to the 1950s, studio directors usually didn't cast their films (there were exceptions, such as John Ford), they were busy directing. They typically did not write the script, pick the location, set the budget, or cast the stars. They rarely edited Westerns. Instead, the studio system decided and controlled what they made.

As a result of pressures on the industry, the old studio system with its assembly-line production of movies declined and was replaced by independent productions. The power in the industry shifted now to the actors and directors. With the change from the traditional studio system with its movie ranches and captive back lots, the new independent producers moved away from filming Westerns at the studios and increasingly went on location.

Part of the reason was financial. It was often cheaper to film on location than to build costly sets or rent facilities at existing studios with expensive overhead costs. The more obvious reason was that filming on location in the outdoors for Westerns had a far more authentic look than filming on a back lot or sound stage. In most cases the scenery would be too difficult or costly to recreate on the back lot.

In addition, overuse of some movie ranches and sets around Los Angeles had made them overly-familiar to audiences. Like Broncho Billy Anderson 50 years earlier, directors were always on the lookout for new, exciting, and unknown locations for their films. *The Ballad of Cable Hogue* (1970), for example, was filmed on location in Arizona, Nevada, and New Mexico because director Sam Peckinpah did not want the familiarity of Hollywood back lots.[7]

The major studios, on the other hand, returned to their home locations and back lots in an effort to cut costs. They still produced Westerns, but now they struggled with rising costs that made it harder to make a profitable product without cutting corners and cheapening the look of the final film. This presented a dilemma, because theater audiences for Westerns were less willing to put up with artificial-looking rear-projection scenes with the actors speaking their lines while standing in front of a movie screen, and with exterior scenes obviously filmed inside a sound stage or on the same old Hollywood back lot.

An example of how this affected the filming of Westerns was *The Man Who Shot*

Liberty Valance (1962), made by veteran director John Ford. The movie was filmed on the back lot at Paramount and consisted almost all of artificial-looking interiors on Paramount soundstages. Also, it was photographed in black and white, instead of Technicolor.

After the movie was released, it was praised for the director's choice of black-and-white photography, which critics felt gave it a haunting, claustrophobic atmosphere, and created a dark and oppressive mood that emphasized the plot. Ford always claimed that he deliberately chose black-and-white film to create the mood he wanted with its ability to create subtle variations in lighting.[8] However, William Clothier, the director of photography, said that the reality was that the movie was filmed in black and white and on an interior soundstage because Paramount was looking for ways to cut costs and filming on the back lot in black and white was much cheaper than filming in color on location. He claimed that Ford agreed to these conditions because it was a case of either accept the terms or not make the film.[9]

Another significant problem that influenced the decline of studio Westerns was that their stables of movie stars were aging and were not the trim, athletic, romantic figures of their younger years. And the remaining studios tycoons were also aging. By the late 1960s the old-time movie moguls who had built the industry, such as Jack Warner, William Fox, and Harry Cohn, were gone. Many of the original employees at the studios were out of touch with what the newer, younger audiences wanted. Changing audience tastes made the traditional movies seem old-fashioned. And the studios themselves were starting to deteriorate physically, as most of them had not expanded or renovated their facilities in a number of years. Most were physically dated and their management teams were not as aggressive and vibrant as they had been 30 or 40 years before when the studios had been founded. A further factor was that during the 1960s unions made it virtually impossible for anyone to obtain employment on a California movie set unless they were a union member.[10]

The result of these various pressures on the traditional film industry was that the 1960s saw the decline and end of the classic Hollywood studio system. The glory days of the "dream factories" were past. After this transition occurred, directors and actors were no longer bound to long-term contracts, and a new wave of independent filmmakers took the place of captive studio productions.

Another result was that the major studios were taken over by multi-national companies run by teams of managers and accountants. Studio back lots were sold and the number of A-Western film productions sank to an all-time low, even though the production of television Westerns had risen. Western productions that would have been made on location in the West in glorious color were instead filmed in the controlled environment of the studio sound stages or back lots. To counteract this, the major studios started to look at other forms of entertainment, such as making television series and made-for-television movies to keep them busy and fill the production void. Westerns for theatrical release and made-for-TV movies were gradually abandoned. Studios started to become financiers and distributors of movies, rather than producers.

Income tax laws meant that top performers found it desirable, as well as more profitable, to incorporate and produce their own films. Instead of paying themselves straight salaries, they now added stock dividends, pension benefits, and corporate profits, which resulted in a lower tax rate burden for them. Actors formed their own production companies, such as Batjac (John Wayne), Joel Productions (Kirk Douglas), and Malpaso (Clint Eastwood). Some companies were in business to do film production, while others financed pictures and contracted with third parties to make the films.[11] The disadvantage was that this new-found freedom was not as simple as it seemed. John Wayne's *The Alamo* (1960), for example, almost sank his company and he had to invest a large amount of his own personal money to complete the film.[12]

The hope in Hollywood was that independent movie production would lead to greater creativity and better movies, but at the same time directors now found that as producer-directors they had additional responsibilities to those who financed them and the distributors who released their pictures. And to the audiences who paid for the tickets.

The time to the release date of a film was of the essence. Producers had to film a popular commercial product within a reasonable amount of time in order to make a reasonable return on their financier's investment. The new independent filmmakers now had to weigh and balance budgets, resources, and production schedules.

Hollywood Westerns

In 1948 approximately 25 percent of the films produced by the major studios were Westerns. In 1953, 92 Westerns were made by Hollywood. By 1963 this was down to only 11. Hollywood production of Westerns held steady for most of the 1960s at about 20 per year. In 1965 the figure was 22 Hollywood films. These figures were not good. They had declined from 27 percent of films in 1953 to 9 percent in 1963. By 1964 this figure had dropped to about 7.5 percent. The number of all Hollywood feature films was in decline, but Westerns declined faster.[13]

Most Western movies have traditionally been action-packed, particularly the serials and B-Westerns of the 1930s and 1940s. The chases and showdowns between the good guys and cattle thieves, desperadoes, rustlers, claim jumpers, cattle barons, and crooked bank presidents (who usually oozed charm and had thin mustaches) had to take place in real mountains, canyons, and prairies. If a scene called for the wide-open spaces of a mountain pass, a canyon rim, or dusty plains with sagebrush and cactus, then that is where it had to be filmed for audience acceptance. The days of outdoor scenes filmed in studio interiors were in the past.

In spite of all their problems, the major studios continued to produce Westerns in the outdoors. *The Comancheros* (1961) started filming in June of 1961 in scenic Professor Valley, northeast of Moab, Utah. Howard Hawks made three Westerns. He started filming *El Dorado* (1967) in October of 1965 at Old Tucson Studios. This film was essentially a replay of the *Rio Bravo* plot with a few twists, and a few years later he basically retold the same story in *Rio Lobo* (1970), though Hawks continued to claim that they were all different films.[14] Perhaps these were not remakes, but they were all filmed at Old Tucson Studios and all three certainly had plot similarities.

Though television took over the production of cheaply-made Western television series, the epic Western movie remained on the wide screen. Western epics, however, definitely had to be filmed on location to look real. For example, 75 percent of the production of *How the West Was Won* (1962) was filmed on location in places such as the Ohio River Valley, the Black Hills of South Dakota, the Uncompahgre National Forest and Gunnison River in Colorado, and the Sierra Nevada Mountains of California.

How the West Was Won (1962), filmed in Cinerama by MGM, was such a large and complex project that it required the talents of three veteran directors, John Ford, Henry Hathaway, and George Marshall, and four directors of photography, to make it. Even with the simultaneous work of all three directors, the production took about 10 months to film. If MGM had used only one director and one cinematographer it would have taken several years to complete.[15]

For maximum effect the film used far-ranging, powerful scenic outdoor locations for backgrounds, such as the snow-capped Sierra Nevada mountains of California and Mount Whitney for the sequence where Zeb Rawlings (George Peppard) meets with Jethro Stuart (Henry Fonda) at his cabin; the rocky sand-flats of Lone Pine, California, for the Indian attack, complete with a wagon overturning and rolling down into a gully; the Colorado Rocky Mountains around Owl Creek Pass near Ridgway (where the final shoot-out in the meadow in *True Grit* [1969] was also filmed) for the wagon train encampment; and Monument Valley for the final scenes where Lilith and Zeb Rawlings drive to Zeb's ranch. This type of magnificent location scenery was not the same when viewed on a television screen, as opposed to the massive wraparound screen of the original Cinerama theaters.

More than a hundred films have been made in locations like this in southwestern Colorado. Among them, *The Naked Spur* (1953), with James Stewart and Janet Leigh, around Silverton and the San Juan Mountains; *Tribute to a Badman* (1956) with James Cagney, filmed around Ridgway; *How the West Was Won* (1962) with scenes filmed around Ridgway, Montrose, Durango, and Silverton; *True Grit* (1969) filmed in Ridgway and on Owl Creek Pass to the east, on top of the mountain range; and *Butch Cassidy and the Sundance Kid* (1969) filmed around Durango, Silverton, and Telluride. *How the West Was Won* (1962) was one of the many films that showed off the beauty of the fall colors in the southwest corner of Colorado, as the aspen leaves turned from the green of summer to yellow and gold in the fall. The courthouse scenes for *True Grit* (1969) used an existing building in Ouray, a small historic town to the south of Ridgway set in a beautiful mountain bowl surrounded by soaring high peaks on three sides.

Across the Border to Mexico

Rising costs of productions filmed in Hollywood during the 1950s and 1960s, coupled with the trend towards independent production, caused much of the filming of Westerns to move to locations outside the United States.

Sharply rising costs made conditions economically sound for producers and directors to begin shooting Western films in Mexico. Mexico had sunny outdoor locations that were relatively close to Los Angeles, production costs for filming were lower than in Hollywood, and parts of Mexico looked very much like directors' visions of the American West. *The Magnificent Seven* (1960), for example, was filmed

In the mid–1950s construction techniques for movie sets changed with the introduction of fiberglass. This plastic material was lightweight, durable, and easier to work with than wood or concrete. Though this building used as the homestead in *The Outlaw Josey Wales* (1976) looks like it was built from adobe bricks, it is lightweight fiberglass that has been spray-painted to give it the appearance of weathered mud.

in Cuernavaca, Mexico. *Hondo* was filmed at Camargo, Mexico, 500 miles south of El Paso, because the director considered the barren and sunbaked terrain to be his ideal background for a Western.[16]

The wide-open landscape and the small existing primitive towns in parts of rural Mexico were ideal for representing the American Southwest of the late 1800s. This was perfect for filming stories that were set in New Mexico, Arizona, or Texas. And so Mexico became the new representation of the Western landscape.

A popular outdoor location for filming Westerns was Durango, Mexico, which was about 600 miles south of El Paso, Texas. Durango as an outdoor film location was first discovered by Hollywood in the 1960s. The landscape was primitive, unspoiled, and isolated, consisting mostly of a combination of sandy desert and arid mountains, which made it a popular location for Western films. Between 1969 and 1972, actor John Wayne made seven Westerns there. They were *The Sons of Katie Elder* (1965), *The War Wagon* (1967), *The Undefeated* (1969), *Chisum* (1970), *Big Jake* (1971), *The Train Robbers* (1973), and *Cahill U.S. Marshal* (1973).

Much of *The Professionals* (1966), though set in Mexico, was filmed in Valley of Fire State Park, near Las Vegas, Nevada, and in Death Valley in California. *The Ballad of Cable Hogue* (1969) was also filmed in Valley of Fire.

In the 1970s, when the production of big-budget Westerns declined drastically, even the use of Durango became too expensive to use as a location.[17]

Westerns Go Overseas

In the late 1950s, while high production costs in Hollywood and the popularity of Western television shows such as *Gunsmoke* and *Rawhide* started to decrease the output of theatrical Westerns at the American box office, the Western genre still remained very popular and profitable in Europe. Hollywood Westerns, such as *The Magnificent Seven* (1960), which at the time of its initial release was only moderately successful in the United States, was very successful in Europe.

To meet a high demand for theatrical Westerns that was not being supplied by the Hollywood studios, several European countries decided to make their own. Thus a dominant trend that emerged in the 1960s was making Westerns on location in Europe. The British, for example, made *The Sheriff of Fractured Jaw* (1958), directed by veteran Hollywood Western director Raoul Walsh, with English actor Kenneth More and American actress Jayne Mansfield. This movie was the first Western made in Spain. This was not a new concept, however, as Europe, specifically Germany, had produced popular Westerns in the 1930s and 1940s.

The production of Westerns was primarily taken over by the Germans and the Italians to meet their domestic markets, as well as for export. Both countries took Westerns seriously, and these films could be made in Europe at a much lesser cost than Hollywood productions. Producers of this new wave of Westerns tried to keep up with the times and seek a wider audience by adding liberal amounts of violence and sex. This new European style of Westerns was terse and violent, but still only partly realistic. The new trend, however, became so popular that Hollywood started making co-production deals with European companies and using American actors as stars.

Several Western movies were filmed in Yugoslavia as German-American co-productions, using magnificent local scenery that looked like the early American frontier landscape, with mountains, lakes, rivers, waterfalls, and pine forests. Ironically, then, this approach brought filming full circle, back to the days when American Westerns were filmed in the lush forests of the East.

The European trend included the Winnetou series. From the late 1870s to 1910, German author Karl May wrote a series of Western novels that described the adventures of Winnetou the Warrior, an Apache chief, and his white friend and blood brother Old Shatterhand, a pioneer. The Winnetou novels are estimated to have sold in the millions, and have been translated into more than 30 languages.

In 1962 a West German company filmed *The Treasure of Silver Lake* (1962), the first of a series of Winnetou films based on May's novels about the American West. French actor Pierre Brice played the Apache warrior Winnetou, and American actor Lex Barker, who had previously played Tarzan, was Old Shatterhand, Winnetou's friend. The film was a huge financial success in Europe. As a result, more Winnetou films were made between 1962 and 1968 in West Germany and at Split in Yugoslavia, near the Adriatic Coast.

Spain and Italy

There was also a resurgence of the Western after the sudden unexpected popularity of three non-traditional Western films made in Italy and Spain by director Sergio Leone. As a result of their imagery, the sunbaked deserts of southeast Spain became the new audience vision of the West.

Making movies in Italy and Spain was not a new practice. In the late 1950s and early 1960s Rome was second only to Hollywood as the international film capital of the world. Cinecittà Studios, in particular, was well-known for producing mass-appeal movies. They made films in an assembly-line type of process, somewhat like the Hollywood B-Westerns of the 1930s. Shooting schedules were typically five to six weeks, sets were used over and over again, and the same pieces of stock action footage showed up in various productions. One big difference from Hollywood filming was that most of the films were shot without sound and then voices were dubbed later in various languages for release in different countries.

The Italian film industry of the late 1950s and early 1960s specialized in historical spectacles, many of them developed around mythic heroes, such as Hercules and Goliath, played by actors such as Steve Reeves, Kirk Morris, and Ed Fury. These burly, muscular men were often ex-Mr. Universe contestants.

Four main heroes appeared commonly in these movies: Hercules, Maciste, Ursus, and Sampson. Two of the first of these "muscleman films" were *Hercules* (1958) and *Hercules Unchained* (1959), starring Steve Reeves as Hercules. They were followed by *Hercules in the Haunted World* (originally titled *Hercules at the Center of the Earth*) (1961) and *The Fury of Hercules* (1962). Other brawny musclemen appeared in movies such as *Ursus* (1960) and *The Revenge of Ursus* (1961).

Often derisively called "sword and sandal" epics by critics, these were the type of film that typically played in double features at the drive-in theaters of the 1960s. The heroes used muscle power to solve all the problems they encountered, often in the manner of today's comic strip heroes. These movies were very successful in the United States and Britain due to strong advertising campaigns by their U.S. distributor, Embassy Pictures.

The villains in these movies were a mix bag, consisting of gladiators, Babylonians, or Atlanteans, and even pirates, vampires, and men-in-the-moon. The genre was popular enough that an entire series of sword-and-sandal epics appeared between 1958 and 1964, many of them made by the directors of the later Spaghetti Westerns.

American film companies had previously made historical spectacles in Spain and many Hollywood epics were filmed in Rome. Examples are *Helen of Troy* (1955), *Alexander the Great* (1956), *The Pride and the Passion* (1956), *Ben Hur* (1959), *Spartacus* (1960), *El Cid* (1961), *King of Kings* (1961), and *55 Days at Peking* (1963).

Sergio Leone, later to become famous for popularizing the Spaghetti Western, helped with the direction on two of the Roman spectacles, *The Last Days of Pompeii* (1959) and *The Colossus of Rhodes* (1960). Leone went to law school in Rome before joining the film industry as an assistant director. He worked with the second unit (which typically films action scenes) on the battle scenes of *Helen of Troy* (1955), the action sequences in *El Cid* (1961), was second unit director on *Sodom and Gomorrah*

(1962), and was an assistant director for the famous chariot race sequence in *Ben Hur* (1959).

El Cid (1961), *King of Kings* (1961), and *Lawrence of Arabia* (1962) were filmed on location in Spain because labor and other production costs were cheaper than in the United States at a time when the major studios were faced with rapidly rising costs in Hollywood. In addition, due to tax implications, money that American companies made in Europe had to be spent in Europe. For this reason, several of the major studios opened subsidiaries in Europe, such as the MGM-British Studios facility at the town of Borehamwood in England, also nicknamed "British Hollywood." This was an entire second MGM studio facility that included seven soundstages and was nearly a hundred acres in size.[18]

The craze for historical epics came to an end in 1962 when expensive historical epics like *The Last Days of Sodom and Gomorrah* (1962) failed at the box office. As a result, American financiers pulled back and the money to make this type of spectacle dried up. As banks stopped extending credit for these movies, the Italian film industry went into the doldrums. By 1963, Roman Empire, the cornerstone of the Italian film industry at Cinecittà Studios in Rome, was starting to disintegrate.

In an effort to develop and exploit the next fad in film genres, Italian filmmakers tried to branch out in various different directions, such as thrillers, horror movies, swashbuckler films, science fiction, and pirate movies.[19]

But then the Italian film industry hit on a new trend.

Spaghetti Mayhem and Violence

One of the influences that started the Italian Western trend was the financial success of *The Treasure of Silver Lake* (1962). This turned out to be one of the most popular releases in Germany, and was a huge commercial success. So the Italian film industry turned to create a new type of Western.

The so-called Spaghetti Westerns of the 1960s began with a series of overlooked Italian-Spanish co-productions that had little impact on audiences until the release of Sergio Leone's *Fistful of Dollars* (1964). Before this success, Italian producers had mostly ignored Westerns, though Spanish directors had made a series of movies based on Zorro, the swashbuckling bandit-hero of Old Spanish California. But with the success of *The Treasure of Silver Lake* (1962) producers jumped on the Western bandwagon. Between 1963 and 1965 a total of 130 Westerns were produced in Europe by Italian filmmakers, in conjunction with various Spanish, French, and West German companies. In 1965, out of a total of 144 Italian-made and financed films, 24 were Westerns. The Western boom continued for the next two years.[20] Italian Westerns were so popular that in the 1960s and 1970s American companies went to Spain and fueled the craze.

The term "Spaghetti Western" was a derisive label applied by American critics to describe the violent Westerns made in Italy and Spain between 1963 and 1977.[21] These new films were different than the traditional Hollywood Westerns. The hero of the Italian Western was not a cowboy, but was an anti-hero gunfighter, a mercenary without scruples who looked out mainly for himself. For example, one of the main characters in *The Good, the Bad, and the Ugly* (1966), Tuco (Eli Wallach), was known for his many crimes, which included murder, armed robbery, rape, arson, perjury, bigamy, and deserting his wife. Another difference in these new Westerns was that the Italian directors had a fascination with violence.

The most famous of these Westerns aimed at American audiences were Sergio Leone's "Dollars Trilogy," consisting of *Fistful of Dollars* (1964), *For a Few Dollars More* (1965), and *The Good, the Bad, and the Ugly* (1966). In them Leone transformed the clean-cut, grinning Rowdy Yates (Clint Eastwood) from the American television series *Rawhide* into a squinty-eyed, terse-lipped, stubble-chinned, cigarillo-smoking anti-hero. In *Fistful of Dollars* (1964) he had no morals as he pitted two gangs against each other. These films made an icon of Eastwood's poncho-clad gunfighter, "the Man with No Name," as the distributor's publicity promoted him.[22]

The real craze for Spaghetti Westerns started in the United States and the United Kingdom in the mid–1960s after the success of Leone's Dollars Trilogy. Distributors such as United Artists, Avco Embassy, and Columbia quickly started buying the rights to Italian Westerns that were successful in Europe and released them in the U.S. Profits were large as United Artists purchased the rights to the first two Dollars movies for only $35,000 and $70,000, respectively.[23]

Leone tried to recreate what he thought was the real West with brutality, blood, and lingering close-ups of ugly villains. The films featured Leone's vision of intense violence, an apparent lack of heroic motivation, and a penchant for sadistic behavior by the protagonist. In spite of all the blood-drenched violence in these movies, Leone claimed that his westerns were "fairy tales for adults."[24]

As Spaghetti Westerns gained in popularity in the mid–1960s, production companies rushed to film and release the same type of movie while the trend was still selling well. More than 500 Spaghetti Westerns were made between 1963 and 1969, with 300 or so released in Italy.[25]

By the late 1960s and early 1970s, films in general, and Western movies in particular, contained more sex, violence, and brutality. The Spaghetti Westerns, along with the offshoots they spawned, contain multiple shootings and assorted scenes of violence. The body count kept creeping higher and higher. *Fistful of Dollars* (1964) showed a brutal beating and screen make-up to match. Leone's *Once Upon a Time in the West* (1968) showed the cold-blooded murder of the entire McBain family, including the father, two sons, and a daughter.

Spaghetti Westerns were predominantly Italian and Spanish-Italian co-productions, with Italian directors filming on location in Spain with international casts. International stars were included to give the films an international appeal. For example, if the Germans were financing a film, they typically wanted a German star somewhere in the cast to increase the film's popularity in the German market.

The custom in Europe was to film Westerns without sound so that the edited movie could be dubbed into various languages in post-production. The soundtrack was dubbed into English, French, German, Spanish, or Italian, depending on the distribution plan. European releases that were not considered economically feasible for dubbing into a separate language were given subtitles.[26]

As an actor in a film might be speaking French, German, Italian, Spanish or English, depending on the actor, a loss of lip synchronization was sometimes visible during the dubbing process. As a result, sound editors often had to make on-the-spot changes to the planned voice script to match the dialog movements on the screen.

By the same token, filming could also be difficult if different nationalities spoke their lines in their native languages. American actors who did not speak German or Spanish commented that this was confusing. They often did not know during dialog scenes when the European actors had finished their spoken lines and when they should speak theirs. One actor wryly commented that this actually helped to create dramatic pauses in some instances while an actor waited to be sure that another actor was finished.[27] For simplicity, one particular actor did not speak his lines from the script during filming, but simply counted from one to 10 with the appropriate facial expressions.[28] By 1967 the directors of Spaghetti Westerns realized that it would be better if the actors all spoke English to ensure maximum distribution of the film, which of course translated into maximum profits.

The names of Italian and Spanish actors (and crew members) were often Americanized to make international audiences feel that this type of movie was a genuine American Western product. Even director Sergio Leone called himself Bob Robertson on the screen for *Fistful of Dollars* (1964). Casts often included European stars with either Anglicized names or an American pseudonym in order to appeal to American audiences. On the other hand, actors might use German names for German audiences. Europeans, particularly the Italians, liked big American star names and the producers wanted the Italians to think that these were real Americans. And Hollywood stars responded. Many acted in Spaghetti Westerns, including Clint Eastwood, Burt Reynolds, Lee Van Cleef, Charles Bronson, Cameron Mitchell, and even a few old timers, such as Alan Ladd, Broderick Crawford, and James Mason. By 1966 the vast majority of these Westerns became vehicles for has-been actors on the way down or were cheap B-movies.

The Italian Westerns were primarily filmed outdoors at movie towns and Western movie town sets on location in the countryside around Rome, with interior scenes filmed in Rome on rented studio sets and sound stages. There were three primary Western town sets near Rome: Cinecittà Studios, Elios Studios, and Dino De Laurentiis's studio complex named Dinocitta. The Cinecittà town set was constructed in 1964 at the studio complex that was known as "Hollywood on the Tiber." Elios Studios was founded in 1962 by Alvaro Mancori. In 1964 a Western village set, the most frequently used Italian Western town setting, was added for *The Last Gun* (1964). An adobe Mexican village was added later. At Dinocitta, De Laurentiis added a Western set built for *The Hills Run Red* (1966).

Outdoor locations at Lazio, the administrative district that surrounds Rome, and Abruzzo, the adjacent region to the northeast containing national parks and protected reserves, were frequently used for location scenes for these low budget westerns. Some of the locations that will be visually familiar to Spaghetti Western fans are the gorge at Tolfa, the quarries at Magliana, Manziana around Bracciano Lake, and Abruzzo National Park. It was rare to burn down or otherwise destroy a set in an Italian Western as the sets were used and re-used so often that this would have been a waste of money.

Filming in Spain

The most distinctive locations for many of these Westerns were outdoor locations in Spain, where Spanish producers had been making Westerns since 1962, because parts of Spain appeared to producers to be very like the American West. Like the Italians, the Spanish constructed several western sets. Balcazar Studios in Barcelona had their own town set at Espluges De Llobregat, that was constructed and used for a series of Spanish Westerns.

The main areas of Spain used for locations for making Westerns were Madrid and Almeria. The province of Almeria (in Andalusia), had a dry, desert landscape where temperatures routinely exceeded 100°F in the summer. Because of this, Almeria, was affectionately known as the "Armpit of Europe."[29] Filming Spaghetti Westerns in Almeria provided movie audiences with a new vision of "the West." They now saw it as the sunbaked deserts of the extreme southeast corner of Spain. The barren rocky desert and the sun-bleached, dusty towns of the Spaghetti Westerns tended to look like the Westerns filmed in Death Valley and the deserts of Utah. By the late 1960s the Almeria area was overrun by film crews shooting Westerns, war movies, and Arabian adventures.

As well as Almeria, another principal location used to film Spanish Westerns was the area around Guadix in the province of Granada. This was popularly used for railroad scenes and those requiring use of the railway station at La Calahorra, which was 11 miles east of Guadix. La Pedriza, 20 or so miles north of Madrid, at the foot of the Sierra de Guadarrama, was used for its scenic rock formations.

Two Western towns were constructed north of Madrid. One was a set at Colmenar Viejo ("Old Beehive," sometimes referred to as Aberdeen City) built for the British Western *The Sheriff of Fractured Jaw* (1958). The other was a Western village near Colmenar Viejo at Hojo De Manzanares, in the Hojo De Manzanares mountains north of Madrid. The Hojo De Manzanares Western village, constructed in 1962 for the earlier series of Zorro movies, was redressed for the movie *Fistful of Dollars* (1964) to become the set for the town of San Miguel. The desert riding sequences were shot in Almeria.

Leone's films featured a dry, dusty desert landscape that came to signify the West as a place of open space for plenty of action. *For Few Dollars More* (1965) was shot in 12 weeks from April to July of 1965. The interior scenes were filmed at Cinecittà Studios in Rome. The Cinecittà back lot Western town set became the town of Santa Cruz. The exteriors were shot mainly in the Almeria desert, where the village of Los Albaricoques ("The Apricots") in the Cabo de Gata-Níjar Natural Park in Andalusia became Agua Caliente. The set for El Paso was designed and built specially for the film near Tabernas. The scenes in the interior of the saloon at El Paso was the set at Tabernas with desert and mountain scenes shot nearby. The Western town at Colmenar Viejo was filmed as White Rock. The New Mexico town of Tucumcari was the redressed set from *Fistful of Dollars* (1964) at Hojo De Manzanares. Leone's depictions of Tucumcari, Agua Caliente, El Paso, and later Sweetwater, presented his vision of the West as full of grime, dirt, and poverty.

The Good, the Bad, and the Ugly (1966) was Leone's epic Western centered around the American Civil War. The plot was loosely based around a real-life incident in 1862 when Gen. Henry Hopkins Sibley led Confederate forces out of Texas to invade New Mexico. His eventual intention was to capture the rich gold fields of Colorado and California as a way to help finance the war for the South. Sibley reached Valverde, New Mexico, and engaged Union troops in what became known as the Battle of Valverde. He then marched northwards towards Santa Fe, seeking to capture the army's Fort Union. His forces were defeated at Glorieta Pass, just east of Santa Fe, in a battle that has been called the "Gettysburg of the West." Part of Sibley's difficult trek north of Valverde went through a long, bleak, open stretch of waterless desert in south-central New Mexico that was named in Spanish times as the *Jornada del Muerto* ("Journey of the Dead Man").

Leone filmed his version of the story from May to July 1966, first at the Elios Studios in Italy, then moved to location shooting in Spain to represent New Mexico and the Sangre de Cristo Mountains. The ghost town in the opening was specially constructed in the hills in Almeria. The set built as El Paso for *For a Few Dollars More* (1965) was redressed to become the town of Valverde. The set at Tabernas was reused for Valverde, Santa Ana, and Santa Fe. The town of Peralta was the Western town at Colmenar Viejo dressed to show shell damage. The railroad station at La Calahorra, near Guadix, became the railroad station. The Civil War battle scenes were filmed at the River Arlanza outside Bargos, north of Madrid. The circular graveyard set at the climax of the movie was built at Carazo, south of the river.

Almeria in the province of Andalusia is the location visually most familiar to fans of Spaghetti Westerns. Almeria is Europe's only desert. It is a stark and barren land, but has plenty of sunshine and clear blue skies for predictable filming weather. Many scenic locations were available to directors in the surrounding area, including the rock formations at La Pedriza (in the Guadarrama Mountains), the reservoir at Santillana, and the landscape of Manzanares El Real. In spite of a certain similarity to New Mexico, though, the landscape and vegetation in the area were typically Spanish and didn't look like the American West. The villages, for example, consisted of low white houses with tile roofs, an architecture that was typical of old rural Spain rather than the West of the United States.

The most inhospitable of the filming locations was the Tabernas Desert in the rain-shadow of the mountain ranges surrounding it. This consisted of treeless plains with rolling hills, punctuated by occasional dried-up gullies and riverbeds. The Western set near Tabernas in 1965 used for filming *For a Few Dollars More* was known through the 1970s as Yucca City, then it became Mini Hollywood (now called Oasys), a Western-themed tourist attraction with Wild West cowboy stunt shows.

Texas Hollywood (now known as Fort Bravo) was constructed in the early 1970s north of Mini Hollywood, half of it as a Western town and the other half as a Mexican pueblo-style village. In 1970 a huge fortress was built west of Texas Hollywood for *El Condor* (1970), but it was in disrepair by 1986. In 1970 film producer and studio owner Dino De Laurentiis built a cavalry fort near Malaga for *The Deserter* (also known as *The Devil's Backbone*) (1971) and a whitewashed prison set near Tabernas for *A Man Called Sledge* (1970). The coast at Cabo De Gata and San Jose had whitewashed villages that if filmed carefully could be made to look like the authentic West.

The third tourist attraction near Tabernas was Western Leone, a smaller Western theme park that was originally built to be the Sweetwater Ranch for Sergio Leone's epic Western *Once Upon a Time in the West* (1968). The movie was filmed from April to July of 1968 in Almeria and a small amount was filmed the United States.

Leone wanted to film part of *Once Upon a Time in the West* (1968) in Monument Valley as a tribute to John Ford, because Leone admired Ford's Westerns. Initial filming took place in Arizona, then Leone ran into difficulties with his American crew and found too much interfering background clutter, such as telephone poles, where he wanted to film. He therefore moved the entire production to the deserts of Almeria and filmed the interiors at Cinecittà in Rome.[30]

The problem then became what to do with the material he had already filmed in Monument Valley. This was the one location that Leone wanted to keep in the film. His solution was to recreate Monument Valley on the back lot at Cinecittà and keep the original footage. When Jill McBain (Claudia Cardinale) and Sam (Paolo Stoppa) drive from the town of Flagstone to Sweetwater in a buggy during a sweeping panning shot, they are driving through the real Monument Valley. Part of the following scenes, where Morton's surveyors try to flag the carriage down as they drive through the railroad construction site, were filmed in front of a gigantic painted backdrop of desert buttes and mesas.[31] Interestingly, then, some aspects of filming had come full circle, back to the days of the Wild West shows and early silent movies that were filmed on back lots with painted backdrops.

The opening of *Once Upon a Time in the West* (1968) was filmed at the railroad station at La Calahorra, near Guadix, with the nearby set for the town of Flagstone unseen in this sequence, though it was next to the railroad tracks. The Flagstone set was a real town with buildings, streets, and alleys, not just back-lot facades, created by production designer Carlo Simi at a cost of $250,000. The set was left standing after filming was complete and was later used for other productions. The Flagstone set did not appear as prominently in the film's U.S. release as in the European version, as the U.S. distributor, Paramount, made cuts to the American version to trim the film to the running length they wanted.[32]

Meanwhile, Almeria continued to be used for other Westerns. For example, *Django* (1966) was filmed on location at Colmenar Viejo and at Manzanares El Real. The Fort Cheriba set in the movie was located near Santillana Reservoir.

Navajo Joe (1966), an action Spaghetti Western starring American actor Burt Reynolds was one of many filmed in Almeria and around Castile. The plot revolved around a group of scalphunters led by a brutal half-breed who killed Indians for the reward on their scalps. This was a grim and violent theme to begin with, but further gruesome activities included graphic depictions of bloody beating, scalpings, whippings, and killings by knife, garotte, and tomahawk. The Colmenar set near Madrid was used for filming and interiors were shot at the Dino De Laurentiis' Dinocitta studio near Rome. The Navajo Indian camp massacre scene was filmed at Tor Caldera in Italy.

This film shows a classic example of the problem of filming in different locations. Desert, forest, and grasslands scenes were filmed at various locations, including the railroad tracks at Guadix. The fictional town of Esperanza where the gang hides out was filmed at the set at Tabernas. The problem was that the two locations that were supposed to be Esperanza did not always match in continuity. Part of the footage showed lush grasslands and other parts were obviously barren desert. At one point the gang rides up a street in Italy and arrives outside the bank in Spain.

In the late 1960s, the craze for spaghetti Westerns was still in full swing. *A Bullet for the General* (1966) was originally supposed to be filmed in Mexico but, due to logistical problems, filming was moved to Almeria. The Mexican settlements were filmed at local villages, such as Polopos standing in for San Miguel. The Guadix railway station was back again to play the rail depot at Cuidad Juarez. Almost the entire film was shot on location, including the interiors.

In *Death Rides a Horse* (1967), Sergio Leone's El Paso set at Tabernas from *For Few Dollars More* (1965) was re-dressed to become Lyndon City. The Lyndon City railway sequences were shot at La Calahorra. Filming also took place at the Western set at Cinecittà and at the Western village at Elios.

Face to Face (1967) was filmed on location in Spain and at Elios Studios in Italy. Again the Spanish landscape of mountains, gullies, dunes, and dried-up riverbeds in Almeria became the American southwest. The train station at Purgatory was La Calahorra, outside Guadix.

Spaghetti Westerns were commonly set in New Mexico because the desert country of Almeria was ideal for portraying the New Mexico landscape. In *A Pistol for Ringo* (1965), the town of Quemado ("burned field" in Spanish) was based on a real town in New Mexico, near the Arizona border. The filming location was the Balcazar Studios' "Wild West" town set at Esplugues De Llobregat, near Barcelona. Location scenes were also shot in the dried-up riverbeds and gullies of Almeria and in San Jose. *The Return of Ringo* (1965), which was set in the New Mexico settlement of Mimbres in the southwest corner of New Mexico, was filmed at Balcazar Studios.

Day of Anger (1967) was set on the borderlands of Arizona and New Mexico. The real town of Clifton was west of the Little Burro Mountains, Bowie was 50 miles to the south, and Stafford was between the other two. For location filming in Spain, Los Albaricoques, which had been Agua Caliente in *For Few Dollars More* (1965), was used for Bowie, and Clifton City was filmed at the Cinecittà Studios in Rome.

Before Leone's *Fistful of Dollars* (1964) was released, only about 25 Italian Westerns had been filmed. After the release of the film in Europe was met with such great success, over 300 Spaghetti Westerns were released in Italy between 1963 and 1969. The peak period for production was 1966–1967 when 66 were made. Fewer than 20 percent of these were distributed internationally, but this ended up overloading the market. By 1969 only seven Italian Westerns were made.[33]

The 1970s: Spaghetti Westerns Return to the U.S.

The popularity of the Spaghetti Westerns eventually created a return of Westerns to locations in the U.S. and Mexico as Westerns were imported back to Hollywood. But they also returned with all the violence of the Spaghetti Western. The new cowboy protagonist (it is hard to think of him as a hero) was a gunfighter rather than a cowboy, and was tough, ruthless, violent, cold-blooded, self-centered, and callous, taking advantage of everyone wherever he could. The beating scene and other violence in *Day of Anger* (1967), for example, was so graphic that several scenes were cut by censors.

Taking a cue from the popularity of the violence in the Italian movies, *The Wild Bunch* (1969), filmed entirely on location in Mexico, ended with five long minutes of violent carnage as seemingly everybody in sight was shot, knifed, machine-gunned, or blown up. These last scenes of graphic violence led to the first R-rating for a Western. Other violence included beatings, knifings, and death by gunfire. Blood spurted rather than dripped. Author Lee Mitchell commented, "In a sneak preview in Kansas City thirty-odd people walked out, some physically ill."[34] Some critics hailed this as a fresh, realistic approach. Others were outraged.

Following this trend, location work for *Two Mules for Sister Sara* (1970) with Clint Eastwood and Shirley MacLaine was entirely filmed in Mexico, except for some work back on the back lot at Universal. Like others influenced by the increasing trend in violence, it also had several scenes of violence that had to be cut to win an acceptable rating in England.

The success of the Spaghetti Westerns ushered in new themes that included extraordinary scenes of brutality, violence, and cruelty. *Butch Cassidy and the Sundance Kid* (1969) ended with a new twist, the death of the heroes. *True Grit* (1969) showed John Wayne in a new light, where he was sadistic instead of fair, enjoyed drinking, and

This is the high desert of New Mexico, south of Santa Fe, with its piñon-juniper ecosystem and the characteristic pointed hills that make movies filmed there easy to recognize. Westerns filmed in the area include *The Man from Laramie* (1955), *Cowboy* (1958), *Butch Cassidy and the Sundance Kid* (1969), *Young Guns* (1988), and *Cowboys and Aliens* (2011).

was motivated by money instead of a desire for justice. *The Shootist* (1976) and *Open Range* (2004) both contained graphic scenes of violent shootouts.

Another film that contained gratuitous violence was *McCabe & Mrs. Miller* (1971). This movie was also notable for using the weather encountered during location filming to create additional atmospheric effects to add to the plot. It was filmed in weather that included the rain and snow that pervades the film and helped to create the gloomy atmosphere that the director wanted. *McCabe & Mrs. Miller* (1971) also used a more true-to-life background as a filming location. The plot supposedly took place in the town of Presbyterian Church, a mining town in the turn-of-the-century state of Washington, though it was filmed in British Columbia, Canada. The setting was a cluttered town, built for and during the film where, as film historian Ted Sennett put it, "wretched people live out their wretched existences."[35]

In contrast to most Westerns, both the landscape and the weather were dreary, which was admittedly realistic for the Northwest, with mud, snow, and water everywhere. The building of the church (which is burned down at the end) was a theme running through the movie and the town was actually built as the movie progressed. Half-built buildings and lumber were seen with trash and rubble everywhere, which gave the impression of the building and development of a mining town as it really happened. This was realistic in terms of the kind of real town that is found in historical photographs of the early West. *McCabe & Mrs. Miller* (1971) contains no blue skies or red buttes of the idealized Monument Valley, only snow and rain.

Some of these 1970s Westerns had an international basis. *My Name Is Nobody* (1973), with Sergio Leone as the producer, was partially filmed in the American West, and partially in Spain. American filming locations included the ghost towns of Cabezón and Mogollon in New Mexico, as well as Acoma Pueblo and White Sands National Monument in the same state. The volcanic plug of Cabezón Peak, which is visible for miles around, appeared in the background of the film.

The ghost town of Cabezón was used for the opening shootout at the barbershop. The saloon where Nobody (Terence Hill, Americanized from Mario Girotti) met Jack Beauregard (Henry Fonda in his last Western) was filmed in the ghost town of Mogollon, a mining town from the 1890s near Glenwood, New Mexico. The general store opposite the saloon was constructed for the film. Other parts of the film were shot in Almeria, using the train station at La Calahorra. Cheyenne City was adapted from Leone's original Flagstone set at La Calahorra. The final battle with the film's Wild Bunch (not to be confused with the Wild Bunch of the Peckinpah film) was shot on the open plains near the Guadix railway line.

My Name Is Nobody (1973) contained a humorous reference to Sam Peckinpah, the director of *The Wild Bunch* (1969), in the graveyard scene shot outside San Esteban Del Rey Mission at Acoma Pueblo, near Grants, New Mexico. Nessuno (Terence Hill) walked past a grave in the Acoma cemetery, then stopped and looked at the name on the wooden cross on one grave marker and said, "Sam Peckinpah. That's a beautiful name in Navajo."

By the early 1970s, a few Spaghetti Westerns were still being cranked out, but the popularity of the genre was in decline as the traditional audience for Westerns turned to thrillers, horror films, and comedies. By the mid–1970s, the European Western had essentially died away. The audience had withered, but producers tried every variation to try to create a continuing market for Westerns. This was a time of Westerns for children, science-fiction Westerns, soft-core pornographic Westerns, and Western parodies.

By the 1970s the traditional Western and audience interest in the Western film genre was in decline again. The 1970s were also the end of the transition period for the major Hollywood studios during which they evolved from kingdoms run by the old-time movie moguls into vast and diversified corporations managed by lawyers and accountants. The studios had mutated from feudal family businesses into corporate conglomerates. New blood and new talent came into the industry, and younger people were making movies for younger audiences. The expense and overhead of shooting in Hollywood turned most of the studios into corporate headquarters. They were used to film pick-up shots that the director and crew had overlooked or forgotten to film on location. Editing, post-production, and soundtrack scoring continued to be mostly done in Hollywood because the existing infrastructure was already there.

The release of Westerns reached a peak between 1969 and 1972 with an average of 24 per year. The high was 19 in 1971, but by 1973 this had fallen to only 13. In 1974 only seven were released. Between 1972 and 1975 Western series also disappeared from television.[36]

The 1970s was a time of renewal in Hollywood with the popularity of blockbuster movies and franchises such as *Star Wars*. These were big-budget, big-star blockbusters that were followed by a string of sequels that translated into big box-office dollars. Fewer films were in production, but the Hollywood mantra was "bigger and better."

In the late 1970s and early 1980s, movies about the occult, science fiction, horror, thrillers, and kung-fu became popular. Outer space themes, such as the *Alien* and *Star Wars* series of movies, were embraced by movie audiences. In spite of this, Western themes continued, though in altered settings. *Outland* (1981), for example, with Sean Connery as a Federal District Marshal investigating a series of murders at a titanium mining colony in outer space, is a classic Western plot in a science fiction setting.

Westworld (1973) was a Western and gunfighter movie also with a decidedly science-fiction twist. One of the characters in the movie who has just returned from Westworld says that when he and his friends played "cowboys and Indians" as kids, they pointed their fingers at each other in the classical gun configuration and went "bang, bang." Now, as an adult, he says he can live out his fantasies shooting cowboy robots that are programmed to look, talk, act, and bleed like real gunfighters.

The 1970s was the end of the John Wayne era with *The Shootist* (1976), set in 1901 and filmed in Carson City, Nevada, and the back lot at Warner Bros/Burbank Studio. Aging gunfighter J.B. Books realizes that he is dying of cancer and enters into a final gunfight. Wayne had made 82 feature-length pictures between 1939 and 1972.

Also by the late 1970s, Westerns had become so stereotyped that they left themselves open to parody in such movies as *The Villain* (1979), which makes fun of the hero (Handsome Stranger), the villain, the girl, and the Indians. Other earlier popular satires were *Cat Ballou* (1965) and *Blazing Saddles* (1974).

The Continued Effect of Television

The Western has always owed much of its popularity to the use of rugged, widespread landscapes for the background, and this wide sweep of the outdoors lost a lot on the small television screen. Westerns, however, were consistently among the top-rated television shows for most of the period from 1955 to 1970. Between 1957 and 1960 there were routinely nine to 12 Westerns in the top 25 shows. During the 1958–1959 season, seven of the top 10 television shows were Westerns. From 1957 to 1961 the top-ranked show was always a Western. The average audience share for Western television series between 1957 to 1961 was about 35 percent. No other genre of action-adventure television show captured such a high share of prime time for so many years.[37]

But by 1960 critics were complaining about all the violence on television. When the surgeon-general announced that there was a relationship between violence on television and in real life, in response the small screen changed to Westerns with less violence, such as *Bonanza*. In *Sugarfoot* (1957–1961) the star, Will Hutchins, shunned violence, playing the part of a pacifist cowboy law student.

By the 1971–1972 season both movies and television had mostly abandoned the Western except for old reruns of theatrical films that were often relegated to a time slot late at night. By the early 1970s, television demographics had become more important than numbers. *The Virginian* (1962–1970), for example, went off the air not because it was not popular, but because most of the audience was rural and working class, and not the affluent middle-aged urban audience that advertisers wanted.[38]

By 1973, when *Bonanza* went off the air, series Westerns had essentially faded from popularity among television viewers.

The 1980s and the Blockbusters

The 1980s were characterized by further growth of the blockbusters. These were formulaic large-budget features enhanced by spectacular CGI (computer-generated imagery) special effects and high concept production design. The successful ones spawned many sequels and were a part of franchises that were popular with audiences.

By the late 1980s the Western had fallen on hard times again. Fewer and fewer were made, and most of them received a lukewarm reception at the box office. *The Long Riders* (1980), the stories of the Younger and James gangs, didn't do well at the box office, nor did *Pale Rider* (1985). Neither did *Silverado* (1985), which was an attempt to bring back the rousing old-fashioned Western. The movie *Young Guns* (1988) spawned a television version in the form of *Young Riders* (1989–1992), and later a movie sequel *Young Guns II* (1990), but none of them generated a tremendous amount of interest among audiences. *Heaven's Gate* (1980) has arguably been called one of the greatest box office disasters of all times. This movie was such a financial and critical failure that it almost bankrupted United Artists and scared other producers and financiers away from making Westerns.[39] As one critic rather unkindly opined, he felt it was "an epic that fairly boggles the mind in its excess and incoherence."[40] Other critics felt that the movie effectively killed the genre of the Western.

Making Westerns was also overwhelmed by corporate juggling. For example, in 1989, Warners and its parent company Warner Communications merged with Time, Inc., and became known as Time-Warner. Time-Warner purchased Lorimar Telepictures, which had been formed in 1969 to produce television shows, including such hits as *The Waltons, Dallas,* and *Knot's Landing.* Lorimar was then incorporated into Warner Television and effectively shut down as a separate entity. Columbia, who was sharing the Warners lot at the time, was purchased by Sony, who now became part owners of The Burbank Studios, which operated the Warners lot. Sony gave up ownership in the Burbank Studios in exchange for the Culver City Studio. And as a result the Columbia Ranch went back to Warners. All this corporate business maneuvering made it difficult for producers of Westerns to keep the players straight and do their job.

The 1990s and On

The 1990s were about the same. The movie remakes of the popular 1960s television shows *Maverick* (1994) and *The Wild Wild West* (1999) did not do well at the box office. *Geronimo: An American Legend* (1993) didn't excite audiences. Neither did *The Mask of Zorro* (1998), *Tombstone* (1993), or *Wyatt Earp* (1994). The 1990s continued the growth of more spectacular CGI effects and major studio blockbusters, such as *Jurassic Park* (1993), *Mission Impossible* (1996), and *Titanic* (1997).

The extreme violence started by the Spaghetti Westerns continued. *Bad Girls* (1994) and *Open Range* (2003) are examples of the increased level of violence dictated by audiences. Though filmed on location in beautiful country, both movies built up to violent, blood-spattered shootouts at the end.

Movie audiences demanded and expected more action and violence, thus the Western kept changing to accommodate this in *The Wild Bunch* (1969), *Unforgiven* (1992), and the *Django* series. The early Django films were not protected by copyright, therefore different versions were filmed by several different directors, totaling more than 30 sequels and derivatives. *Django Kill* (1967) was arguably one of the most gruesome and violent of the Spaghetti Westerns. In a touch of irony, *Django Unchained* (2012) used one of Ennio Morricone's themes from an earlier Spaghetti Western.

Dances with Wolves (1990), on the other hand, which told its story from an Indian viewpoint, depicted the white man as being corrupt and the Indian way of life in harmony with nature as superior. The movie, beautifully filmed on location in the Black Hills of South Dakota to show off the vast scope of the land and the open horizons of the West, won seven Academy Awards and set off new craze for Westerns.

Other Westerns filmed in the early 2000s included *The Alamo* (2004) and *The Missing* (2003). HBO's *Deadwood*, which focused on Wild Bill Hickok, Calamity Jane, and Al Swearengen (owner of the real Gem Theater in Deadwood, South Dakota), was gritty, violent, and foul-mouthed. *Brokeback Mountain* (2005) focused on the love between two 1960s cowboys as they herded sheep in Wyoming.

Silverado (1985), *3:10 To Yuma* (2007), *Cowboys and Aliens* (2011), *The Magnificent Seven* (2016), and others took extensive advantage of the stunning cliffs, canyons,

The stunning red-and-white striped cliffs, canyons, and broad grassy flats around the Ghost Ranch in the heart of Georgia O'Keeffe country north of Abiquiu, New Mexico, were a popular background for Westerns. Seen here are one of the cabins and the remaining corral that are still standing from the modern Western *City Slickers* (1991).

and broad grassy flats around The Ghost Ranch, located north of Abiquiu, New Mexico. The ranch was also used for *City Slickers* (1991), a modern Western. Two cabins, a two-story barn, and several corrals were built for the production, with one of the cabins and a corral still standing.

It was indeed spectacular country for a filming location. In 1937 noted artist Georgia O'Keeffe, who lived at the ranch, said, "[It is] perfectly mad-looking country—hills and cliffs and washes too crazy to imagine and thrown up into the air by God and let tumble where they would. It was certainly as spectacular as anything I've ever seen..."

And perhaps that should sum up the West of the movies.

Postscript

Of all sound films made between about 1920 and 1970, approximately 25 percent were Westerns. Indeed, during this time, much of the stability of Hollywood was due to the production of routine bread-and-butter Westerns, which guaranteed a theater audience and a steady income for the studio.

Part of the reason was the gorgeous scenery of the American West. In popular culture, the Hollywood visual image is what dominates, and thus the image of "the West" in the minds of movie audiences has emerged as consisting of barren and lonely deserts, rather than the lush green forests of the East that appeared in the first Western films.

As the preceding chapters have described, changes the motion picture industry from about 1900 to 1970, along with changing audience preferences and tastes, affected how and where Westerns were filmed, whether inside on a studio soundstage, on the back lot, at some rugged outdoor location in the West, or overseas in Spain and Italy. As the industry evolved, the visual perception of the West changed as filmmaking matured during the first 70 years of movies, and the original center of movie production in New York moved westwards to flourish in Los Angeles.

Just as there was not one "West" for a filming location, there was not one "Western." Western movies changed and evolved along with the tastes and desires of their audiences. Movies, like any product manufactured for public consumption, are intended to make money. In the last analysis, a movie has to appeal enough for its audience to pay hard-earned dollars to see it. Movies are judged not necessarily solely on the basis of artistic merit or technical achievements, but by their success at the box office. They have to cater to the popular audience tastes of the times. When circumstances and popular tastes change, so also must a filmmaker in order to survive.

For viewing audiences of the early 1900s, the lush forests of the East were considered to be the real "West." By the 1940s and 1950s audience perceptions changed this image into the open landscapes of the real West of New Mexico, Colorado, Wyoming, Montana, South Dakota, Nevada, and Texas. In the 1960s, the West became the dry, lonely, sunbaked deserts of Mexico and southern Spain.

In 1989 Mauduy and Henriet analyzed 191 Western films and found that the majority had been filmed about equally in Utah, Arizona, and California, with the second largest number being filmed in Mexico.[1]

Iconic Images of the Movie West #10: Death Valley, California. **Death Valley National Park was used as a filming location until the 1960s for productions such as** *Escape from Fort Bravo* **(1953),** *The Bravados* **(1958),** *The Law and Jake Wade* **(1958),** *The Professionals* **(1966), and of course the long-lived television anthology series** *Death Valley Days.* **The raw setting of Death Valley, with its dry, seemingly barren desert landscape and surrounding mountains, presents a bleak image that is an appropriate background for some of the bleak plots used in Westerns.**

The West of the Tourist

Today, fans of Western movies still try to find the "real West" and recreate the visions they have seen filmed in movie locations. To this end, some towns in the West use their past history and lurid images to capitalize on tourism. Tombstone re-creates the Gunfight at the O.K. Corral daily for the entertainment of the tourists flocking to the town to find the real West. Dodge City has a re-creation of Front Street, where cattle herds and drovers gathered at the end of the trail from Texas. Deadwood entertains tourists with a re-creation of the trial of Jack McCall after he shot and killed Wild Bill Hickok. Prescott, Fort Worth, Cheyenne, and Cody add their images of the Old West. Western-themed festivals, such as Covered Wagon Days, Frontier Days, Pioneer Days, Helldorado Days, and other similar annual events keep the spirit and vision of the Old West alive with rodeo, riding wild horses and steers, calf roping, and bulldogging contests.

The first Helldorado Days festival was staged in Tombstone, Arizona, in October 1929. The event was held during the week of the gunfight at the O.K. Corral, which occurred on October 26. The festival was named after the book *Helldorado* (1928) by former Tombstone deputy sheriff Billy Breakenridge. The name supposedly originated in a remark that appeared in the *Daily Nugget* of July 1881, when an old prospector said he came to find "El Dorado," but found "Hell Dorado" instead.

The Helldorado festival offered re-enactments of shootouts, hangings, killings, lynchings, stagecoach robberies, and a bevy of fancily-dressed saloon ladies. However, John Clum, former editor of the *Epitaph* newspaper of Tombstone said that this image did not resemble the Tombstone he lived in and remembered. It was, rather, an image that the tourists expected from the movies. During the time Clum was there, he remembered only one street battle and one lynching.[2] Ed Garrett, a previous lawman who advised director John Ford on period details in his Western films, said that in Tombstone he never saw flashy clothes and dance-hall girls in short skirts, as are commonly portrayed in Western films.[3] And he was correct. Though a discussion of the subject is outside the scope of this book, Victorian-era women—even saloon girls—did not wear the type of clothing, or reveal the amount of cleavage or leg that is shown on the shady ladies in Westerns. That would have been considered unthinkable at the time. But, nevertheless, movie-makers and literary legend-makers continued to embellish and distort the facts in movies such as *Tombstone: The Town Too Tough to Die* (1942) with Richard Dix and Victor Jory, and *Gunfight at the O.K. Corral* (1957).

One of the locations highlighted in the Helldorado festival was Boot Hill, a popular feature from Westerns as the name for the cemetery that often formed part of the background in movie plots. Boot Hill was a popular generic name for the cemetery in Tombstone, Arizona, though the original name was the more prosaic Tombstone Cemetery. The name arose from the idea that villains in the West died in gunfights and were buried with their boots on, as opposed to dying peacefully at home in bed with their boots off, like respectable folks. There were actually two cemeteries in Tombstone. The original Boot Hill cemetery was so quickly filled with gamblers, cutthroats, thieves, and prostitutes that some of the more respectable people did not want their loved ones buried in such a place. So they banded together and started a second cemetery.

For the first Helldorado festival in 1929, the organizers found that the original Boot Hill cemetery had fallen into ruins. Most of the original markers had been wooden boards and the wood had rotted away, fallen down, or been stolen by souvenir hunters. Thus many of the graves were not marked. Though many of the existing graves could not be identified from public records, new headboards were erected with succinct and catchy epitaphs painted on them, many of which were fictional or borrowed from other Boot Hills around the West.

In the 1950s the citizens of Dodge City capitalized on their own past notorious reputation and built Dodge City's Front Street Replica and carved a similar Boot Hill out of the hillside that was the south slope of the original cemetery. The life of the original Boot Hill in Dodge City, on a hill just northwest of Front Street, was short-lived and it was used by only a few. If the deceased had enough money, they were buried at nearby Fort Dodge. If they had none, they were buried quietly out on the Kansas prairie. Like Tombstone, Dodge City's Boot Hill is a mock graveyard with comic headboards. But tourists still flock to see the fake graves with their made-up epitaphs. They are going to see a vision induced by the movies of a place in the West that never was.

Perpetuating the Myth

An interest question that has perplexed those who study Western film is whether Hollywood takes its visual cues from the real world, or whether it is the other way around. After *The Virginian* was published in 1902, even real cowboys started to incorporate features from the book into their own lives to reflect what they felt was their image of themselves as tough individuals.[4] Many working cowhands even adopted the clothing styles and look of the screen stars. As one old-time cowboy remarked, "Well, maybe we didn't talk that way before Mr. Wister wrote his book, but we sure all talked that way after the book was published."[5] Rancher Carey McWilliams remembered that cowboys on his father's Colorado ranch read Western pulp novels and tried to imitate the cowboy heroes described in them.[6]

Like any other form of entertainment, Western movies build on what has gone before. Many Westerns therefore replicated what had previously been seen in Westerns, and thus many Western movies tended to look like previous Western movies. Wayne Sarf has commented that Sergio Leone's Spaghetti Westerns, for example, did not reflect so much the appearance of a specific time and place in the American West as reproduce much of what had been seen previously in American Westerns.[7]

The Myth on Film Today

Out-of-state tax incentives, along with a search for cheaper material and labor costs, have led producers to make films in locations other than Hollywood. At the present time, much of the location filming of Westerns is affected by the size of the financial and other incentives that film companies can negotiate with various state and local governments, and rebates are now an important factor in the decision of where to film. The old-time studios have become the financiers and distributors of movies, with less and less of the production performed in-house. Full-service studios, such as ABQ Studios in Albuquerque, are available for rent in cities other than traditional Hollywood.

In 1997 Canada started marketing its scenery as a lower cost alternative for filmmakers willing to make movies outside the Hollywood system. And they added tax breaks and other financial incentives for doing so. As of this writing Vancouver, British Columbia, has the fourth largest film and television production industry in North America. Ahead of it are Los Angeles, New York, and Toronto. This has given Vancouver the nickname of "Hollywood North."

Previously, the major studios acted like an assembly line, with a stable of stars and permanent production crews. For the new independent producers, each film now becomes a new project. A new production line has to be created, and talent and crew hired specifically for each movie. Support services, such as lab work and post-production, are contracted out. At the end of the film, everyone is laid off and has to be re-hired for the next movie.[8]

Just like Broncho Billy Anderson and the other early Western filmmakers, directors and producers still try to find new and exotic locations to use for the backgrounds to their films. Examples are *Willow* (1988) and the *Lord of the Rings* movies that were filmed against the stunning backdrop of New Zealand, *The Scorpion King 3: Battle for Redemption* (2012) that was filmed in Thailand, and *The Scorpion King: Book of Souls* (2018) that was filmed in South Africa. Another factor in the search to outdo other films in terms of location is the use of "digital backlots," which are virtual film sets created inside a computer. One example of this is *How the Grinch Stole Christmas* (2000), where all the backgrounds were created digitally.

Monument Valley continues to be popular for filming television commercials and advertising photographs, which perpetuates that particular image of "the West." The rugged landscape of Monument Valley is what moviegoers feel that the real West should look like. As one example, when the animated feature *Rango* (2011) wanted to depict the iconic West of the Westerns, one background setting used was a cartoon version of Monument Valley. Other cartoons that used the same type of background to denote the West were *An American Tail: Fievel Goes West* (1991) and Warner Brothers' series of Road Runner stories.

Western movies have always distorted the reality of the landscape and history of the American West into the directors' and producers' versions of "real" history to enhance their entertainment value. So too, Western movies have presented an idealized vision of the plains, deserts, and magnificent landscapes of the American West. A long shot of a horse and its rider against a huge backdrop of mountains, vast spaces of grassy range land, or the emptiness and loneliness of the reddish desert provide unforgettable images. As a result, the audience concept of "the West" developed over the years into a type of mythic image of "Western" geography that often consists of a sweeping view of Monument Valley, with a background of immense blue skies and puffy white clouds, and red sandstone buttes and mesas towering over the actors.

And that's not all bad.

Chapter Notes

Preface

1. Quoted in Stanton, *Where God Put the West*, 1.
2. Readers wishing to study criticism of Western films might enjoy books such as *Western Films 2: An Annotated Critical Bibliography from 1974 to 1987* by Jack Nachbar, Jackie R. Donath, and Chris Foran (New York: Garland Publishing, 1988) or *The American West in Film: Critical Approaches to the Western* by Jon Tuska (Westport: Greenwood Press, 1985).
3. Jack Weston, *The Real American Cowboy* (New York: New Amsterdam Books, 1985), 209.

Chapter One

1. Nachbar, *Focus on the Western*, 2.
2. Hamilton, *Thunder in the Dust*, 13.
3. Kitses and Rickman, *The Western Reader*, 90–91.
4. McDonald, *Shooting Stars*, 28.
5. An amusing incident occurred when a friend of the author's moved from Colorado to New York to live. When she showed color photographs of where she grew up, some of her friends back East would not believe that the West really had the incredibly blue skies shown in the pictures, but insisted that the photographs had been digitally enhanced.
6. Hamilton, *Thunder in the Dust*, 155.
7. In two of my previous books I have explored history as presented by the movie industry versus the real history of the West (*The Old West in Fact and Film: History Versus Hollywood*, McFarland, 2012) and the creation of the cowboy as a mythic heroic image (*The Creation of the Cowboy Hero: Fiction, Film and Fact*, McFarland, 2015). Interested readers may wish to consult one or both of these volumes for further background on the creation of mythic aspects of the West versus the historical reality.
8. For more information on this subject, see Jeremy Agnew, *The Age of Dimes and Pulps* (Jefferson: McFarland, 2018).
9. The term "Manifest Destiny" was coined in 1845 by the editor of the *New York Morning News*, John L. O'Sullivan, as a rallying cry to justify the concept that Americans had the moral obligation to settle the vast empty areas of the West between the Mississippi and the Pacific Coast.
10. James Sullivan, *Jeans: A Cultural History of an American Icon* (New York: Gotham Books, 2006), 48.
11. Wallis, *The Real Wild West*, 434.
12. Reddin, *Wild West Shows*, 76.
13. Mangan, *Colorado on Glass*, 19.
14. Mangan, *Colorado on Glass*, 232. As one example of the confusion this could cause, the only verified photograph of Billy the Kid, believed to have been taken in Fort Sumner, New Mexico, in 1879 or 1880, is a full-length portrait that shows him with a holstered Colt single-action revolver on his left hip. Because of this photograph, he has been theorized to have been left-handed, which was the inspiration for the title of the movie *The Left-Handed Gun* (1958). However, because the photograph was a tintype, the image was reversed, and the holster was actually on his right hip. As further confirmation, firearms expert Robert Wilson has pointed out that the loading gate for the Winchester carbine shown in the photograph appears on the left side of the rifle, whereas in reality it would be on the right side of the gun (Robert L. Wilson, *Winchester: An American Legend* [New York: Random House, 1991], 46).
15. Mangan, *Colorado on Glass*, 100.
16. Kitses and Rickman, *The Western Reader*, 122–123.
17. Mangan, *Colorado on Glass*, 102.
18. Celluloid is the trademark name for a clear flexible plastic material used as a base for motion picture and X-ray film.
19. Mangan, *Colorado on Glass*, 207.
20. Allen, *Horrible Prettiness*, 260.
21. Mangan, *Colorado on Glass*, 323. For those interested in technical information, film speed is a measure of a film's sensitivity to light. A high numerical speed number, known as the exposure index, is more sensitive to light than a film with a low speed number. Film speed in the United States is designated by the American Standards

Association (now renamed ANSI, the American National Standards Institute) and is specified as an ASA number. Film speeds for amateur film for general-purpose daylight use in film cameras in the 1960s and 1970s typically ranged for color film from ASA 25 to ASA 160 and for black-and-white film from ASA 125 to ASA 400, or even up to ASA 1600 for use with low light levels. For comparison, Kodak's Ektachrome-X color film of the 1970s for making slides had an ASA rating of 64 and High-speed Ektachrome was ASA 160. In Europe the rating for film speed is given as a DIN number, which stands for *Deutsches Institut für Normung*.

22. Due to a biological phenomenon called persistence of vision, if individual photographs are viewed at a rate of more than about 16 per second, our eyes will not distinguish the individual pictures, but will perceive them to be in continuous motion. This minimum viewing rate is called the "flicker rate." Indeed an older slang name for motion pictures was "the flickers." When sound was introduced, the standard projection speed for 35mm movies was increased from 16 to 24 frames per second to eliminate variations in sound quality. Thus, when viewed today, many early movies have a speeded-up, jerky quality. The reason is that early movies were shot with hand-cranked mechanisms that exposed 16 frames per second. When replayed on projectors that ran at 24 frames per second, the film (and the action on it) is indeed speeded up, resulting in the frantic motion we associate with old-time comedy films.

23. The same type of mythology appears in films about British India. They were always conceptually set in the 1890s, which was a time that conveniently summarized British rule in India.

24. Cowie, *John Ford and the American West*, 191.

Chapter Two

1. Spencer, *Hollywood of the Rockies*, 14.
2. Allen, *Horrible Prettiness*, 265.
3. This would be about $200 in 2019 dollars.
4. David Shipman, *The Story of Cinema* (New York: St. Martin's Press, 1982), 36.
5. Goetzmann and Goetzmann, *The West of the Imagination*, 306.
6. Smith, *Shooting Cowboys and Indians*, 39.
7. Smith, *Shooting Cowboys and Indians*, 9.
8. *Sioux Ghost Dance* (1894) was filmed only four years after the emergence of the real Ghost Dance ceremony that was a contributing factor in the tragic battle between the U.S. army and Sioux Indians at Wounded Knee Creek in South Dakota in 1890 that essentially ended the Indian wars.
9. At the time Cripple Creek was the location of a rich gold strike in Colorado. The reserve of gold ore at Cripple Creek was so big that gold is still actively being mined there. First developed in 1890, it was the biggest strike in the United States and to date has yielded over 23 million ounces of gold.
10. The decidedly masculine-looking bartender probably was a man, as men often played the roles of women in early movies.
11. Bingen, *Warner Bros.*, 96.
12. O'Neil, *The End and the Myth*, 206. The length of *The Great Train Robbery* (1903) has been given as nine minutes, 10 minutes, or 12 minutes, depending on the reference consulted. The author's copy runs 11 minutes and 30 seconds, with an additional 15 seconds of actor Justus Barnes blasting away at the audience with his six-gun in a close-up, to be spliced in at the beginning or the end of the film, as the distributor preferred. No matter, it was one reel long.
13. Goetzmann and Goetzmann, *The West of the Imagination*, 302.
14. Fenin and Everson, *The Western*, 50.
15. Smith, *Shooting Cowboys and Indians*, 11–12.
16. Smith, *Shooting Cowboys and Indians*, 39.
17. Mangan, *Colorado on Glass*, 201.
18. Smith, *Shooting Cowboys and Indians*, 15.
19. Smith, *Shooting Cowboys and Indians*, 13.
20. Smith, *Shooting Cowboys and Indians*, 9.
21. Spencer, *Hollywood of the Rockies*, 43.
22. At several places in the movie there is a curious banner attached to trees that sports a diamond design with the initials "WNS" inside. Harry Buckwater put this identifying flag with Col. Selig's initials in several scenes of his movies to prevent unauthorized copying and exhibiting of Selig films. This was a common practice among film companies at the time.
23. Smith, *Shooting Cowboys and Indians*, 22.
24. Kitses and Rickman, *The Western Reader*, 115.
25. Jones and Jones, *Buckwalter*, 143.
26. Kitses and Rickman, *The Western Reader*, 42.
27. Etulain and Riley, *The Hollywood West*, 2–4.
28. Smith, *Shooting Cowboys and Indians*, 26.
29. Golden, Colorado, was to have later strong ties to Western history when showman Buffalo Bill Cody was buried in a steel vault under two tons of cement on June 17, 1917, on top of Lookout Mountain, which overlooks the town.
30. Goetzmann and Goetzmann, *The West of the Imagination*, 303.
31. George-Warren, *Cowboy*, 46.
32. Buscombe, *The BFI Companion to the Western*, 24.
33. Garry Wills, *John Wayne's America: The Politics of Celebrity* (New York: Simon & Schuster, 1997), 311.
34. Tuska, *The Filming of the West*, 13.
35. Tuska, *The Filming of the West*, 6.
36. Buscombe, *The BFI Companion to the Western*, 28.

37. George-Warren, *Cowboy*, 51.
38. Wallis, *The Real Wild West*, 342.
39. Wallis, *The Real Wild West*, 344.
40. Smith, *Shooting Cowboys and Indians*, 43–45.
41. Smith, *Shooting Cowboys and Indians*, 55.
42. This practice for shooting on location did not change for a long time. When John Ford was filming in Monument Valley in the 1940s, he had to use a private plane to ship exposed film daily to Los Angeles for processing.
43. Smith, *Shooting Cowboys and Indians*, 51.
44. In the early days of movie distribution, prints of films were purchased by exhibitors rather than being rented. "Exchanges" were businesses where exhibitors traded or sold films after they had shown them to other exhibitors who needed new material. Later, copies of films were rented instead of purchased, and exchanges became wholesalers who purchased films from production companies and then rented copies to theaters.
45. Smith, *Shooting Cowboys and Indians*, 80.
46. Tuska, *The Filming of the West*, 7.
47. Wallis, *The Real Wild West*, 365.

Chapter Three

1. Smith, *Shooting Cowboys and Indians*, 21.
2. Buscombe, *The BFI Companion to the Western*, 24.
3. Smith, *Shooting Cowboys and Indians*, 105–106.
4. Simmon, *The Invention of the Western Film*, 9.
5. Simmon, *The Invention of the Western Film*, 34.
6. Smith, *Shooting Cowboys and Indians*, 54.
7. Tuska, *The Filming of the West*, 37.
8. For those with a technical interest, the speed of the film used was on the order of ASA 10. See Chapter Note 21 for Chapter 1 for more information about ASA.
9. Smith, *Shooting Cowboys and Indians*, 135–136.
10. Tuska, *The Filming of the West*, 17.
11. Cowboy movie stars Tom Mix, Hoot Gibson, Buck Jones, Ken Maynard, and others performed with the show before they became famous on film.
12. Wallis, *The Real Wild West*, 358–359.
13. Fred J. Balshofer and Arthur C. Miller, *One Reel a Week* (Berkeley: University of California Press, 1967), 76.
14. Eyman, *Print the Legend*, 27.
15. Wallis, *The Real Wild West*, 371.
16. Smith, *Shooting Cowboys and Indians*, 106.
17. Eyman, *Print the Legend*, 27.
18. Wallis, *The Real Wild West*, 374.
19. Smith, *Shooting Cowboys and Indians*, 161.
20. George-Warren, *Cowboy*, 58; Nachbar, *Focus on the Western*, 5.
21. Jon Tuska, *The American Western Cinema: 1903-Present*, quoted in Nachbar, *Focus on the Western*, 33.
22. Wallis, *The Real Wild West*, 235.
23. Horwitz, *They Went Thataway*, 74.
24. Reddin, *Wild West Shows*, 204.
25. Goetzmann and Goetzmann, *The West of the Imagination*, 303.
26. Slotkin, *Gunfighter Nation*, 64.
27. Wallis, *The Real Wild West*, 237.
28. Wallis, *The Real Wild West*, 602.
29. Reddin, *Wild West Shows*, 191.
30. Fenin and Everson, *The Western*, 111.
31. Tuska, *The Filming of the West*, 51.
32. Fenin and Everson, *The Western*, 112.
33. Reddin, *Wild West Shows*, 190.
34. Bingen, *Warner Bros.*, 208.
35. Reddin, *Wild West Shows*, 195.
36. Krefft, *The Man Who Made the Movies*, 323.
37. The name "cliff-hanger" was derived from the practice of putting the hero in a perilous situation at the end of each chapter of a serial, so that the audience had to return the next week and watch the next chapter to see how he escaped. A typical cliffhanger showed the hero fighting the villain in a speeding car without a driver or on top of a runaway stagecoach as the vehicle careened towards a cliff.
38. Goetzmann and Goetzmann, *The West of the Imagination*, 304.
39. *Motion Picture World*, April 26, 1913, 367.
40. Wallis, *The Real Wild West*, 368.
41. Tuska, *The Filming of the West*, 43.
42. Wallis, *The Real Wild West*, 395. Thomas Ince died at his home on November 19, 1924, at age 42, after being taken ill on the *Oneida*, the luxury yacht of newspaper magnate William Randolph Hearst. The official cause of death was heart failure, but in true Hollywood fashion, unconfirmed rumors in the *Los Angeles Times* for November 16, 1924, hinted that he had actually died of a gunshot wound (Wallis, *The Real Wild West*, 439–440).
43. Buscombe, *The BFI Companion to the Western*, 38.
44. Smith, *Shooting Cowboys and Indians*, 164–166.
45. Smith, *Shooting Cowboys and Indians*, 82–83.
46. Jensen, *The Movie Railroads*, 78.
47. Tuska, *The Filming of the West*, 60.
48. Bingen, *Warner Bros.*, 5.
49. Kenneth Anger, *Hollywood Babylon II* (New York: E.P. Dutton, 1985), 40; Wallis, *The Real Wild West*, 403.
50. Krefft, *The Man Who Made the Movies*, 2, 286.
51. Krefft, *The Man Who Made the Movies*, 703.

52. Bingen, *Warner Bros.*, 6–7.
53. Bingen, *Warner Bros.*, 17, 208.
54. As the authors of *M-G-M: Hollywood's Greatest Backlot* humorously pointed out, if the names had been combined the other way, the company would have been Selfish Pictures.
55. Bingen, Sylvester and Troyan, *M-G-M*, 18.

Chapter Four

1. Cowie, *Seventy Years of Cinema*, 55.
2. Tuska, *The Filming of the West*, 131.
3. Buscombe, *The BFI Companion to the Western*, 36.
4. Krefft, *The Man Who Made the Movies*, 366.
5. Griffith and Mayer, *The Movies*, 120.
6. Krefft, *The Man Who Made the Movies*, 1.
7. Kenneth Anger, *Hollywood Babylon II* (New York: E.P. Dutton, 1985), 41.
8. Bingen, *Warner Bros.*, 16.
9. Smith, *Shooting Cowboys and Indians*, 179.
10. The film was based on the real-life foiling of a train robbery by Dick Gordon, as related by Paul Leicester Ford in his book *The Great K & A Train Robbery*, originally published as a serial in *Lippincott's Monthly Magazine* in 1896.
11. Jones and Jones, *Buckwalter*, 151.
12. John Wayne's introduction to the film business was when he worked at Fox Studios as a prop man in the late 1910s, where he met Tom Mix. Wayne was part of the Mix unit that went to Colorado to film *The Great K & A Train Robbery* (1926) as a prop boy. Mix gave him some work as an extra in the film (Munn, *John Wayne*, 17).
13. The beginning of the film states that the exterior filming was done in "The Royal Gorge of Colorado." Filming actually took place along the Colorado River in Glenwood Canyon, just east of Glenwood Springs, Colorado. Today the name "Royal Gorge" is traditionally applied to a ten-mile stretch of rugged canyon along the Arkansas River, just west of Cañon City, Colorado.
14. Wallis, *The Real Wild West*, 448.
15. Reddin, *Wild West Shows*, 195.
16. Krefft, *The Man Who Made the Movies*, 363.
17. Jensen, *The Amazing Tom Mix*, 111.
18. Krefft, *The Man Who Made the Movies*, 323.
19. Tuska, *The Filming of the West*, 88.
20. This is the correct spelling for the corporation; however, the hyphens were never used in the screen logo (Bingen, Sylvester, and Troyan, *M-G-M*, 19).
21. Krefft, *The Man Who Made the Movies*, 386.
22. Bingen, *Warner Bros.*, 11.
23. Bingen, *Warner Bros.*, 209.
24. An entertaining parody of the time of transition from silent pictures to talking movies is the MGM musical *Singin' in the Rain* (1952), which delightfully satirizes the difficulties that two of the main characters undergo during the change, including problems with sound pick-up, the use of a camera "sweat-box," the pitfalls of dubbing and synchronization of voices, and the realization that not all actors had voices suitable for the talkies.
25. Bingen, *Warner Bros.*, 15.
26. Fox also developed a first-class news reporting organization under the name of *Movietone News* for theatrical release of newsreels.
27. Krefft, *The Man Who Made the Movies*, 438.
28. Etulain and Riley, *The Hollywood West*, 5.
29. Krefft, *The Man Who Made the Movies*, 489–490.
30. Stanfield, *Hollywood, Westerns and the 1930s*, 25–26.

Chapter Five

1. Tino Balio, *Grand Design: Hollywood as a Modern Business Enterprise, 1930–1939* (New York: Charles Scribner's Sons, 1993), 15–17.
2. Garry Wills, *John Wayne's America: The Politics of Celebrity* (New York: Simon & Schuster, 1997), 312.
3. Stanfield, *Hollywood, Westerns and the 1930s*, 124.
4. Buscombe, *The BFI Companion to the Western*, 39.
5. The promotional technique of giveaways to attract audiences, such as Bank Night and drawings for various prizes, continued through the 1960s.
6. Slotkin, *Gunfighter Nation*, 255–256.
7. Buscombe, *The BFI Companion to the Western*, 39.
8. Simmon, *The Invention of the Western Film*, 100. There are several collections of old B-Western movies that have been re-issued on DVD. A good way to get a feel for them is to watch one of these collections, such as "Cowboys and Bandits" from Mill Creek Entertainment, a collection of 50 movies, a 12-disc set consisting of 47 hours and 40 minutes of features, mostly from the 1930s, with a few from the 1940s and three similar ones from the 1950s.
9. Tuska, *The Filming of the West*, 88.
10. Buscombe, *The BFI Companion to the Western*, 37.
11. Tuska, *The Filming of the West*, 349.
12. Tuska, *The Filming of the West*, 425.
13. George-Warren, *Public Cowboy No. 1*, 160–161.
14. George-Warren, *Public Cowboy No. 1*, 138.
15. McDonald, *Shooting Stars*, 30.
16. George-Warren, *Public Cowboy No. 1*, 129.
17. *The Phantom Empire* (1935) was one of the oddest of the singing B-Westerns. The bizarre

plot is more understandable if the reader knows that Wallace McDonald, one of the writers, claimed that the idea came to him while he was under the influence of laughing gas at the dentist (George-Warren, *Public Cowboy No. 1*, 131). Odd as *The Phantom Empire* (1935) was, it was a great success, particularly among rural audiences, and its success may have encouraged the filming of the science-fiction films *Flash Gordon* (1936) and *Buck Rogers* (1939).

18. Tuska, *The Filming of the West*, 408.
19. McDonald, *Shooting Stars*, 90.
20. Smith, *Shooting Cowboys and Indians*, 205.
21. *Canon City Record*, October 11, 1911.
22. Beale's Cut became obsolete as a roadway when the nearby Newhall Tunnel was completed. The tunnel was then eliminated when the Sierra Highway was widened and improved. The remains of Beale's Cut today is located northwest of Newhall, just off the east side of the Sierra Highway, approximately one mile south of San Fernando Road and a half-mile north of the junction of the Golden State and Antelope Valley freeways, where Interstate 5 and Highway 14 split just south of Newhall. In 1998 a rockslide that was the result of an earthquake filled much of the remaining cut.
23. Tuska, *The Filming of the West*, 163.
24. Fenin and Everson, *The Western*, 292.
25. Fenin and Everson, *The Western*, 293.
26. Mitchum, *Hollywood Hoofbeats*, 15.
27. O'Neil, *The End and the Myth*, 201.
28. Mitchum, *Hollywood Hoofbeats*, 63.
29. Munn, *John Wayne*, 7–8, 13.
30. Etulain and Riley, *The Hollywood West*, 36
31. Munn, *John Wayne*, 56.
32. Tuska, *The Filming of the West*, 379.
33. Eyman, *Print the Legend*, 185.
34. Anne Hillerman, *Rock with Wings* (New York: Harpercollins, 2015), 16.
35. Aitchison, *A Traveler's Guide to Monument Valley*, 41.
36. Anne Hillerman, *Rock with Wings* (New York: Harpercollins, 2015), 59.
37. Aitchison, *A Traveler's Guide to Monument Valley*, 30.
38. Cowie, *John Ford and the American West*, 187.
39. Moon, *Tall Sheep*, 150–151
40. Cowie, *John Ford and the American West*, 186.
41. Miller, *Hollywood Censored*, 126–127.

Chapter Six

1. Buscombe, *The BFI Companion to the Western*, 38.
2. Bingen, *Warner Bros.*, 67; Colorado Springs Utilities, "Renewable Energy Projects Break Ground," *Connection*, July, 2019.
3. Bingen, *Warner Bros.*, 69.
4. Bingen, Sylvester, and Troyan, *M-G-M*, 48.
5. Bingen, *Warner Bros.*, 69–70.
6. Tuska, *The Filming of the West*, 378.
7. Eyman, *Print the Legend*, 476.
8. Eyman, *Print the Legend*, 180.
9. *The Searchers* (1956) resulted in Ford having to wear an eye-patch in real life. He went into hospital for removal of cataracts before filming the movie, but took the bandage off one eye prematurely and, as a result, lost the sight in it completely (Cowie, *John Ford and the American West*, 99)
10. Cowie, *John Ford and the American West*, 166.
11. John Mack Farragher, "The Tale of Wyatt Earp," in Mark C. Carnes, ed., *Past Imperfect: History According to the Movies* (New York: Henry Holt and Company, 1995), 154
12. Burns, *Tombstone*, 29.
13. Cowie, *John Ford and the American West*, 59.
14. Eyman, *Print the Legend*, 292–294.
15. Eyman, *Print the Legend*, 96, 318.
16. Eyman, *Print the Legend*, 314.
17. Tuska, *The Filming of the West*, 516.
18. Eyman, *Print the Legend*, 313
19. Cowie, *John Ford and the American West*, 182.
20. Munn, *John Wayne*, 177–178.
21. Eyman, *Print the Legend*, 421.
22. Lana Wood, *Natalie: A Memoir by Her Sister* (New York: G.P. Putnam, 1984), 23.
23. Cowie, *John Ford and the American West*, 195.
24. Tony Hillerman, *Sacred Clowns* (New York: HarperPaperbacks, 1993), 143–144.
25. Eyman, *Print the Legend*, 190.
26. Eyman, *Print the Legend*, 331.
27. Eyman, *Print the Legend*, 190
28. Stanton, *Where God Put the West*, 15.
29. Lawton, *Old Tucson Studios*, 59.
30. Stier, *The First Fifty Years of Sound Western Movie Locations*, xi
31. D'Arc, *When Hollywood Came to Town*, 140.
32. D'Arc, *When Hollywood Came to Town*, 172.
33. The "Rat Pack" was originally an informal group of influential actors, first organized by Humphrey Bogart and later led by Frank Sinatra (Murray, *Cinema Southwest*, 8–9)
34. U.S. Route 66, also known as the Main Street of America and the Mother Road, was established in 1926 to go from Chicago to Los Angeles. It was one of the most famous roads in the United States and rose to almost cult status after it was obsoleted by the present Interstate Highway system.
35. At 14,494 feet, Mount Whitney is the highest peak in the continental United States.
36. "On Location With Gunga Din." Special

feature on *Gunga Din* (1939) DVD. Turner Entertainment, 2004.

37. George White's ranch today is the location of Red Cliffs Lodge, which houses an excellent museum commemorating movies filmed around Moab

38. Stanton, *Where God Put the West*, iii.

39. D'Arc, *When Hollywood Came to Town*, 233

40. Las Vegas & San Miguel County Visitors Guide 2016, 19.

41. Tuska, *The Filming of the West*, 509–510.

42. Buscombe, *The BFI Companion to the Western*, 40.

43. Wilson and Wilson, *Mass Media/Mass Culture*, 206

44. Wilson and Wilson, *Mass Media/Mass Culture*, 194

45. Miller, *Hollywood Censored*, 146.

46. Bingen, *Warner Bros.*, 28.

Chapter Seven

1. Barbour, *Saturday Afternoon at the Movies*, 156.

2. Goetzmann and Goetzmann, *The West of the Imagination*, 337.

3. Bingen, Sylvester, and Troyan, *M-G-M*, 105.

4. Smith, *Industrial Light and Magic*, 145.

5. Smith, *Industrial Light and Magic*, 190–191.

6. Bingen, *Warner Bros.*, 114.

7. Michael F. Blake, *Code of Honor: The Making of Three Great American Westerns*. (Lanham: Taylor Trade Publishing, 2003), 77.

8. Tom Reilly, *The Big Picture* (New York: Thomas Dunne Books, 2009), 56.

9. D'Arc, *When Hollywood Came to Town*, 92.

10. Eyman, *Print the Legend*, 70.

11. Tuska, *The American West in Film*, 52.

12. Charles C. Poling, "Movie Magic: Santa Fe's Transformative Role in Cinematic History." *Santa Fean*, February/March 2014.

13. Bingen, *Warner Bros.*, 224.

14. Bingen, *Warner Bros.*, 235.

15. "Destination Yuma." Special feature on *3:10 to Yuma* (2007) DVD. Lionsgate, 2004.

16. The ranch has a museum open year-round, and one weekend a year the entire ranch is open to the public during the Cowboy Poetry & Music Festival held at the end of April.

17. Horwitz, *They Went Thataway*, 218.

18. In 1968 and 1969 the Spahn Ranch was occupied for a while by Charles Manson, the cult-leader and criminal, and his followers known as The Family.

19. The rugged mountains around the ranch were the main filming location for the original *M*A*S*H* (1970) and the subsequent *M*A*S*H* television series.

20. Bingen, *Warner Bros.*, 27.

21. Bingen, *Warner Bros.*, 175.

22. Bingen, *Warner Bros.*, 119.

23. Tuska, *The Filming of the West*, 218.

24. Wallis, *The Real Wild West*, 388.

25. Stier, *The First Fifty Years of Sound Western Movie Locations (1929–1979)*, ix.

26. George-Warren, *Cowboy*, 189.

27. Jackson, *Classic TV Westerns*, 17.

28. McDonald, *Shooting Stars*, 218.

29. Jackson, *Classic TV Westerns*, 19.

30. Bingen, *Warner Bros.*, 177, 180.

31. Fenin and Everson, *The Western*, 310.

32. Fenin and Everson, *The Western*, 302.

33. The first cathode ray tubes for television sets were round, specified by their diameter, and only later did they become rectangular. The size of the rectangular tubes was measured from one corner to the opposite diagonal corner to maintain a consistent specification with the diameter measurement of the round tubes. This was long before today's flat-screen solid-state televisions.

34. Bingen, Sylvester, and Troyan, *M-G-M*, 235.

35. Today program length is shorter to allow for more commercials, which equates to more revenue earned.

Chapter Eight

1. Jensen, *The Movie Railroads*, 5.

2. Osterwald, *Cinders & Smoke*, 9.

3. The track of a narrow-gauge railroad is built with 3 feet between the rails, as opposed to a standard gauge track, which is laid with 4 feet 8–1/2 inches between the rails. The advantage of the narrow-gauge is that it is cheaper to build and can be laid with sharper curves than standard gauge, thus allowing more curves and a steeper rate of climb in mountainous terrain than the equivalent standard gauge.

4. Osterwald, *Cinders & Smoke*, 6.

5. Lucius Beebe and Charles Clegg, *Narrow Gauge in the Rockies* (Berkeley: Howell-North, 1958), 17–21.

6. Jensen, *The Movie Railroads*, 87.

7. Jensen, *The Movie Railroads*, 26.

8. Jensen, *The Movie Railroads*, 42.

9. Jensen, *The Movie Railroads*, 96.

10. Robert A. LeMassena, *Colorado's Mountain Railroads* (Denver: Sundance Books, 1984), 239–242.

11. Lawton, *Old Tucson Studios*, 109.

12. Jensen, *The Movie Railroads*, 152.

13. Bingen, Sylvester, and Troyan, *M-G-M*, 176–177.

14. Jensen, *The Movie Railroads*, 144.

Chapter Nine

1. Bingen, Sylvester, and Troyan, *M-G-M*, 271–272.

2. Lawton, *Old Tucson Studios*, 9.
3. Bingen, *Warner Bros.*, 178.
4. Bingen, Sylvester, and Troyan, *M-G-M*, 237.
5. Bingen, Sylvester, and Troyan, *M-G-M*, 286–289.
6. Smith, *Shooting Cowboys and Indians*, 177.
7. Bingen, *Warner Bros.*, 178.
8. Cowie, *John Ford and the American West*, 193.
9. Stone, *The 50 Greatest Westerns*, 157; Munn, *John Wayne*, 232.
10. Bingen, *Warner Bros.*, 33.
11. Griffith and Mayer, *The Movies*, 440.
12. Munn, *John Wayne*, 209.
13. Buscombe, *The BFI Companion to the Western*, 48.
14. Munn, *John Wayne*, 263.
15. Metro-Goldwyn-Mayer, *How the West Was Won*, 25.
16. Tuska, *The Filming of the West*, 548.
17. Jensen, *The Movie Railroads*, 115.
18. Bingen, Sylvester, and Troyan, *M-G-M*, 140.
19. Hughes, *Once Upon a Time in the Italian West*, xi.
20. Fenin and Everson, *The Western*, 343.
21. A list of all the Italian westerns made between 1963 and 1969 may be found in Alice Goetz and Helmut Banz, *Aspekte der Italienischen Films*, Vol. 2, *Der Italo-Western* (Society of German Film Clubs, 1969), 256.
22. Though Eastwood's character is called "Joe" in a couple of places, "Manco" in *For a Few Dollars More* (1965), and "Blondie" in *The Good, the Bad and the Ugly* (1966), the U.S. distributors, United Artists, tried to keep his character anonymous for marketing purposes.
23. Frayling, *Spaghetti Westerns*, 73.
24. Hughes, *Once Upon a Time in the Italian West*, 254.
25. Frayling, *Spaghetti Westerns*, 256.
26. Hughes, *Once Upon a Time in the Italian West*, 194.
27. Hughes, *Once Upon a Time in the Italian West*, 7.
28. Frayling, *Spaghetti Westerns*, 69.
29. Hughes, *Once Upon a Time in the Italian West*, 2.
30. Frayling, *Spaghetti Westerns*, 198.
31. Frayling, *Spaghetti Westerns*, 198.
32. Hughes, *Once Upon a Time in the Italian West*, 243.
33. Frayling, *Spaghetti Westerns*, 256.
34. Mitchell, *Westerns*, 315.
35. Sennett, *Great Hollywood Westerns*, 253.
36. Slotkin, *Gunfighter Nation*, 627.
37. Slotkin, *Gunfighter Nation*, 348, 723.
38. George-Warren, *Cowboy*, 197.
39. Garfield, *Western Film*, 7. *Heaven' Gate* (1980) escalated from an original $10 million budget to $36 million. United Artists was only saved by their next James Bond film, which fortunately for them made $192 million worldwide.
40. Sennett, *Great Hollywood Westerns*, 255.

Postscript

1. Jacques Mauduy and Gérard Henriet, *Géographies du Western* (Paris: Nathan, 1989), 23.
2. Faulk, *Tombstone*, 201.
3. Sarf, *God Bless You, Buffalo Bill*, 26.
4. Sarf, *God Bless You, Buffalo Bill*, 77.
5. Murdoch, *The American West*, 81.
6. Carey McWilliams, "Myths of the West." *North American Review*, Vol 232, November 1931, 428.
7. Sarf, *God Bless You, Buffalo Bill*, 26.
8. Bingen, *Warner Bros.*, 198.

Bibliography

Agnew, Jeremy. *The Age of Dimes and Pulps; A History of Sensationalist Literature 1830–1960.* Jefferson: McFarland, 2018.

Agnew, Jeremy. *The Creation of the Cowboy Hero: Fiction, Film and Fact.* Jefferson: McFarland, 2015.

Agnew, Jeremy. *The Old West in Fact and Film: History Versus Hollywood.* Jefferson: McFarland, 2012.

Aitchison, Stewart. *A Traveler's Guide to Monument Valley.* Stillwater: Voyageur Press, 1993.

Allen, Robert C. *Horrible Prettiness: Burlesque and American Culture.* Chapel Hill: University of North Carolina Press, 1991.

Alter, Judy. *Wild West Shows: Rough Riders and Sure Shots.* New York: Franklin Watts, 1997.

Autry, Gene. *Back in the Saddle Again.* Garden City: Doubleday, 1978.

Barbour, Alan G. *Saturday Afternoon at the Movies.* New York: Bonanza Books, 1986.

Berg, Jeff. *New Mexico Filmmaking.* Charleston: History Press, 2015.

Bingen, Steven. *Warner Bros: Hollywood's Ultimate Backlot.* Lanham, MD: Taylor Trade Publishing, 2014.

Bingen, Steven, Stephen X. Sylvester, and Michael Troyan. *M-G-M: Hollywood's Greatest Backlot.* Solana Beach, CA: Santa Monica Press, 2011.

Burns, Walter N. *Tombstone.* New York: Doubleday, 1927.

Buscombe, Edward, ed. *The BFI Companion to the Western.* New York: Atheneum, 1988.

Calder, Jenni. *There Must Bbe a Lone Ranger: The American West in Film and in Reality.* New York: Taplinger Publishing, 1975.

Cameron, Ian, and Douglas Pye, eds. *The Book of Westerns.* New York: Continuum Publishing, 1996.

Carmichael, Deborah A., ed. *The Landscape of Hollywood Westerns.* Salt Lake City: University of Utah Press, 2006.

Cowie, Peter. *John Ford and the American West.* New York: Harry N. Abrams, 2004.

Cowie, Peter. *Seventy Years of Cinema.* Cranbury: A.S. Barnes, 1969.

Culhane, John. *Special Effects in the Movies: How They Do It.* New York: Ballantine Books, 1981.

D'Arc, James V. *When Hollywood Came to Town: A History of Moviemaking in Utah.* Layton: Gibbs Smith, 2010.

Debarbieri, Lili. *Location Filming in Arizona: The Screen Legacy of the Grand Canyon State.* Charleston: History Press, 2014.

Dykstra, Robert R. *The Cattle Towns.* New York: Alfred A Knopf, 1968.

Eppinga, Jane. *Tombstone.* Charleston: Arcadia Publishing, 2003.

Etulain, Richard W., and Glenda Riley, eds. *The Hollywood West: Lives of Film Legends Who Shaped It.* Golden, CO: Fulcrum Publishing, 2001.

Everson, William K. *A Pictorial History of the Western Film.* New York: Citadel Press, 1969.

Eyman, Scott. *Print the Legend: The Life and Times of John Ford.* New York: Simon & Schuster, 2015.

Faulk, Odie B. *Tombstone: Myth and Reality.* New York: Oxford University Press, 1972.

Fenin, George N., and William K. Everson. *The Western: From Silents to the Seventies.* New York: Grossman Publishers, 1973.

Frayling, Christopher. *Once Upon a Time in Italy: The Westerns of Sergio Leone.* New York: Harry N. Abrams, 2005.

Frayling, Christopher. *Spaghetti Westerns: Cowboys and Europeans from Karl May to Sergio Leone.* London: I.B. Taurus, 1998.

French, Philip. *Westerns: Aspects of a Movie Genre.* New York: Viking, 1973.

Garfield, Brian. *Western Film.* New York: Rawson Associates, 1982.

George-Warren, Holly. *Cowboy: How Hollywood Invented the Wild West.* Pleasantville, NY: Reader's Digest Association, 2002.

George-Warren, Holly. *Public Cowboy No. 1: The Life and Times of Gene Autry.* New York: Oxford University Press, Inc., 2007.

Goetzmann, William H., and William N. Goetzmann. *The West of the Imagination.* New York: W.W. Norton, 1986.

Griffith, Richard, and Arthur Mayer. *The Movies.* New York: Simon & Schuster, 1970.

Hamilton, John R. *Thunder in the Dust: Classic Images of Western Movies.* New York: Stewart, Tabori & Chand, 1987.

Harris, Charles W., and Buck Rainey, eds. *The*

Cowboy: Six-Shooters, Songs, and Sex. Norman: University of Oklahoma Press, 1976.

Horwitz, James. *They Went Thataway.* New York: Thomas Congdon Books, 1976.

Hughes, Howard. *Once Upon a Time in the Italian West.* London: I.B. Taurus, 2004.

Jackson Ronald. *Classic TV Westerns.* New York: Carol Publishing Group, 1994.

Jensen, Larry. *The Movie Railroads.* Burbank: Darwin Publications, 1981.

Jensen, Richard D. *The Amazing Tom Mix: The Most Famous Cowboy in the Movies.* Lincoln, NE: iUniverse, 2005.

Jones, William C., and Elizabeth B. Jones. *Buckwalter: The Colorado Scenes of a Pioneer Photojournalist, 1890–1920.* Boulder: Pruett Publishing, 1989.

Kasson, Joy S. *Buffalo Bill's Wild West.* New York: Hill and Wang, 2000.

Kitses, Jim. *Horizons West.* Bloomington: Indiana University Press, 1969.

Kitses, Jim, and Gregg Rickman. *The Western Reader.* New York: Limelight Editions, 1998.

Krefft, Vanda. *The Man Who Made the Movies: The Meteoric Rise and Tragic Fall of William Fox.* New York: HarperCollins, 2017.

Lahue, Kalton C. *Riders of the Range: The Sagebrush Heroes of the Sound Screen.* Cranbury: A.S. Barnes, 1973.

Lawton, Paul J. *Old Tucson Studios.* Charleston: Arcadia Publishing, 2008.

Lloyd, Ann, ed. *They Went That-A-Way.* London: Orbis Publishing, 1982.

Maltin, Leonard. *Movie and Video Guide.* New York: Penguin-Putnam, 1998.

Mangan, Terry W. *Colorado on Glass: Colorado's First Half Century As Seen by the Camera.* Silverton, CO: Sundance, 1975.

McClure, Arthur F., and Ken D. Jones. *Western Films: Heroes, Heavies, and Sagebrush of the "B" Genre.* New York: A.S. Barnes, 1972.

McDarrah, Fred W., and Gloria S. McDarrah. *The Photography Encyclopedia.* New York: Schirmer Books, 1999.

McDonald, Archie P., ed. *Shooting Stars: Heroes and Heroines of Western Film.* Bloomington: Indiana University Press, 1987.

McVeigh, Stephen. *The American Western.* Edinburgh: Edinburgh University Press, 2007.

Metro-Goldwyn-Mayer. *How the West Was Won.* Culver City: Metro-Goldwyn-Mayer, 1963.

Miller, Frank. *Censored Hollywood: Sex, Sin & Violence on Screen.* Atlanta: Turner, 1994.

Mitchell, Lee C. *Westerns: Making the Man in Fiction and Film.* Chicago: University of Chicago Press, 1996.

Mitchum, Petrine D. *Hollywood Hoofbeats.* Irvine, CA: i-5 Publishing, 2014.

Moon, Samuel. *Tall Sheep: Harry Goulding, Monument Valley Trader.* Norman: University of Oklahoma Press, 1992.

Munn, Michael. *John Wayne: The Man Behind the Myth.* New York: New American Library, 2003.

Murdoch, David H. *The American West: The Invention of a Myth.* Reno: University of Nevada Press, 2001.

Murray, John A. *Cinema Southwest: An Illustrated Guide to the Movies and Their Locations.* Flagstaff: Northland, 2000.

Nachbar, Jack, ed. *Focus on the Western.* Englewood Cliffs: Prentice-Hall, 1974.

O'Neil, Paul. *The End and the Myth.* Alexandria: Time-Life Books, 1979.

Osterwald, Doris B. *Cinders & Smoke.* Lakewood, CO: Western Guideways, 1982.

Osterwald, Doris B. *Narrow Gauge to Cumbres: A Pictorial History of the Cumbres and Toltec Scenic Railroad.* Lakewood, CO: Western Guideways, 1972.

Pinteau, Pascal. *Special Effects: An Oral History.* New York: Harry N. Abrams, 2004.

Quick, John, and Tom LaBau. *Handbook of Film Production.* New York: Macmillan, 1972.

Reddin, Paul. *Wild West Shows.* Urbana, University of Illinois Press, 1999.

Robinson, David. *From Peep Show to Palace: The Birth of American Film.* New York: Columbia University Press, 1995.

Rollins, Peter C., and John E. O'Connor, eds. *Hollywood's West: The American Frontier in Film, Television, & History.* Lexington: University Press of Kentucky, 2005.

Rosenblum, Naomi. *A World History of Photography.* New York: Abbeville Press, 2007.

Sandler, Martin W. *Photography: An Illustrated History.* New York: Oxford University Press, 2002.

Sarf, Wayne M. *God Bless You, Buffalo Bill.* East Brunswick: Associated University Presses and Cornwall Books, 1983.

Sennett, Ted. *Great Hollywood Westerns.* New York: Harry N. Abrams, 1990.

Shipman, David. *The Story of Cinema.* New York: St. Martin's Press, 1982.

Simmon, Scott. *The Invention of the Western Film: A Cultural History of the Genre's First Half-Century.* Cambridge: Cambridge University Press, 2003.

Sklar, Robert. *Film: An International History of the Medium.* New York: Harry N. Abrams, 1993.

Slotkin, Richard. *Gunfighter Nation: The Myth of the Frontier in Twentieth-Century America.* New York: Atheneum, 1992.

Smith, Andrew B. *Shooting Cowboys and Indians: Silent Western Films, American Culture, and the Birth of Hollywood.* Boulder: University Press of Colorado, 2003.

Smith, Thomas G. *Industrial Light and Magic: The Art of Special Effects.* New York: Ballantine, 1986.

Speed, F. Maurice. *The Western Film Annual.* London: MacDonald, 1954.

Spencer, Michael J. *Hollywood of the Rockies: Colorado, The West & America's Film Pioneers.* Charleston: History Press, 2013.

Stanfield, Peter. *Hollywood, Westerns and the 1930s.* Exeter: University of Exeter Press, 2001.

Stanfield, Peter. *Horse Opera: The Strange History of the 1930s Singing Cowboy.* Urbana: University of Illinois Press, 2002.

Stanton, Bette L. *Where God Put the West: Movie Making in the Desert.* Moab: Canyonlands Natural History Association, 1994.

Stier, Kenny. *The First Fifty Years of Sound Western Movie Locations (1929–1979).* Corriganville, CA: Corriganville Press, 2006.

Stone, Barry. *The 50 Greatest Westerns.* London: Icon Books, 2016.

Thomson, David. *Warner Bros: The Making of an American Movie Studio.* New Haven: Yale University Press, 2017.

Tuska, Jon. *The American West in Film: Critical Approaches to the Western.* Westport: Greenwood Press, 1985.

Tuska, Jon. *The Filming of the West.* Garden City: Doubleday, 1976.

Varner, Paul, ed. *Western: Paperback Novels and Movies From Hollywood.* Newcastle, England: Cambridge Scholars Publishing, 2007.

Verhoeff, Norma. *The West in Early Cinema.* Amsterdam: Amsterdam University Press, 2006.

Walker, Janet, ed. *Western: Film Through History.* New York: Routledge, 2001.

Wallis, Michael. *The Real Wild West: The 101 Ranch and the Creation of the American West.* New York: St. Martin's Press, 1999.

Warren, Louis S. *Buffalo Bill's America: William Cody and the Wild West Show.* New York: Alfred A. Knopf, 2005.

Whitlock, Cathy. *Designs on Film: A Century of Hollywood Art Direction.* New York: itbooks, 2010.

Wilson, James R., and Stan L. Wilson. *Mass Media/Mass Culture.* New York: McGraw-Hill, 1998.

Wilson, Robert L., and Greg Martin. *Buffalo Bill's Wild West: An American Legend.* New York: Random House, 1998.

Wright, Will. *Six Guns and Society: A Structural Study of the Western.* Berkeley: University of California Press, 1975.

Index

Numbers in **_bold italics_** indicate pages with illustrations

A-Westerns 90, 99, 109, 126, 138, 140, 184
Abiquiu, New Mexico **_8_**, 202, **_202_**
Acoma, New Mexico 128, 198
actualities 30
Agoura, California 147, 155, 156, 160, 162
Alabama Hills, California 6, 128–130
Anchorville 130
Anderson, Gilbert *see* Broncho Billy Anderson
anti-trust action 84–85, 108, 135–136, 180
Apacheland Studio 148
Aronson, Gilbert *see* Broncho Billy Anderson
ASA film speed 24, 112, 209–210, 211
Autry, Gene 75, 93, 96–99, 109, 129, 130, 138, 147, 154, 156, 158, 163

B-Westerns 86–99, 102–103, 129, 138, 146, 154, 158, 160–164, 185, 189, 212–213
back projection *see* rear projection
Balshofer, Fred 45–47, 54–56, 64
Baltimore & Ohio Railroad 174
Baumann, Charles 45, 46, 64
Beale's Cut 100, 101, 213
Bell Moving Picture Ranch 148
Bierstadt, Albert 7, 10–11
big screen technology 144–145
Big Sky Movie Ranch 149
The Big Trail 84, 88, 104, 123
Billy the Kid 38, 88, 90, 107, 121, 122, 123, 128, 132, 150, 177, 182, 209
Biograph studio 33, 37, 41, 46, 47–49, 53, 54, 61, 98, 160
Bison 101 films 64–65
black-and-white: filming 27, 93, 112, 128, 164, 184; photography 10, 17–23, **_22_**, **_23_**, 107, 210
Black Maria studio 29–30, **_29_**, 31, 55

Boggs, Francis 35–36, 40, 43, 60
Bonanza Creek Ranch 149–150
Boot Hill 205, 206
Borehamwood studio, England 190
Brackettville, Texas 140
Breakheart Pass 176
Broncho Billy Anderson 36–40, 44–45, 53–54, 59, 97, 102, 183
Bronson Canyon 118, 160–161
Brownie camera 22, **_22_**
Buckskin Joe, Colorado **_92_**, 151
Buckwalter, Harry 33, 35, 36, 40, 74
Buntline, Ned 13–14

California School of Art 10
California State Railroad Museum 172
Camas Prairie Railroad 176
Camel Rock, New Mexico **_149_**, 150
cameras, movie 79–82, 89, 112–113, 144
Canutt, Yakima 102–103, 105
Cat Ballou 151, 175, 199
cavalry trilogy 116–117
Cheyenne Autumn 113, 114, 118–119, 131, 146
Cheyenne Social Club 149, 152, 153, 178
Cinemascope 111, 134, 144
Cinerama 111, 144–145, 186
Cisco Kid 83, 126, 129, 154, 158; *see also In Old Arizona*
City Slickers 8, **_8_**, 202, **_202_**
cliff-hanger 63, 94–95, 211
Clothier, William 184
Cody, Buffalo Bill 13–17, 29, 40, 59, 98, 210
color photography 13, 20, 23–24, 111–113, 116, 117, 118, 122, 126, 184, 210; *see also* Technicolor
Columbia studio 86, 91, 97, 120, 136, 138, 154, 163, 178, 182, 191, 201; ranch 93, 151–152, 201
Consolidated Film Industries (CFI) 96, 111

Corriganville 116, 147, 152, 158, 162
The Covered Wagon 72, 76–77, 90, 132, 172
Cripple Creek Bar-Room Scene 31
Culver City 64, 65, 118, 201
Cumbres & Toltec Scenic Railroad 170–171, **_171_**

deadman's fall *see* horse falls
Death Valley, California 111, 130–131, 187, 193, 204, **_204_**
Death Valley Days 124, 130, 148, 204
Delaware and Lackawanna Railroad 32
DeMille, Cecil B. 66, 88, 140, 177
Denver & Rio Grande Railway 33, 73, 151, 166–170, 175
The Depression *see* The Great Depression
Dickson, W.K.L. 29, 31, 41, 55
dime novels 13–17, 40, 50, 51, 59
Dollars Trilogy *see* Leone, Sergio
Don Juan 79, **_79_**
double feature 89–90, 189
Dover, New Jersey **_27_**, 32
dubbing *see* sound dubbing
Durango, Colorado 166–170, 175, 186
Durango, Mexico 187–188
Dwan, Dorothy 73–74

Eastern locations 25, 26, **_27_**, 37, 48, 52, 188, 203
Eastman, George 21–22, 112
Eastman Kodak Company 21, 112
Eastmancolor 112
Eaves Movie Ranch 120, 149, 152–153, **_153_**, 178
Edendale, California 43–44, 46, 54, 62, 64, 66, 67, 94, 162
Edison, Thomas 26–27, 29–36, 41, 47, 48, 55, 78
Edison Trust *see* Motion Picture Patents Company

El Rancho Hotel 126–127, *126*
Emma Sweeny 167, *168*, 173
Empire Ranch, Arizona 109, *110*, 134–135
Essanay Film Manufacturing Company 37–40, 44, 46, 47–48, 49, 52, 54, 66, 84
exchanges, film *see* film exchanges

Fairbanks, Douglas, Jr. 130
film: exchanges 45, 47, 64, 67, 96, 211; geography 110–111
filming weather *see* weather
First National Pictures 67, 71, 83, 89, 155
Ford, John 13, 56, 77, 87, 100, 103, 105–108, 113–116, 120, 131, 146, 161, 183–184, 186, 195, 205; cavalry trilogy 116–117
Fort Apache *106*, 116, 118, 152
Fox, William 67, 75, 77, 78
Fox studio *see* Twentieth Century-Fox studio

Gallup, New Mexico 26–28, *47*, *65*, 69, 111, 112, 119, 126–128, *127*, 139, *139*, 150
Ghost Ranch, New Mexico 202, *202*
Glenwood Canyon, Colorado 73–74, *73*, 169, 212
Golden, Colorado 36, 45, 210
Golden Gate Mountain 6, *51*, 120
Golden Gate Park 57
Golden Oak Ranch 158–159
Goulding, Harry 107–108
Goulding Trading Post 106–108, *106*, 116–117, 119
Grafton, Utah 83, *83*, 125–126
Grandeur 70 process 84
The Great Depression 57, 85, 86–87, 89, 90–91, 93, 99, 106–107, 109, 126
The Great K&A Train Robbery 72–74, *73*, 212
The Great Train Robbery 27, 32–33, 34, 36, 102, 165, 210
Great Western Railway 175–176
Griffith, D.W. 40–41, 53, 65, 127, 160, 183
Griffith Park 46, 160–161

Hadleyville 151–152, 173
Hart, William S. 58–59, 62–63, 65, 72, 84, 97, 159, 183
Hartville 65
The Harvey Girls 107, 177, 182
Heaven's Gate 176, 200, 215
Helldorado festival 204–205
Hoch, Winton 13, 117
Homestead Act 8–9
horse falls 64, 102–103; *see also* stunts
How the West Was Won 102, 107, 130, 132, 145, 166, 168, 174, 178, 182, 186
Hudson River School 10

iconic images of the movie West *8*, *27*, *51*, *70*, *87*, *110*, *139*, *166*, *181*, *204*
In Old Arizona 78, 82–84, 88, 123, 126; *see also* Cisco Kid
Ince, Thomas 54–58, 64, 65, 67, 72, 211
Inceville 54, 56–57, *56*, 64–65
Independent Moving Picture Company (IMP) 46–47, 54, 64
infra-red film 116
The Iron Horse 77, 90, 100, 103, 146
Italian film industry 52, 113, 188–196, 215
Iverson Movie Ranch 93, 147, 152, 153–154, 162

Jack Ingram Movie Ranch 147, 154–155, 162
Jackson, William 18, 20–21
Jamestown, California 119, 151, 171–173, *173*
The Jazz Singer 80–81
Jersey scenery 52
Johnson Canyon, Utah 123–124, *123*

Kanab, Utah 25, 112, 122–125, 131
Kerkorian, Kirk 180, 182
Kessel, Adam 45, 46, 64
Keystone Film Company 64, 161
Kinetophone 78
Kinetoscope 26, 33
Kodak: camera 21–22, *22*; company 49, 112, 210

Laemmle, Carl 46, 54, 64, 67, 89
Lasky, Jesse 66–67, 85, 107, 122
Lasky Ranch 155, 162
Las Vegas, New Mexico 61, 126, 132–133, 150
The Left Handed Gun 209
Leone, Sergio 189–196, 198, 206; Dollars Trilogy 190–194
lighting, artificial 53, 79, 112
locations: in the East *see* Eastern locations; non-matching 45, 110–111, 145–146, 195–196
Loew, Marcus 66, 68, 77
Loew's Inc. 68, 70, 136, 180
Lone Pine, California 6, 25, *70*, 128–130, 186
Longmire 133–134, *134*, 150
Los Angeles State and County Arboretum 161
Lubin Manufacturing Company 37, 45, 49, 52, 61, 132–133
Lucerne Lake, California 105, 161

Lucky Baldwin Ranch 161
Lumière Brothers 24, 27

Magma Railroad 174
major studios 66–67, 71, 84, 86, 136; *see also* Seven Sisters
make-up 53, 116, 146, 191
The Man Who Shot Liberty Valance 25, 162, 183–184
Manifest Destiny 11, 18, 165, 209
Manson, Charles 214
May, Karl 188
Mayer, Louis B. 67, 77–78, 89, 180
McCabe & Mrs. Miller 198
Melody Ranch *see* Monogram Ranch
Mescal, Arizona 121, 182
Metro-Goldwyn-Mayer (MGM) studio 67, 68, 70, 83, 84, 86–89, 112, 123–124, 138, 143, 180–183; dismantling of 180–182; MGM England 190; studio railroad 176–177
Metrocolor 112
Mexican National Railroad 174–175
Mexico as a filming location 186–188
Miller Brothers *see* 101 Ranch
mis-matching locations *see* locations, non-matching
The Mittens *87*
Mix, Tom 6, 43, 59–63, 72–76, 86, 97–100, 123, 133, 155, 165, 211, 212; death 76; lifestyle 74–75
Mixville 62, 162
Moab, Utah 114, 116, 122, 131–132, 185
Mojave Desert 82, 158, 161
Monogram Ranch 93, 147, 155–156, 162
Monument Valley 6, 25, 69, *87*, 104, 105–108, 113–120, 125, 128, 131–132, 141, 144, 186, 195, 207; discovery 107–108
Moran, Thomas 10–12, *12*
Motion Picture Patents Company 48–49, 64, 78
Mount Whitney 213
Mountain of the Holy Cross 11, *12*
movie camera *see* camera, movie
Movie Flats *70*, 129
movie railroads *see* railroads, movie
movie ranches 147–160; *see also* specific studio
movie stunts *see* stunts
movies: 1980s 200–201; 1990s 201–202
Movietone 78–81
music 9, 16, 26, 43, 78–80, 89, 97, 118, 132

Index

musical Westerns *see* singing Westerns
Muybridge, Eadweard 24, 26
My Darling Clementine 114–117
the mythic West 6, 7–25, 30, 52, 62, 75, 115, 206, 207; *see also* iconic images of the movie West

Navajo 57, 87, 106–108, 113, 116, 118–120, 126, 128, 146, 195
New Mexico Film Office 150
New York Motion Picture Company 43, 45–48, 54–55, 64–66, 160
Newhall Cut *see* Beale's Cut
nickelodeon 7, 28–29, 34, 37, 45, 48, 49, 64, 65, 67, 68, 71, 84
Niles, California 37, 54
nitrate film 31–32

Old Tucson Studios 6, 25, *51*, 111, 115, 119, 120–121, 140, 160, 177, 180, 182, 185
101 Ranch 41–43, 54–58, 60
The Outlaw Josie Wales **187**
Owl Creek Pass, Colorado 166, *166*, 186

Paramount studio 67, 69, 72, 77, 85, 86, 93, 94, 107, 111, 122, 128, 138, 144, 147, 164, 178, 182, 184; ranch 93, 156–158, *157*; studio railroad 177–178; theater chain 67, 70, 85, 136, 156, 162
Paria, Utah 125, 142
Patents Trust *see* Motion Picture Patents Company
Peckinpah, Sam 183, 198
persistence of vision 24, 26, 210
The Phantom Empire 212–213
photography: black-and-white *see* black-and-white photography; color *see* color photography
Pioneertown 147, 158
pit shot 103
Porter, Edwin 31–33, 36, 41
Poverty Row 93–96
problems of sound *see* sound problems
production figures *see* Westerns, number of
The Professionals 130, 175, 176, 187, 204
projection speed 210
Pyramid Rock, Gallup **65**, 128

railroads, movie 18, 20, 25, 32–36, 45, 60, 73–74, 77, 90, 106, 119, 126–127, 132, 151, 165–179, 193–195; narrow gauge 214; track width 214; wrecks 169, 170, 172, 174

Railtown 1897 Historic Park 172, 179
Rat Pack 125, 213
rear projection 90, 105, 107, 143, 183
Red Hills Ranch 158
Red Rock Canyon, California 25, 161
Red Rock Park, New Mexico **65**, 128, **139**
reel length 28, 32, 94, 210
Remington, Frederic 9, 11, 13, 14, 117
Republic Pictures 94–96, 99, 102, 105, 111, 122, 138, 154, 155, 163; studio ranch 158–159
Rio Grande 114, 116, 131
RKO studio 67, 71, 86, 118, 182; studio ranch 93, 147, 159, 162
Rogers, Roy 75, 93, 97, 99, 103, 109, 129, 138, 154, 158, 163
Romanticism in art 9–10
Roosevelt, Theodore 14, 41, 60
Rosita, Colorado 151
Route 66 126, 127, 213
Royal Gorge, Colorado 33, 60, **61**, 169, 175, 212
running insert 82, 103, 163
running W *see* horse falls
Russell, Charles 9, 11, 13

Saddle the Wind 151
saguaro cactus 51, **51**, 52, 102, 115, 120–121, 162, 174
San Bernardino Mountains 46, 158, 161
Santa Fe, New Mexico 149, 150, 152–153, 194, **197**
Schary, Dore 180
Schenck, Nicholas 180
The Searchers 113, 114, 117–118, 119, 120, 144, 213
Sears-Roebuck films 28
Sedona, Arizona 121–122, **181**
Selig, William 33, 36–37, 39, 40, 41, 43, 46–49, 52, 55, 60–62, 66, 74, 84, 98, 133, 210; copyright flag 210
Selig Polyscope *see* Selig, William
serial Westerns 94–95, 98, 104, 109, 154, 172, 185
series Westerns 71–72, 94–95, 97, 109
Seven Sisters 67–68
She Wore a Yellow Ribbon 13, **106**, 114, 116–117, 119
Sierra Railway *see* Jamestown, California
Silver Lake, California *see* Edendale
Silverton, Colorado 113, 166, **166**, 167–170, 186
singing cowboys *see* singing Westerns

singing Westerns 59, 89, 98–99, 104, 109, 134, 138, 212
Sonora, California 158, 171–172
sound 28, 77, 78–84, 89, 98; on disc *see* Vitaphone; dubbing 89, 145–146, 178, 189, 191–192; effects 78–79, 89, 145; on film 80–81; introduction 78–82; problems 78, 88–89, 140, 145–146, 212
spaghetti Westerns 190–199
Spahn Movie Ranch 148, 152, 159, 162, 214
Spain as a filming location 25, 188–198
special effects 63, 124–125, 140–144, 169–170
Spoor, George 36–37, 44, 54
Stagecoach 88, 90, 100, 103–108, 113, 114, 141, 161
stagecoach, runaway 74, 211
stationary W *see* horse falls
stereographic images 22–23, 45
stereoscope 22–23, **23**
Stout, Archie 116
stunt double 98, 100, 103
stunts 43, 55, 57, 59, 60, 63–64, 73, 74, 91, 99–103, 105, 130, 169; horse falls 102–103
sweat box 80, 212

Technicolor 111–112, 117, 122, 126, 128, 138, 164, 178, 184
television 15, 109, 136–137, 138, 162–164, 200; tube size 214
theater chains 67–68, 69–71, 84–85, 108, 127, 136, 147, 203; *see also specific studio*
theater divestiture *see* anti-trust action
30 mile rule 147
3-D movies 111, 122, 145
3-D photographs *see* stereographic images; stereoscope
A Ticket to Tomahawk 167–168, **167**, 173
Tombstone 110, 121, 153, 201
Tombstone, Arizona 111, 114, 115–116, 117, 121, 156, 204–205
The Tourist West 204–206
Tracked by Bloodhounds 35
tracking shot *see* running insert
trains *see* railroads
The Treasure of Silver Lake 188, 190
Triangle Motion Picture Company 65–66, 67
Trucolor 111, 122
True Grit 113, 150, 166, 186, 197
Turner, Ted 182
Twentieth Century–Fox studio 43, 59–60, 62, 67, 74, 84,

86, 93, 144, 159, 162, 179, 182, 212; studio railroad 179; studio ranch 150

United Artists 67, 107, 138, 182, 183, 191, 200, 215
Universal Film Manufacturing Company *see* Universal studio
Universal studio 49, 64–65, 67, 86, 89, 136, 138, 155, 160, 182; studio railroad 178–179; studio ranch 160

Valles Caldera, New Mexico 119, 133–134, *134*
Vasquez Rocks 93, 162
vaudeville 17, 27–30, 33, 34, 45, 66, 67, 68, 71
Victorville, California 102, 105, 161
Virginia & Truckee Railroad 176–178
Vistavision 111, 144
Vitagraph Studios 36–37, 47, 49, 62, 78, 84
Vitaphone 78–81
Vitascope projector 27

Wanger, Walter 107
Warner Brothers studio 62, 67, 71, 78–82, *79*, 86, 89, 98, 112, 145, 163, 182, 201; studio ranch 93, 151–152, 155, 160, 162; studio railroad 178; theater chain *79*, 136; TV westerns 163–164
Wayne, John 3, 96, 98, 102, 103–104, 108, 116–117, 140, 185, 199, 212
weather 37, 41, 44–45, 49, 53, 113, 116–117, 146, 171, 198

Westerns, number of 7, 39, 50, 52, 87, 90, 109, 185, 190, 191, 196, 199
White, George 114, 131, 214
wide screen processes 84, 111, 134, 144–145, 186
The Wild Bunch 175, 197, 198
Wild West shows 15–17, 24, 34–35, 40, 41–43, 45, 50, 51, 54–58, 59, 62–63, 86, 98, 102, 195
Wildwood Regional Park 162
Winnetou 188
Wood, Lana, 118
Wood, Natalie 118
Wortley Hotel *38*

Yates, Herbert 96, 99
Yugoslavia locations 188

Zukor, Adolph 66–67

www.ingramcontent.com/pod-product-compliance
Lightning Source LLC
Chambersburg PA
CBHW060342010526
44117CB00017B/2929